**PRIMA GAMES®** **WE ARE STRATEGY**

FREE eGUIDE!

Enter this code at primagames.com/code to unlock your FREE eGuide:

F3UC-RR62-C4MP-7YCN

Mobile Friendly

Access your eGuide on any web-enabled device.

Searchable & Sortable

Quickly find the strategies you need.

Added Value

Strategy where, when, and how you want it.

Check Out Our Complete eGuide Library at primagames.com!

PRIMA® GAMES

www.primagames.com

The Prima Games logo and Primagames.com are registered trademarks of Penguin Random House LLC, registered in the United States. Prima Games is an imprint of DK, a division of Penguin Random House LLC, New York.

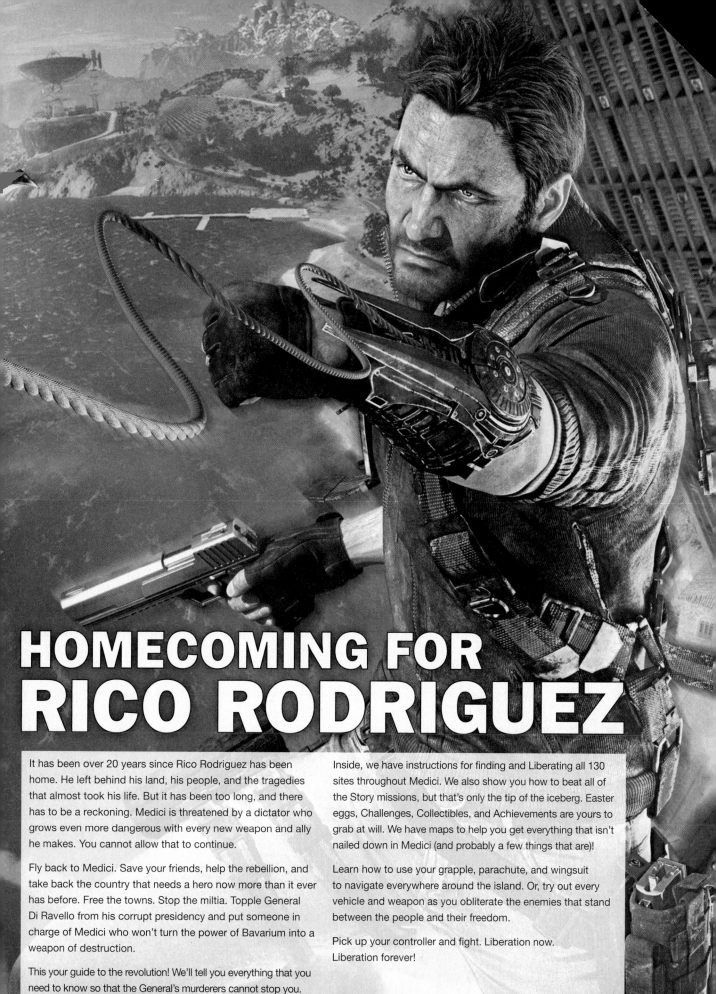

HOMECOMING FOR RICO RODRIGUEZ

It has been over 20 years since Rico Rodriguez has been home. He left behind his land, his people, and the tragedies that almost took his life. But it has been too long, and there has to be a reckoning. Medici is threatened by a dictator who grows even more dangerous with every new weapon and ally he makes. You cannot allow that to continue.

Fly back to Medici. Save your friends, help the rebellion, and take back the country that needs a hero now more than it ever has before. Free the towns. Stop the miltia. Topple General Di Ravello from his corrupt presidency and put someone in charge of Medici who won't turn the power of Bavarium into a weapon of destruction.

This your guide to the revolution! We'll tell you everything that you need to know so that the General's murderers cannot stop you.

Inside, we have instructions for finding and Liberating all 130 sites throughout Medici. We also show you how to beat all of the Story missions, but that's only the tip of the iceberg. Easter eggs, Challenges, Collectibles, and Achievements are yours to grab at will. We have maps to help you get everything that isn't nailed down in Medici (and probably a few things that are)!

Learn how to use your grapple, parachute, and wingsuit to navigate everywhere around the island. Or, try out every vehicle and weapon as you obliterate the enemies that stand between the people and their freedom.

Pick up your controller and fight. Liberation now. Liberation forever!

CHARACTERS

THE STORIES AND PEOPLE OF MEDICI

In this chapter we talk about the beginning of the story and the people who take part in it. Don't worry, we won't give anything away, so you can read this whenever you like.

OUR STORY

Medici is an island nation with a wealth of a special material known as Bavarium. Discovery of this powerful compound has rocketed Medici's international importance and power, but it has also brought great woe to the country. It is currently under the boot of a vile dictator known as General Sebastiano Di Ravello. The people have little say in their government, their work, and sometimes even their lives. Things are desperate for many, and there needs to be change!

What could be more of a just cause than that?

Our hero, Rico Rodriguez, was born in Medici but left quite some time ago. In his people's hour of need, he returns to try and free them from tyranny. Using his courage, and a massive arsenal of weapons and gadgets, he might very well succeed in changing the course of history!

RICO RODRIGUEZ

Age	40s
Born	Mexico
Profession	Revolutionary
Ethnicity	Medician/Mexican
Hair	Brown
Eyes	Hazel
Height	6'0"
Weight	180 lbs.

HISTORY

Rico grew up in Medici after leaving Mexico with his parents when he was only a small baby. His family lived a semi-rural life on the edge of a minor town, but Rico found a way to distinguish himself as a young racecar driver. Rico seemed to be driven by a different fire than just winning. Even when he was leading races by several seconds, he continued to push as if some demon burned at his back. Rico became a local hero, but also began attracting the attention of a young military general with his eye on power.

During a Medician championship race, where Rico was clearly winning the field, he wrecked his car and had to be taken to the hospital. That same night, President Antonio Dante was assassinated and his murder blamed on the popular socialist leader, Rosa Manuela. In the ensuing chaos, what would later be termed 'The Night of the Bonfires,' General Di Ravello grabbed control of the country in a brutal military coup. Rico, with only minor injuries, escaped from the hospital, but too late. He returned home to find it in flames and his family murdered. His best friend, Mario, smuggled him away from the scene to the last boat to leave Medici. Rico escaped, having lost everything he cared about in one night.

On the boat ride across the Atlantic, Rico met Sheldon, who worked for an American government secret agency. He joined up with this new path in life, eventually ending up working as a freelance go-between for The Agency. From there, his continued training in the art of regime destabilization solidified his role as an indispensable agent. His known assignments included overthrowing dictators in the Caribbean nation of San Esperito and the Southeast Asian nation of Panau. At some point, his service allowed him to gain US citizenship, though he never really considered the US as his home. He always kept sporadic contact with his old friend Mario. When he received news that Mario and the rebellion was nearing defeat, he decided to put a lifetime of training to personal use and right the wrongs of his past.

MARIO FRIGO

HISTORY

As a child, Mario compensated for his lack of physical stature with a talent for making friends. One weekend, he found himself watching an F1 race on TV with the head mechanic of a local garage. Mario was enamored with the drivers' skills, and when he realized that many of them were as small as he was, he was hooked. He soon became the mechanic's assistant and found himself working on the car of Medici's prodigal race driver, Rico Rodriguez. They became fast friends, literally, but things went badly for Rico on the night that General Di Ravello seized power, and Mario helped his friend escape Medici when the rest of his family perished.

At 18, Mario took a job as a bus boy in a restaurant frequented by local Mafiosi. An older gentleman who was impressed by Mario's devotion to even unimportant duties invited him to train for a position in a leading crime family. Mario jumped at the opportunity to improve his precarious financial situation, but his progress was soon impaired; Di Ravello began to favor other, less scrupulous, mafia families: organizations that in turn funneled money to his regime, without regard for the effect their horrific acts had on the nation.

Before long, Mario's crew merged with a growing Medician rebellion. The rebel movement has been active for some time, but it's been losing ground lately. Without outside help, they're doomed to fall against the superior numbers, force, and financial power of the general's militia.

Age	Early 30s
Born	Colle Salrosa, Medici
Profession	Mafia Fixer
Ethnicity	Medician
Hair	Brown
Eyes	Brown
Height	5'6"
Weight	160 lbs.

DIMAH

HISTORY

A gifted mathematician and scientist, Dimah Ali Umar al-Nasri never intended to work with nuclear weaponry. At Cairo University, she studied nuclear physics under Sameera Moussa, the nuclear scientist known as the "Mother of Atomic Energy," who nurtured in Dimah a fervent belief that atomic energy would change the world for the better. Dimah's thesis centered around the use of Bavarium for safer nuclear energy, which she hoped would ease the burdens of developing nations. She fervently believed that her research would yield benefits for humanity no matter her vocation. Upon graduating at the top of her class, she joined a military hardware manufacturer.

Age	70s
Born	North Africa
Profession	Physicist
Ethnicity	Egyptian
Hair	Black
Eyes	Brown
Height	5'5"
Weight	150 lbs.

Her clever inventions caught the attention of the Agency, who spirited her away to serve as a gadget and weapons inventor for several decades. During this time, she met and equipped a young Rico Rodriguez with his signature grappling hook and parachute. She also invented a number of gadgets the Agency determined were too risky for operatives to utilize, including the stripped-down wingsuit that she would later give to Rico. When Sebastiano Di Ravello, dictator of the Bavarium-rich island nation of Medici, became an ally of the United States, the Agency gave him Dimah to help develop and research Bavarium; in return, Di Ravello allowed the Agency (limited) access to his research.

In Medici, Dimah made incredible sprints of progress where teams of brilliant scientists had slogged before her. Di Ravello superficially supported her interest in generating energy and curing illness with Bavarium, but simultaneously directed her toward what he saw as more *useful* goals: mining, refinement, and weaponization. The more time she spent in Di Ravello's oppressed nation, the more she bore witness to the terrors of his regime: failure rewarded with torture and death. Petty crime punished by lifelong labor in the mines that produced the very Bavarium she weaponized. She grew to understand Di Ravello's increasingly clear schemes for the imperial conquest of the Mediterranean.

Seeing how her work with Bavarium fit into the collage of turmoil that transformed the once-beautiful Medici into a ruin, she finally began to ask whether her years of dedicated research were really yielding benefits for humanity; she did not like the answer. A rift grew between Dimah's passion for research and invention, and Di Ravello's greed for novel new weapons of mass destruction.

Seeking repentance for her contributions to Di Ravello's progress, Dimah fled and sought asylum from Mario Frigo's rebellion.

ANNIKA SVENSSON

HISTORY

Annika Svensson grew up rich in Stockholm, lived the party life for a while, then decided she wanted "adventure" without really knowing what that meant. At 24, she sailed out of Stockholm on her 35-foot sail yacht accompanied by her lover of the moment, a professional archaeologist. The first destination on their around-the-world tour was Medici.

Their trip was cut short when Medician outlaws hijacked her boat and held them for ransom. She was never in real danger, or at least she didn't feel like it. These pirates just wanted money, and why not? Here was her privilege, her peers' privilege, exposed; these pirates, as she learned, were both dirt-poor and also unwelcome in their own country's society. She convinced them to release her lover (who was not worth nearly as much), then promptly fell in love with the outlaws' leader, Paulo de Silva, and became increasingly sympathetic to their cause. When her parents refused to pay her ransom, she just took the money from the bank account herself and chose to stay.

After Paulo was killed by Di Ravello's troop s during a raid, Annika couldn't bear to see the crew he'd built disintegrate because of a lack of leadership, so she became their de facto captain instead.

Age	Late 20s
Born	Sweden
Profession	Outlaw/Pirate
Ethnicity	Caucasian
Hair	Blonde
Eyes	Blue
Height	5'10"
Weight	140 lbs.

TEO

HISTORY

Born in the small town of Aiyetoro, Teo quickly learned the ropes of piracy from the locals who patrol the Gulf of Guinea. Decades spent pillaging holds, abducting ransoms, and narrowly escaping the military educated Teo in the subtleties of brawling and economics, in shipping lines and naval combat, in fight or flight. Many of his friends started calling him the professor, as he often would bring back all the books he could find from the ships they took. Though not widely known in the rest of the gang, Teo possessed a near photographic memory. The long days and nights at sea, Teo would immerse himself in philosophy, mechanical schematics, Jules Verne, and any other book or source of knowledge he could get his hands on.

Soon, his insatiable thirst for knowledge sent him exploring the waterways of the world. Selling his skills as a sailor and a warrior, he came into the employ of Paolo de Silva. Paolo was a charismatic pirate who specialized in harassing the Medician army and ransoming wealthy tourists who came to soak in the warmth of Medici's sunlight, oblivious to the suffering that engulfed the rest of the country. Medici, so full of history and filled with modern technology, captured Teo's imagination. He quickly ascended the ranks until he was Paolo's right-hand man and closest companion.

Years passed, when one day the pirates abducted a young Swedish aristocrat named Annika. She was quickly more than a match for Paolo's leadership skills and both fell into a fiery relationship. Even in the short time, the couple became a much-loved institution among the pirates, and were seen as the soul of their crew, even if Teo had become the will. One fateful day, Paolo perished at the hands of Di Ravello's militia on a routine raid, and much to Teo's surprise, the crew rallied to Annika. Trusting Paolo's judgment, Teo served her as though she were his friend's reincarnation.

As the years passed, much of the crew got absorbed into the revolution or died. Soon, Annika and Teo found themselves as two smugglers against the world. Annika quietly supported Teo's constant search for knowledge and Teo in turn never doubted her leadership, thus forging their unbreakable friendship.

Age	Late 30s
Born	Kismaayo, Somalia
Profession	Outlaw/Pirate
Ethnicity	Somali
Hair	Bald
Eyes	Brown
Height	5'10"
Weight	230 lbs.

TOM SHELDON

HISTORY

Tom Sheldon is a longtime Agency operative who first came into Agency employ in the sixties. Sheldon was active during the various Agency black ops of the Vietnam War (including ops in Laos and Cambodia). Sheldon was active in the South American Theatre during the eighties and also played an important role in the operations that led to the election of the framed 'Papa Panay' of Panau, who was later deposed by Rico Rodriguez. His involvement in General Di Ravello's coup of Medici led to the assimilation of Rico Rodriguez into The Agency.

Age	66
Born	Abilene, TX on July 4th
Profession	Agency Operative
Ethnicity	American
Hair	Silver
Eyes	Blue
Height	6' 2"
Weight	220 lbs.

ROSA MANUELA

HISTORY

Rosa Manuela first came to public attention as a prominent lawyer. With WWII far in the rearview mirror, Europe was changing, and Medici along with it. A conciliatory voice like Manuela, was just what both sides of the country needed. Although Manuela was first elected to the Medician parliament as an unimportant member of a minor party, she soon came to lead a coalition of opposition parties. During this time, her husband was killed in a car accident. Many said that the killing was meant as intimidation; it left Manuela to raise her young son alone.

Age	60s
Born	Medici
Profession	Lawyer
Ethnicity	Salirosan
Hair	Brown
Eyes	Brown
Height	5'4"
Weight	110 lbs.

After Manuela led the opposition for a few years, she looked likely to unseat the government of the sitting president, Antonio Dante, in the next election. If she won, she would be Medici's first female leader. This could be proof that, like other European democracies, Medici was becoming comfortable with diversity. But when president Dante was assassinated shortly before the election, General Sebastiano Di Ravello blamed Manuela for the crime; the general roused a mob to harass Manuela's supporters. Manuela fled into exile the Night of the Bonfires, and has lived in South America ever since, lobbying with world leaders for the freedom of Medici from General Di Ravello and biding her time until it is safe to return to lead her homeland.

ZENO ANTIKYTHERA

HISTORY

Zeno Antikythera never really intended to move from Greece to Medici permanently; he relocated after learning about Bavarium and scheming to make a fortune on Bavarium tchotchkes. One thing led to another, and soon Zeno found himself in the employ of the dictator of Medici, who was quick to use psychological and physical harm to manipulate the frail and weak-minded scientist. Zeno spent some time working with Dimah, who saw him as mostly useless.

Age	70s
Born	A Greek island
Profession	Physicist
Ethnicity	Greek
Hair	White
Eyes	Blue
Height	5'5"
Weight	170 lbs.

GENERAL SEBASTIANO DI RAVELLO

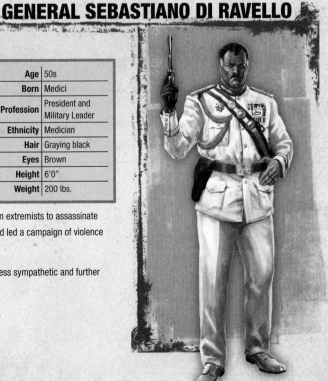

HISTORY

Sebastiano Di Ravello was born to a lower-middle-class Medician family and worked his way up to the highest echelons of the military; because he pulled himself up from near poverty, he has little sympathy for others who haven't done the same. Several decades ago, as he watched Rosa Manuela leading her people toward a more prominent place in Medician society, he decided she was forcing Medici in the wrong direction. To his eyes, she was promising prosperity to people who hadn't earned it and devaluing the accomplishments of honest Medicians.

Age	50s
Born	Medici
Profession	President and Military Leader
Ethnicity	Medician
Hair	Graying black
Eyes	Brown
Height	6'0"
Weight	200 lbs.

Because of this he took drastic measures to protect his country. To prevent Manuela from winning the election, Di Ravello induced several Medician extremists to assassinate the president. He then personally drew up documents that blamed Manuela, and led a campaign of violence against her supporters.

For decades, he has led Medici with an iron fist; over time he has grown even less sympathetic and further limited the people's rights.

BASICS

This section provides you with everything you need to free Medici of oppression!

HUD

Your Heads Up Display or "HUD" constantly updates the player on the status of critical things such as ammo, objectives, and health.

HEALTH

While there is no "Health Bar" visible on the screen, taking damage slowly causes the green to turn red before changing to a black and white perspective when near death.

NEAR DEATH

When you're near death, you enter slow motion and the environment changes to black and white, leaving your enemies in full color.

> ### Fight or flight!
> If only a few enemies remain, the near death state makes killing them easy, but in most cases you should still flee the area.

Use your tether to pull yourself away from the fight, activating your parachute to escape quickly. However, raising yourself into the air may make you easier to hit. Using your wingsuit when near death is not recommended as striking any object results in death.

WEAPON SELECTION

Press and hold the D-Pad to bring up the Weapon Selection screen. Tapping any direction on the D-Pad quickly selects the weapon.

- ✛ Special Weapon
- ✛ Two-Handed Weapon
- ✛ Dual Wield Weapon
- ✛ GE-64 Explosives

AMMO COUNT

Your current gun and amount of ammo is displayed in the bottom-right corner of the screen. The left number is the amount of ammo left before you need to reload, the number to the right is the amount of ammo left in your reserve.

DETECTOR

The detector is a multi-stage icon that begins to glow when you're near the objective, which is then highlighted with a white circle that marks its exact location.

This initially works for collectibles. When using the Vehicle Detector, the same effect happens when you're close to a vehicle that you have not brought back to your garage yet.

GRAPPLE CROSSHAIR

The Grapple crosshair appears in the center of the screen on the object you are aiming at, or the furthest possible object you can grapple. When you initiate a dual grapple, half of the crosshair illuminates while the other half remains dark until you release the second grapple.

HEAT

Heat is the amount of attention you have attracted from Di Ravello's military. This appears as a row of five stars that light up as you hit each level of Heat. Each Heat level comes with a different response from the enemy, sending stronger units as you increase in level.

Aside from each level of stars, the Heat Meter also lets you know when you're in view of Authorities, which means you will be immediately met with resistance if you decide to do anything violent. While in a Combat Zone, all enemies immediately begin to attack without warning.

During engagements, the enemy begins to call reinforcements. Eliminate all enemies in the area to prevent the reinforcements from being called, or escape the area to avoid the fight. Once they have lost visual, the heat meter turns white and a small circle indicates the amount of time remaining before your Heat clears. This meter resets if you are spotted.

Enemy Response by Heat Level

	LAND	SEA	AIR
★	Military Jeep/Private	Light Patrol Boat/Private	N/A
★	Military Jeep/Private	Light Patrol Boat/Private	N/A
★	Military bike/Scout	N/A	N/A
★	Military Jeep/Private	Light Patrol Boat/Private	Machine gun helicopter/helicopter pilot
★	Military bike/Scout	Heavy Patrol Boat/Private	N/A
★	Military Jeep/Private	Light Patrol Boat/Private	Machine gun helicopter/helicopter pilot
★	Military bike/Scout	Heavy Patrol Boat/Private	Rocket helicopter/helicopter pilot
★	Military mounted gun Jeep/Elite, Private	N/A	N/A
	Small tank/tank driver	N/A	N/A
	Military Jeep/Private	Light Patrol Boat/Private	Machine gun helicopter/helicopter pilot
★	Military bike/Scout	Heavy Patrol Boat/Private	Rocket helicopter/helicopter pilot
★	Military mounted gun Jeep/Elite, Private	Corvette	Machinegunner helicopter/helicopter pilot
★	Small tank/tank driver	N/A	N/A
★	Medium tank/tank driver	N/A	N/A

MENUS

Press Touchpad/View to summon the menu. From here, you can check out the Map, Gear Mods, Leaderboards, and your overall progress in the game. Switch between the different sections by pressing L1/LT or R1/RT.

MAP

The map lets you quickly view liberated areas, as well as find challenges, resupply points, missions, and collectibles once they are discovered. You can toggle what's visible on the map by pressing Square or X to open the Legend and select which options you'd like to see.

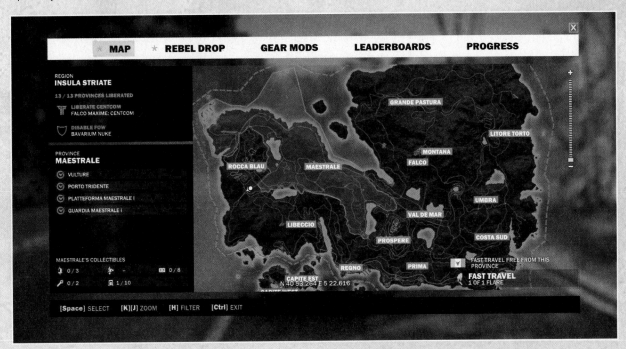

Move around the Map with Left Stick and zoom in with Right Stick Up/Down.

Liberated areas of the map appear as blue, with the oppressed areas showing up as red. Challenges are accessible only in liberated areas.

FAST TRAVEL

You can fast travel from the Map, assuming you have a flare on hand. To do this, press X/A on a challenge, settlement, or base, then select Fast Travel. Once the load to your location completes, you will be standing on the side of a helicopter.

Leap of Faith

The helicopter that drops you off when you fast travel cannot be hijacked, leaving you to jump off above your location.

Freedom!

A Province is liberated by freeing all settlements and destroying all bases within its borders.

Flares can be resupplied by picking them up at different resupply points, which are marked on the map and unlocked by liberating areas and completing random encounters.

SETTING A WAYPOINT

Set a waypoint by pressing X/A and selecting Set a Waypoint.

MOVEMENT

Standard movement is done by moving the Left Stick. There is no sprinting, but this isn't a problem when you have a tether and a parachute.

TETHERING

Tap L1/LT to grab the wall, ground, or object in front of you and rapidly pull yourself toward it. If you haven't pulled your parachute or activated your wingsuit, you'll be attached to the object via the grapple.

WINGSUIT

The wingsuit allows you to fly across the map at high speeds. Activate it by pressing Triangle/Y while you're in the air.

You can adjust your pitch and yaw while in Wingsuit mode by using the Left Stick. Getting low to the ground before pulling up allows you to best maintain your speed. Staying low to the ground is risky since hitting a building or tree puts you in a near-death state instantly.

The tether can be used while in your wingsuit. Press L1/LT to grab the object in front of you, causing you to sling shot past it even faster than before. Using this tether method, you can keep yourself in the air indefinitely—unless you hit an object, of course!

PARACHUTE

The parachute is a life saver, allowing you to avoid death in its multiple forms.

When falling from the sky, activate the parachute by pressing X/A, then control your descent with the Left Stick.

If you're in a vehicle that's heading for an explosive end, hold X/A to deploy your parachute from inside, immediately ejecting you from the vehicle.

While parachuting, you can use your tether on the ground or another object to pull yourself forward. Aiming directly in front of you grants the most speed when pulling yourself toward the tether point. Rico automatically lets go as you move past the spot you tethered.

Find yourself about to smack into a wall while you have your wingsuit activated? Quickly activate your parachute to soften the blow.

VEHICLES

Vehicles provide a varying degree of transportation around the world. Mixing vehicles with your parachute, tether, and wingsuit allows you to traverse the world quickly.

AIRPLANES

While airplanes are the fastest way to travel around, they are also just a one-way ticket unless you're planning on landing them at an airport. If you're bringing a plane to an outpost, slam it down into one of the larger objects that you need to destroy to start the attack while you safely parachute in.

LAND VEHICLES

Cars are everywhere in a variety of types. You'll find anything from a Vespa to a fully loaded tank with Bavarium Powered armor. Remember when you jump out of a moving car, it is likely to explode on the next object it hits, so if you want to keep it park it somewhere safe.

If you're driving a car on the road with a waypoint set, arrows appear on the road showing the way to the objective you have marked. These directions only use main roads, so a more direct path may be possible.

HELICOPTERS

While helicopters are slower than planes, they allow you to land almost anywhere and they're incredibly easy to use in combat.

Military Helicopters can make short work of any outpost, just beware of the AA that lines bigger bases. Either hack the AA systems or use the outpost maps to locate the Anti-Air rockets and destroy them before they destroy you.

BOATS

Stranded between Islas? Tether onto somebody's boat and drive yourself to shore. Jet Skis make for quick travel from Isla to Isla, but they are incredibly vulnerable to attack, which makes them a poor option if you're surrounded by enemies.

Only one military boat allows Rico to operate the gun and drive: the Rebel Corvette.

COMBAT

Whether it's an enemy, vehicle, or a deer in the middle of the road, you must fight your way through all of the enemies in *Just Cause 3*, and this section tells you how.

FINDING WEAPONS/AMMO

Weapons storage can be found and raided for grenades and ammo within police stations and other fortified structures. During combat, you can collect ammo by running over a weapon with the same type of ammo. For example, if you're using a shotgun, kill an enemy holding this weapon, then run over the gun to pick up the ammo.

Weapons can be switched out for your currently equipped gun by pressing Triangle/Y. Switching weapons to something that is compatible with your enemy's ammo type keeps you in the fight longer.

Grenades can also be collected during combat. They have a floating grenade icon above their location. Simply run over the grenade to collect it.

MELEE

Pressing Circle/B unleashes a highly damaging elbow on your enemy, knocking them back with the ability to kill them.

TETHER

Your tether can be used for traversal, combat, stunting, and destructive fun. The tether could be considered the highest damage weapon since it can one-shot kill most enemies by throwing them or tossing objects at them.

TETHER KICK

Tap L1/LB to tether an enemy just like you would tether to an object you want to pull yourself toward. This sends Rico flying feet first at the enemy, kicking the enemy a short distance leaving Rico standing and ready to fight the next enemy.

TETHER THROW

Tether an enemy to an object, then increase the tension (L2/LT) before pressing Circle/B to send your enemy flying off into the direction of the other object you had tethered.

You can also tether pieces of the environment to the ground near the enemies, pulling towers of explosive barrels down onto the them. This is extremely helpful when you're out of ammo or grenades.

DUAL TETHER

Tether two enemies together by firing the first tether hook, then release while aiming at the second target. Once you have the enemies connected, increase the tension.

TWO-HANDED

Two-handed weapons are great against infantry. They hold a medium amount of ammo, but can make short work of fuel tanks and armored infantry. Since two-handed weapons carry less ammo, make every shot count. Headshots are extremely effective with these weapons. Choose between assault rifles, an LMG, or shotguns.

ASSAULT RIFLES

Assault rifle choices vary, each offering different benefits for their use. The U-39 Plechovka and CS Predator provide fully automatic rates of fire, but inflict less damage than the others. If you're a more accurate shot, consider taking the CS37 Misfortune. It allows for three-shot bursts. The UPM61, another good choice, fires one shot with each pull of the trigger.

LMG

The Urga Vdova 89 is your LMG. While you're likely to miss a load of shots while using it, this isn't a problem because this machine gun carries a ton of ammo. It's great against enemies and destroying bases, but ammo is sometimes hard to come across so you may find yourself searching for a new weapon when you run out.

SHOTGUNS

Shotguns have the most damage of all two-handed weapons. This comes at a price, however. They are effective only at close range, which means you must tether your way in close to the enemies to deal damage. You have the choice between a semi-automatic U-96 Kladivo or the fully automatic Automat U12.

DUAL-WIELD

Dual-wield weapons are your standard fare. Ammo for these guns is easily found on enemies and inside weapon racks. They excel at close range engagements, but can still prove to be a threat at mid-range if accurately used.

PISTOL

Pistols are semi-automatic, meaning that only one shot is fired each time you pull the trigger. They deal more damage than SMGs, but require precision and a quick trigger finger to dispatch groups of enemies.

SMG

Submachine guns, or SMGs, are automatic handheld weapons, firing their entire clip if the trigger is not released. Firing in controlled bursts helps conserve ammo. Due to their lower accuracy, get in close before spraying bullets at your target.

EXOTIC

There are two very different weapons in the Exotic weapons section, and both are unlocked by collecting vintage parts.

The CS44 Peacebringer is a high powered revolver. It is easily the best mid-range option in the Dual-wield section. Landing headshots at range is the best way to eliminate enemies with this gun, as its slow fire rate loses most close range battles.

The U-24 Zabijak is the only shotgun in the Dual-wield tree. You need a long to mid-range weapon like an assault rifle equipped in your two-handed slot to help you work your way in close against the enemies. While the U-24 can take down destructive objects, it may not be the best choice as you will be very close to the explosive or other object you're destroying.

SPECIAL

Special weapons are in the Destruction wing of the weapon sets. These guns are meant to deal large amounts of damage quickly. Use Special weapons against groups of enemies, vehicles, and destructible objects.

ROCKET LAUNCHERS

While rocket launchers are easily the best weapons for taking down buildings and vehicles, ammo is scarce in most places. Even with gear mods, you still carry a very limited amount of ammo.

Rocket launchers should be used primarily against armored vehicles and larger structures, leaving your grenades and other weapons to destroy light infantry vehicles and their occupants.

GRENADE LAUNCHERS

Grenade launchers deal less damage and are less accurate than rocket launchers, but those effects are countered by the increased ammo count.

Use grenade launchers to kill groups of enemies at a time, aiming for the center of the group and letting splash damage do the rest of the work.

LAUNCHING GRENADES

Grenade launchers are easier to aim when parachuting as they act much like mortars. They do travel slower than bullets and rockets, though, so you may need to lead a moving target to score a kill shot.

Aim for weak points of larger destructive objects, such as support beams or exposed panels, to get the most out of every shot.

SNIPER RIFLES

While sniper rifles allow you to kill most human enemies with a single shot, you need to use the scope and aim for headshots on the tougher ones.

Sniper rifles can also be used to destroy objects from far away. Carefully plot out every shot. For example, to destroy a water or radio tower, you must aim for the support beams, taking them out until the structure is critically damaged and begins to collapse.

EXOTIC

The sole Exotic of the Special weapons family is the Urga Stupka-210. This initially can only be found behind Ancient Tombs after you've paid your respects. Once you've visited every Ancient Tomb, the Urga Stupka-210 becomes available for Rebel Drops.

The Urga Stupka-210 is a hand-held mortar that packs quite a punch.

Look Up!

The explosive rounds from the Urga Stupka-210 must fire up into the air before returning down to the ground to hit their target. This means any small roof or object overhead can block the projectiles path and deal a large amount of damage to Rico and his allies.

Aiming this weapon is a little bit of a challenge. There is no clear indicator where the round will land, so you must adjust by aiming up or down to increase and decrease the range that the mortar round flies before impacting a target.

You can use it at close range for the greatest success, but this will most likely knock Rico over during the ensuing blast. Taller object make easy targets for the Stupka-210 so use it on things like radio towers or statues.

FOW

FOW Weapons are easily the strongest, most destructive weapons in the game. Each one is rewarded as a prize for completing different missions.

Dionysus PLDS-H: Unlocked after completing Missile Cowboy mission, this weapon grants you the assistance of a fighter jet that drops a payload of bombs on any target or location you mark.

The Thunderbird: This weapon can disable vehicles and Bavarium shields from long distances and becomes available after completing the Tangled Up in Blue mission.

M488: Fire the M488 from a distance and watch a small apocalypse happen on its target. Much like a rocket launcher, this weapon fires a rocket straight at its targets, but this one has a Bavarium powered warhead!

GRENADES

Grenades are a great choice when taking on groups of infantry. Using them against larger groups of enemies conserves lots of ammo, helping to ensure you never have to run from battle.

When parachuting down into an area, you can use grenades to take out pieces of equipment or some emplaced enemies to make your landing area much safer. Grenades can be upgraded in the Mods menu.

GE-64 (PLANTED EXPLOSIVES)

After completing the second mission, you are awarded with the GE-64 explosives. These can take a variety of forms, depending on the Mods you've equipped. They give you a fighting chance against tanks and other heavy vehicles, regardless of any other weapons you've equipped.

Use them to destroy anything and everything that gets in your way. Set up a trap for the enemy by placing them in the road or on a wall, then lure your foe toward the explosives.

Place them on some destructible objects like fuel tanks, billboards, or statues, then move away from the area before blowing them up to make yourself a bit harder to find.

THE ENEMY

Besides gravity and environmental hazards, there are three groups of enemies hunting you down as you travel Medici.

THE MILITARY

These guys have strength in numbers, attack vehicles, and weapons to hunt you with. They are normally found around bases and outposts, but are known to run checkpoints along the road in oppressed provinces.

THE DRM

The DRM is the local police force commonly found in towns. They lack the weaponry and vehicles of their military brothers, making towns much easier to take over. However, raise your heat too high and the military will still show up for the fight!

THE BLACK HAND

These guys are the cream of the crop, providing the greatest challenge in defeating them. Use heavy weapons, environmental items, grenades, vehicles, and anything else you can throw at them.

ADVANCING THE STORY

With so much to do in *Just Cause 3*, you might be wondering how the story advances. How do you actually retake Medici from General Di Ravello? Let's talk about that!

There are two major ways in which you conquer the island: Story missions and Liberations. Accomplishing challenges and grabbing collectible items can help you in this process because they have their own rewards, but neither of those is an essential part of the main story.

STORY MISSIONS

Look for a bull's head icon on your map. That's the sign that there's a story mission available to you. If the icon is gray, you might need to do some preliminary work before starting the mission; your in-game map displays any requirements before you even need to take a step, so always look ahead of time to see what's going on.

Once a Story mission is fully ready to go, it shows up in yellow. Then all you need to do is to travel there and interact with the objective marker to begin. There's always an introductory movie, setting the stage for your action, and then you're placed into the mission itself.

Objectives appear in the upper-right corner of the screen when you're playing a Story mission. These identify your main goal at all times. Yellow objective markers then help you locate the targets involved in those actions (whether they're locations, enemy targets, or allies that you need to reach/assist).

There's a fair amount of variety in the Story missions, so you won't have a one size fits all approach to them. Always resupply before starting your missions, and bring your favorite weapons along.

Feel free to read ahead in the Story mission walkthrough to see what type of fighting is coming up. This lets you know which weapons to request from a Rebel Drop so that you're armed to the teeth. Close quarters fighting ahead? Get fast, high damage weapons. For long-range, go for accuracy. Tons of vehicles? Okay, make sure your explosives are at their best. You get the idea. Also request the appropriate vehicles and gear for each mission to start with everything you need.

Although you can lose during a Story mission, it's impossible to permanently fail one of them. You always get to retry each section until you succeed. Afterward, you're let loose on the island again and can run around doing whatever you want until starting the next Story mission. You're never forced to run these one after the other, nor are you ever locked into a specific area. That's nice, because it allows you to take breaks from the story whenever you want.

The one thing that stops you from advancing is a need for more territory; that's a prerequisite for a number of missions. As such, we can't talk about advancing the story without also looking heavily into…

LIBERATIONS!

Liberations are the fuel that drives your Story missions. That's why we talk about them together, even though they are very different activities. Liberations let you free occupied areas from militia control. It's all about finding critical infrastructure and destroying it so that the military loses control of the area.

Story missions are done in a fairly specific order, as you see the characters develop and work toward their goals. Liberations are different because they can start at any time. Walk into a place that's under enemy control and begin destroying everything that's theirs. Lo and behold, you'll soon liberate the area.

RED IS NEVER A GOOD SIGN

You can tell if an area is occupied by looking at the map. Occupied areas are surrounded by a dotted red line to let you know that they are dangerous locations.

Liberations have many rewards. You reduce Di Ravello's control over Medici, unlock Challenges, get easier access to collectible items (because the military isn't shooting at you every moment you explore), and gain access to future Story missions.

Besides all of that, Liberations are also incredibly fun! You're getting rewarded for fighting, blowing up everything you can, and the people still love you for doing it!

The mechanics of Liberations are somewhat involved. Look in the upper-left corner of the screen when you enter a new area. If the settlement is occupied, a number of icons pop up. These let you know what you need to complete to secure the settlement.

Pause the game and highlight an occupied area on the map. This displays a list of those icons and what they mean. You also find out which rewards Rico receives for completing the Liberation.

Go through the area, locate the required areas/targets, and do whatever needs to be done. Our Liberations chapter takes you through each of these actions so that you know how things are completed (and also, how to survive these encounters).

GEAR MODS

Different mods are unlocked by earning the required amount of gears in their field. This is done by completing challenges; each one can award up to five gears, based on your performance.

Mods can be toggled on and off by pressing X/A while you have them highlighted in the Gear Mods menu.

Every challenge affects a different section of Mods. A full breakdown of these is available in the Mod section.

DESTRUCTION MODS

Destruction Mods are aimed at increasing your destructive capabilities by upgrading your grenades. Gears are earned by completing destruction frenzies with a total of 100 of 125 available to gain every Mod.

EXPLOSIVES MODS

Complete Crash Bomb Challenges to earn Gears for Explosives Mods. This set helps increase the effectiveness of your GE-64 Explosives. You need 45 of the 60 available gears to unlock all Mods in this section.

WEAPON MODS

Weapon Mods are unlocked by completing Shooting Galleries. This increases the amount of ammo you can carry for Special weapons, as well as providing access to precision aim and faster restocking on Rebel Drops. Only 20 of the 25 available gears are needed for all upgrades.

TETHER MODS

Scrapyard Scrambles provide the gears necessary for Tether Mod Upgrades. These allow you to deploy more dual tethers while also increasing their pulling strength and endurance.

TRAVERSAL MODS

Completing Wingsuit Courses unlocks gears for Traversal Mods. While the name may make you think that all of these are just for moving, a few of them actually increase the amount of damage you deal with your tether kick, and reduce the amount of damage you take from physical impacts. Only 105 of the 135 gears available are needed to unlock all of the Mods.

LAND VEHICLE MODS

Land Vehicle Mods are unlocked by completing Land Races. These only affect land vehicles acquired by Rebel Drops. The Vehicle Detector is also available in this skill tree; this tool helps you locate cars that you haven't yet collected. Be warned, though; gathering the different collectibles becomes a bit harder with this enabled as the detector shows up in the same way on the HUD.

Another feature in this tree that's important to note is the ability to increase the number of Beacons you can keep on hand. This allows you to call multiple drops without worrying about finding more Beacons.

For all of the Mods in this section, 70 of the 90 available gears are necessary.

AIR VEHICLE MODS

Air Race Challenges award gears for Air Vehicle Mods when completed. These have the standard Nitrous boost and restock speed increase, but also those that allow you to carry more Fast Travel Flares. This comes in handy early on when much of the map is oppressed. Only 40 of the 60 possible gears are needed to unlock all Air Vehicle Mods.

SEA VEHICLE MODS

Complete Sea Races to unlock gears toward Sea Vehicle Mods, which allow your vehicle to boost forward and/or jump into the air to avoid obstructions.`

LEADERBOARD

The Leaderboard is all about bragging rights. Complete different Feats, set high scores, and call out your friends to beat your scores.

TRACKING A FEAT

Press Square/X on any Feat to set yourself up to track it in-game. This causes the Feat to show up the moment you begin to perform it. Tracking a Feat is useful for either practicing one or watching your progress from the lower end of the leaderboard.

CALLING OUT A PLAYER

Once you have a Feat selected, press Triangle/Y and then select their name from the list. You can challenge any player, regardless of their rank on that leaderboard, even if they haven't set a record in that section yet.

COLLECTIBLES

REBEL SHRINES

Small candlelit shrines in memory of fallen rebels. Light them to collect them.

DI RAVELLO TAPES

Hear the story of Di Ravello how he would tell it. Collect all of the tapes covering his rise to power all the way to present day.

VINTAGE PARTS

Vintage parts to guns and vehicles are hidden throughout each region. Dig them all up to gain their rewards.

DAREDEVIL JUMPS

Grab a vehicle and go flying off the ramps marked on the map to collect these jumps.

ANCIENT TOMBS

Ancient Tombs belonging to great people from long ago. These are found only in Isla Striate and grant you a hand-held mortar once you've paid your respects.

REBEL DROPS

Rebel drops become unlocked after completing the "Mario's Rebel Drops" mission. They allow you to receive weapons and vehicles anywhere on the map.

Mario: but we can only supply what you can find, so get cracking!

BEACONS

Beacons are needed to call in Rebel Drops. These can be found at gas stations or awarded for helping pedestrians and clearing outposts.

DROP CONTENTS

Each drop can contain a vehicle of any type, a Two-handed weapon, a Dual-wield weapon, and a Special weapon. This allows you to completely change your entire load out and mode of transportation on the fly. Until you have unlocked upgraded Mods, each weapon takes a short amount of time before it can be requested again.

UNLOCKING MORE DROP ITEMS

Additional items can be unlocked for Rebel Drops by advancing in the story and meeting other requirements.

GARAGE BLUEPRINTS

Blueprints are gathered from any vehicle brought to the garage. The only vehicles that cannot be chopped up for Blueprints are military units.

MILITARY UNITS

Military Units unlock by clearing bases with the different provinces. Once the base is clear, you are notified that the vehicle is now available for Rebel Drops. No further action is needed.

SPECIAL

Special items are unlocked by completing missions and challenges, and by gathering the different collectibles. A small icon next to a locked item indicates what's needed to unlock the item.

CHALLENGES

Feel like the enemy is gaining the upper hand? Complete some Challenges to earn gears and unlock Mods to improve your game.

WINGSUIT COURSES

Wingsuit through the rings to earn points. Earn bonus points by flying through red rings or by skimming the ground.

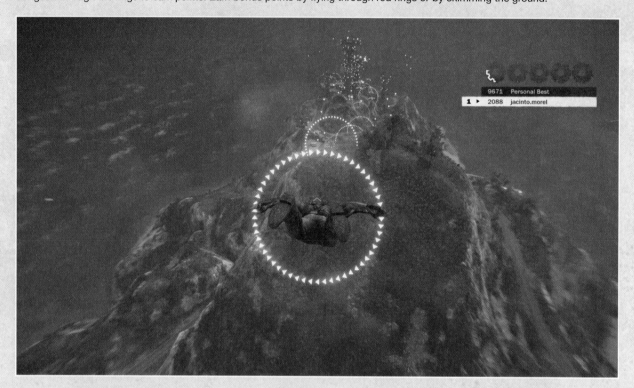

LAND RACES

Drive your car through all the checkpoints, finishing before time runs out.

SCRAPYARD SCRAMBLES

Gather as much Bavarium as you can, using Dimah's patented Bavarium Attractor. Earn more time by delivering Bavarium to the pit in large quantities.

CRASH BOMBS

Your vehicle is a bomb that goes off if you stay below the speed threshold for too long. Crash into the target. Fast runs and big explosions earn greater rewards.

SHOOTING GALLERIES

Shoot as many targets as you can before time runs out. Hits increase your score multiplier while misses reset it.

DESTRUCTION FRENZIES

Destroy everything! Keep the destruction flowing to keep your multiplier up and maximize your reward.

SEA RACES

Sail through all of the checkpoints in a race against the clock.

AIR RACES

Fly through all the checkpoints and reach the finish line as fast as you can.

WEAPONS

THE PERFECT ARSENAL

This chapter features all of the weapons that are available in *Just Cause 3*. To get the most out of your tools, you need to know what they're capable of doing.

TWO-HANDED WEAPONS

ASSAULT RIFLES

Assault Rifles are a comfortable blend of range, speed, and firepower. They're more versatile than LMGs and Shotguns, so they're an excellent choice when you don't know what to take on an upcoming mission.

U-39 PLECHOVKA	
DAMAGE	
ACCURACY	
STABILITY	
FIRE RATE	
CAPACITY	

The Plechovka is a light hitter when it comes to Assault Rifles; don't expect it to wade through your targets with reckless abandon. It's a middle-of-the-road weapon that has a very good rate of fire. Keep your target in your sights and whittle them down.

CS PREDATOR	
DAMAGE	
ACCURACY	
STABILITY	
FIRE RATE	
CAPACITY	

The Predator is almost a full-out improvement over the Plechovka. Its boosts in Accuracy and Stability make it a delightful weapon to shoot; you hit your targets quite well at most ranges. The drop in Firing Rate and Capacity is a small price to pay for most applications.

CS27 MISFORTUNE

DAMAGE	
ACCURACY	
STABILITY	
FIRE RATE	
CAPACITY	

The Misfortune does high damage and has very reliable Accuracy, as well. This gun is a killer, and it lets you have many of the advantages of a normal Assault Rifle while still approaching the Accuracy of a Sniper Rifle.

UPM61

DAMAGE	
ACCURACY	
STABILITY	
FIRE RATE	
CAPACITY	

Similar to the Misfortune, this gun can keep shots on targets like a pro. Amazing Accuracy has a price in this case, and the UPM61 loses enough of its Firing Rate that its total damage output suffers a little. Choose this when you need an Assault Rifle with unparalleled Accuracy, but think about the Misfortune or Predator when you're simply trying to keep the damage pouring.

LIGHT MACHINEGUNS

Light Machineguns (LMGs) offer serious stopping power with sustained fire. They're a joy to use, especially if you know that you're going to be defending a position.

URGA VDOVA 89

DAMAGE	
ACCURACY	
STABILITY	
FIRE RATE	
CAPACITY	

For extended firefights, this weapon comes out on top. It doesn't have the sniping potential of the Assault Rifles (or Sniper Rifles, obviously). However, it's made to keep putting shots on target in prolonged bursts. When you're taking down large groups, this excels.

SHOTGUNS

Shotguns give you massive damage at close range. They're a weaker choice if you're going to be outside, fighting enemies with rifles of any sort. However, they're the best two-handed choice if you're assaulting a base, or going into a city environment (with lots of potential for sudden ambushes).

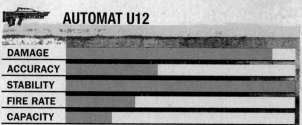

U-96 KLADIVO

DAMAGE	
ACCURACY	
STABILITY	
FIRE RATE	
CAPACITY	

You won't get anything good out of the Kladivo if you start a fight at medium or long range. This Shotgun is entirely designed to eliminate a single target quickly at almost point-blank range. That's what it's for. That's what it does well.

AUTOMAT U12

DAMAGE	
ACCURACY	
STABILITY	
FIRE RATE	
CAPACITY	

The U12 improves heavily on the basic nature of the Kladivo and gives you a weapon with more potential. It retains the catastrophic damage, but gives you more time to fire. You still take this for close quarters battles, but it can handle heavier single targets or even small groups of targets in its ideal range.

DUAL-WIELD WEAPONS

PISTOLS

Pistols are a controlled choice for your Dual-wield slot. They are easy to use, hit their targets often, and don't have a big downside. However, they lack the ability to slice through groups like SMGs. And the Exotic Dual Wield options are superior when it comes to firepower.

U-55S POZHAR

DAMAGE	
ACCURACY	
STABILITY	
FIRE RATE	
CAPACITY	

You aren't going to be very happy with the Pozhar unless you don't have any other options; it's a mediocre weapon that doesn't have any use compared to its alternatives.

CS SPECTRE MARK V

DAMAGE	
ACCURACY	
STABILITY	
FIRE RATE	
CAPACITY	

The Spectre barely gives up anything from its other stats to deal major damage compared to the Pozhar. It's a much better weapon choice for anyone who wants to stay with Pistols. It's still usurped by the Peacebringer, but you won't be disappointed when you're using it!

SUBMACHINEGUNS

Submachineguns (SMGs) have all the firing rate you'll ever need. They really help to kill off groups of lighter enemies at short range.

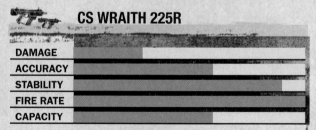

PRIZRAK U4

DAMAGE	
ACCURACY	
STABILITY	
FIRE RATE	
CAPACITY	

The Prizrak is a fast-firing SMG that has weaker secondary stats. It's quite nice when you're fighting enemies that can be staggered (because your Firing Rate is too high for them to handle). Against anything else, it's a poor choice.

CS WRAITH 225R

DAMAGE	
ACCURACY	
STABILITY	
FIRE RATE	
CAPACITY	

The Wraith lays things to waste at short range. It's a viable weapon at almost any time in the game, and is at its best when destroying groups of weaker targets.

CS9 PDW-K

DAMAGE			
ACCURACY			
STABILITY			
FIRE RATE			
CAPACITY			

The CS9 handles quite differently compared to the other SMGs. It's much slower and has very high damage.

You won't obliterate groups of weaker targets quite as well because of the loss in Firing Rate, but you can still put the hurt on them and the damage often makes up for it.

The CS9 pays for itself the most when you take on heavier, single targets. The extra damage is most noticeable there, when you're fighting Elites, Commanders, and other big-ticket enemies.

EXOTICS

The Exotic guns in the Dual-wield category are there to let you bring massive pain to a battlefield. These heavy hitters take out big targets with prejudice.

CS44 PEACEBRINGER

DAMAGE			
ACCURACY			
STABILITY			
FIRE RATE			
CAPACITY			

Speaking of high-health targets, that's what the Peacebringer is made to take out. This pair of Revolvers is able to give a knock-down punch to your most worrisome targets. Match it with a two-handed weapon that can take on groups so that you have one gun for soft enemies and another for the big guys.

U-24 ZABIJAK

DAMAGE			
ACCURACY			
STABILITY			
FIRE RATE			
CAPACITY			

Another option for destroying heavy enemies is the Zabijak. Pair these Shotguns and ambush your targets around corners. Though weak out in the field, this weapon combo is amazing when you're fighting inside bases or in other close quarters situations.

SPECIAL WEAPONS

ROCKET LAUNCHERS

You don't always have the time or inclination to commandeer a vehicle. That's where Rocket Launchers come into play. These ranged weapons deliver unstoppable damage. They help you take out Tanks, APCs, Helicopters, Planes, and everything in between. If you're going into a vehicle-based mission or situation, make sure that you have some type of Rocket Launcher with you.

UVK-13

Your most basic Rocket Launcher is the UVK-13. It's fine for taking out individual vehicles, but it doesn't have the truly murderous power of the Fire Leech or the Capstone Hydra.

FIRE LEECH

The Fire Leech gives you a Rocket Launcher with much more spread. You can target and attack up to eight targets at once with this. Though some aiming and lock-on time are required, this weapon lets you pepper an area with explosives. Very nice for Liberations or defensive Story missions.

CAPSTONE HYDRA

Your Capstone Hydra fires five rockets at a time. When you're taking on the heaviest Tanks and Helicopters, it helps to have this thing packed away

GRENADE LAUNCHERS

Clear groups of targets quickly with a Grenade Launcher. The more enemies the General sends, the more valuable your launcher is going to be. Rocket Launchers are superior for anti-vehicle work, while Grenade Launchers excel at anti-personnel applications. Both can cross over and work in either situation, but you get the most out of your launchers when you use them against their ideal targets.

 CS NEGOTIATOR

Infantry elimination is good enough with the Negotiator. It takes out a decent spread and does moderate damage.

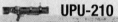 **UPU-210**

Firing a wave of grenades, the 210 annihilates weaker troops, letting you clear a field without much delay.

SNIPER RIFLES

Sniper Rifles give you a wonderful option for taking out high-end enemy targets. Commanders, Black Hand troops, Elites, and Assault Troops are all great examples of enemies that are better killed before they have a chance to shoot at you. Sniper Rifles make that a reality. You give up quite a bit of vehicle/building destruction to take one of these, but it's worthwhile if you're having trouble with higher-end infantry.

USV 45 SOKOL

DAMAGE	
ACCURACY	
STABILITY	
FIRE RATE	
CAPACITY	

The Sokol murders high-end infantry. It has a nasty recoil and takes more time to aim because of that weak point, but you aren't supposed to use it when you're under pressure. Save this for long-range fights, especially when the targets have massive health.

CS110 ARCHANGEL

DAMAGE	
ACCURACY	
STABILITY	
FIRE RATE	
CAPACITY	

The Archangel fills a similar niche to the Sokol, but it does away with the latter's weak point. This Sniper Rifle is smooth and clean with its shots, so you won't have to lose as much time adjusting between shots. It's a lovely weapon.

EXOTICS

The only Exotic here is a Mortar, and it's great at breaking up parties.

URGA STUPKA-210

The Stupka-210 is similar to the Grenade Launchers; it's there to take out waves of weaker targets. This is very nice for Story missions where there are battlefields with many targets.

FOWS

These special weapons are unlocked throughout the Story. Each of them has different functions, so we'll address them individually to get a really good idea about them.

DIONYSUS PLDS-H

This weapon designates a site for attack from the air. Allied airplanes fly in and bomb the location that you select. Take this during Liberations so that you can do even more damage to hardened buildings.

THE THUNDERBIRD

The Thunderbird disables Bavarium shields and enemy vehicles. It's fine for select Story missions, but is often a somewhat limited option. Most of the other special weapons are more versatile, so only take this when you know that shielded targets are involved in the coming battles.

M488

Last, but never least, the M488 destroys whatever it hits. Even Bavarium-shielded Tanks/Helicopters are destroyed in a single shot as long as you fire when the shields are down.

VEHICLES

Now we'll go through all of the vehicles that are found throughout Medici. Civilian and military equipment can (and should) be commandeered so that you get around the island quickly and take out anything that tries to stop you.

Being a rebel is all well and good, but no one is saying that you can't get around in style!

MOTORCYCLES

Motorcycles are fast and agile. They're some of the better land vehicles for getting you around Medici, but they aren't much to write home about during combat. You don't have any protection, and you might crash into any number of targets while zipping around. It's fun but dangerous to use these vehicles during missions (though they're wonderful for sight-seeing).

MV402

SPEED		
POWER		
AGILITY		
ARMOR		
COMBAT		

With an open-throttle speed over 260 km/h, the MV402 is not recommended for novice riders. Only experts need apply.

'69 STRIA SUSSURRO

SPEED		
POWER		
AGILITY		
ARMOR		
COMBAT		

Stria's easily-maintained and gas-friendly vintage moped has long been a favorite of Medicians looking for fast transport without the hassle of a car.

MUGELLO FURIA MS-316

- SPEED
- POWER
- AGILITY
- ARMOR
- COMBAT

When you think Mugello, you think fast, and this high-end sports bike delivers. Speed trials have clocked it at an unreal 200 km/h.

STRIA RISATA

- SPEED
- POWER
- AGILITY
- ARMOR
- COMBAT

The Stria Risata offers all the reliability and economy of the Sussuro with a more robust engine that makes longer trips more practical. Top speed is 120 km/h.

STRIA GIOVANNI

- SPEED
- POWER
- AGILITY
- ARMOR
- COMBAT

The myth of the open road is alive and well when you're cruising on a Stria Giovanni, Stria's crowning achievement in the realm of motorcycle engineering.

VINTAGE STRIA M7

- SPEED
- POWER
- AGILITY
- ARMOR
- COMBAT

Classic design and growling power are the defining characteristics of the Stria M7. The model enjoys a cult following among Medici's gearheads.

PAVOUK U-15

- SPEED
- POWER
- AGILITY
- ARMOR
- COMBAT

When the road gets rocky, rely on the Pavouk U-15. This expertly crafted cycle aces even the hairiest of off-road missions.

OFF-ROAD

Off-Road vehicles give you more freedom to explore the areas off the beaten path. They're perfect if you're hunting for collectibles, or if you're simply wandering around and don't want to worry whether you stay on the road or drive off into the hills.

Most of these are not sensible for combative purposes, though the Monster Truck is a fun choice as long as there aren't any heavy weapons or vehicles in your way.

GESCHWIND V3000

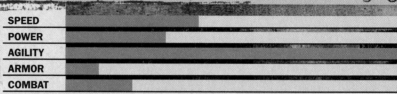

SPEED	
POWER	
AGILITY	
ARMOR	
COMBAT	

As capable as a Medician mountain goat at tackling tough terrain, the Geschwind is a favorite of Medician smugglers, revolutionaries, and teenagers.

CUSTOM GESCHWIND

SPEED	
POWER	
AGILITY	
ARMOR	
COMBAT	

This upgrade of the popular Geschwind V3000 is a zippy, more powerful mountain goat for any revolutionary's off-roading needs.

AUTOSTRAAD KLETTERER 300

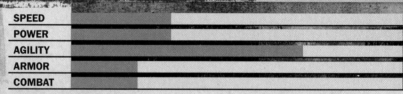

SPEED	
POWER	
AGILITY	
ARMOR	
COMBAT	

The Kletterer 300 pairs off-roading fun with Autostraad's signature reliability to make beaches, mountains, and backroads an adventurer's playground.

CUSTOM KLETTERER 300

SPEED	
POWER	
AGILITY	
ARMOR	
COMBAT	

This custom modification of Autostraad's capable off-roader features a beefier engine, improved maneuverability, and an excessively patriotic paint job. Vive Medici!

INCENDIARIO MONSTER TRUCK

SPEED	
POWER	
AGILITY	
ARMOR	
COMBAT	

Why sit in traffic when you can just roll over it? This beastly Incendiario monster truck turns sports cars into speed bumps.

VINTAGE CARS

Vintage Cars don't have combative oomph or much in the way of off-roading potential. Instead, these are the best cars to pick when you're in the mood for style over substance. What the vehicles lack in direct capabilities, they make up for in their visual flair.

WEIMARANER W3

SPEED	
POWER	
AGILITY	
ARMOR	
COMBAT	

They don't look like much, but these military surplus off-roaders are known for their reliability and durability, making them a staple for island-hopping adventures.

'63 AUTOSTRAAD WELTBUS

SPEED	
POWER	
AGILITY	
ARMOR	
COMBAT	

The '60s survive in Medici, thanks to the prevalence of these vintage camper vans by Autostraad. Great for clam bakes or solving mysteries; terrible for racing.

STRIA CUCCIOLA

SPEED	
POWER	
AGILITY	
ARMOR	
COMBAT	

What the Cucciola lacks in size, it makes up for in economy. It's a smart pick for gas mileage, and thrives in the car-friendly climate of the Mediterranean.

STRIA INFIMO S

SPEED	
POWER	
AGILITY	
ARMOR	
COMBAT	

Don't expect the Infimo S to get you anywhere in a hurry. These old compacts are best enjoyed with the steering wheel in one hand and a choice cigar in the other.

STRIA CARERA STANDARD

SPEED	
POWER	
AGILITY	
ARMOR	
COMBAT	

Relive college poverty in the Stria Carera hatchback, where it doesn't matter what you spill on the upholstery. It comes complete with a jammed tape deck

STRIA CARERA G

SPEED						
POWER						
AGILITY						
ARMOR						
COMBAT						

When two doors just aren't enough, pack your roommates in the back of Stria's Carera G to see your friend's band across town. Hey, what's that smell?

MODERN CARS

Modern Cars offer fairly good acceleration and handling. They're good vehicles all around, though they still won't have the survivability of a military vehicle. Use these when you want to get to places quickly and easily, but don't need heavy protection.

AUTOSTRAAD D90

SPEED						
POWER						
AGILITY						
ARMOR						
COMBAT						

Voted number one luxury sedan by Medici Auto Monthly, the D90 is the preferred status symbol of the nation's wealthy, pairing high-end performance and durability.

STRIA JOIA

SPEED						
POWER						
AGILITY						
ARMOR						
COMBAT						

The Joia combines responsive handling and reliability in an economic model sedan. Offers surprisingly reliable off-road performance.

STRIA KAVALA

SPEED						
POWER						
AGILITY						
ARMOR						
COMBAT						

Limited in top speed and acceleration, the Kavala's virtue lies in its handling, whether you're taking the kids to soccer or ramming your enemies off the road.

STRIA GIOCO

SPEED						
POWER						
AGILITY						
ARMOR						
COMBAT						

Stria's Gioco offers surprising pep for its size, with top speeds approaching 200 km/h on straightaways. It's particularly evasive in roadblock situations.

STRIA TORO

SPEED	
POWER	
AGILITY	
ARMOR	
COMBAT	

The heavy-duty Stria Toro handles any task thrown its way, with a towing capacity of 26,000 pounds, a max payload over three tons, and mountain-road handling.

SPORTS CARS

Sports Cars have all of the zip and style that you'd ever need. They have great top speeds, handle wonderfully, and are the kings and queens of the road. They splatter if you take them into combat, though.

The only reason to avoid Sports Cars for non-combat duty would be if you're going off-road or if you have trouble controlling these beauties and you keep crashing them.

MUGELLO RAFFINATI VITESSE

SPEED	
POWER	
AGILITY	
ARMOR	
COMBAT	

The Raffinati Vitesse's elegant exterior belies the raw power the 1960s could offer, with top speeds exceeding 170 km/h and handling to match.

WINDHUND 4

SPEED	
POWER	
AGILITY	
ARMOR	
COMBAT	

Autostraad's Windhund 4 has earned a reputation in Medici's underground racing circuit as a turn-hugging speedster built for drifting. It has a top speed of 240 km/h.

AUTOSTRAAD D700

SPEED	
POWER	
AGILITY	
ARMOR	
COMBAT	

The Autostraad D700 features robust off-the-line accelerations and top speed for its class. It's prone to handling issues after sustaining damage.

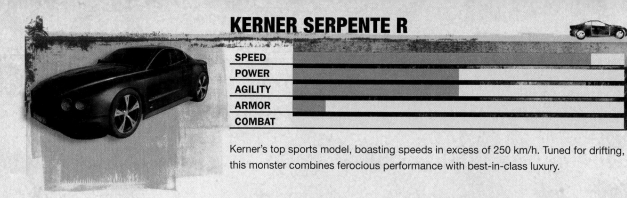

KERNER SERPENTE R

SPEED
POWER
AGILITY
ARMOR
COMBAT

Kerner's top sports model, boasting speeds in excess of 250 km/h. Tuned for drifting, this monster combines ferocious performance with best-in-class luxury.

'13 VIGUEUR

SPEED
POWER
AGILITY
ARMOR
COMBAT

Kerner's 2013 Vigueur combines a powerful drivetrain and classic styling into one of the most elegant and capable luxury vehicles touring Medici today.

MUGELLO VISTOSA

SPEED
POWER
AGILITY
ARMOR
COMBAT

Capable for surpassing 300 km/h, the Mugello Vistosa embodies everything you could want in an Italian supercar: passion, beauty, and exhilaration. For experts only!

MUGELLO QUIPOZZA F

SPEED
POWER
AGILITY
ARMOR
COMBAT

The original head-turner. This pristine '70s machine weds flawless mechanics and sex appeal with heart-stopping power. Capable of topping 250 km/h.

VERDELEON 3

SPEED
POWER
AGILITY
ARMOR
COMBAT

Only a handful of these eco-friendly supercars were ever imported. All were confiscated by jealous customs agents, hidden away in remote warehouses, and forgotten.

MUGELLO FARINA DUO

	SPEED	POWER	AGILITY	ARMOR	COMBAT

Mugello's most recent foray into circuit racing brings us the Farina Duo, driven by Sergio Flores to eight victories this season, including the Medici Grand Prix.

STRIA GHEPARDO 3S

	SPEED	POWER	AGILITY	ARMOR	COMBAT

The Stria Ghepardo, with its throaty roar and classical good looks, is a choice roadster for the discerning Medici driver.

UTILITY VEHICLES

Though large and lumbering, many Utility Vehicles have increased armor and can push things around. Instead of avoiding blockades, you drive right through the middle when you're in these (except for the Rustico; that's just there for pure silliness!).

AUTOSTRAAD REISENDER 7

	SPEED	POWER	AGILITY	ARMOR	COMBAT

Built to haul the heaviest loads, Autostraad's Reisender 7 is Medici's number one name in commercial driving. It also makes a fine battering ram.

'05 CHARMANT

	SPEED	POWER	AGILITY	ARMOR	COMBAT

What the Kerner Charmant lacks in speed and handling, it makes up for in sophistication. A favorite of the few Medicians who can afford this luxury.

STADT TRESOR ST 8530

SPEED		
POWER		
AGILITY		
ARMOR		
COMBAT		

Marked by its cumbersome handlings and limited top speed, the Tresor is most effective when throwing its weight around on the open road.

NASHORN 6100

SPEED		
POWER		
AGILITY		
ARMOR		
COMBAT		

This behemoth of industry is used to remove debris in large-scale mining operations. Once it gets rolling, don't get in its way.

CITISPEED ECO 75

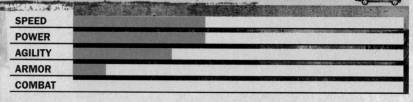

SPEED		
POWER		
AGILITY		
ARMOR		
COMBAT		

Recently incorporated into Medici's public transportation system, the environmentally-conscious Citispeed Eco performs best when kept above 80 km/h.

STRIA SWITZO AMBULANCE

SPEED		
POWER		
AGILITY		
ARMOR		
COMBAT		

If you're ever injured and you hear the Stria Switzo Ambulance coming your way, consider yourself lucky they responded at all. Tipping ensures quality service.

STRIA SWITZO

SPEED		
POWER		
AGILITY		
ARMOR		
COMBAT		

The workmanlike Switzo is the backbone of Medici's diminishing blue-collar work force, combining dependable service with ease of maintenance.

STRIA OBRERO

SPEED	
POWER	
AGILITY	
ARMOR	
COMBAT	

The Stria Obrero is an industrial workhorse, slow to hit top speed and impossible to push off the road. It's great for transporting wine.

STRIA RUSTICO

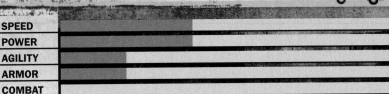

SPEED	
POWER	
AGILITY	
ARMOR	
COMBAT	

The Stria Rustico is the chariot of the honest farmer, keeping mouths fed across Medici. It's best when paired with nitrous, because why not?

STRIA CAMPANIA 115

SPEED	
POWER	
AGILITY	
ARMOR	
COMBAT	

The Stria Campania 115 is the oldest member of Medici's transit fleet, still chugging after decades of reliable service. It's great for creative stunting.

MILITARY CARS

Military Cars have improved armor, may have weapons of their own, and are some of the best things that you can take into Liberations and Story missions. These vehicles dramatically improve your chance of survival because they take the early hits for you, provide an opportunity for attack using any of their turrets, and can help you transport additional allies into the area while they too are protected.

WEIMARANER

SPEED	
POWER	
AGILITY	
ARMOR	
COMBAT	

The general purpose vehicle for military and rebel forces alike. Suitable for all terrains, it is especially capable in off-road situations.

STRIA FACOCERO

	SPEED	POWER	AGILITY	ARMOR	COMBAT

Co-opted by rebels from the DRM militia, the Stria Facocero is ideal for quick strike operations and truck bed shootouts.

STRIA OBRERO

	SPEED	POWER	AGILITY	ARMOR	COMBAT

The Stria Obrero is an industrial workhorse, slow to hit top speed and impossible to push off the road. It has been retrofitted for tactical transport by the rebellion.

CS BALTDJUR

	SPEED	POWER	AGILITY	ARMOR	COMBAT

The Baltdjur APC marks a watershed in siege warfare, capable of delivering reinforcements by land or sea to the most hectic combat areas. Its mounted gun excels in heavy combat.

URGA OGAR 7 V8

	SPEED	POWER	AGILITY	ARMOR	COMBAT

The lightning quick Urga Ogar 7 V8 buggy is the ideal vehicle for reconnaissance missions, harassment strikes, and off-road pursuit of targets.

STRIA FACOCERO W/ TURRET

	SPEED	POWER	AGILITY	ARMOR	COMBAT

Co-opted by rebels from the DRM militia, the Stria Facocero is great for quick strike operations and truck bed shootouts. It has been equipped with a machine gun mount.

URGA SZTURM 63A

SPEED	POWER	AGILITY	ARMOR	COMBAT

If you want to be king of the road, get behind the wheel of the Urga Szturm 63A. This armored vehicle perfectly blends defense, speed, and assault capabilities.

URGA FURA 570

SPEED	POWER	AGILITY	ARMOR	COMBAT

The burly Urga Fura 570 is built to take the hits and keep on rolling. Its rear cabin comfortably accommodates up to 12 soldiers for timely reinforcement.

TANKS

All Tanks have supreme survivability and lethal combat potential. They have machine guns and heavy cannons, and take many hits before being disabled. Your only loss in taking a Tank is that they aren't as fast or maneuverable as your other land vehicle choices, so it's better to commandeer or request one of these when you're already close to a major combat area.

CS ODJUR

SPEED	POWER	AGILITY	ARMOR	COMBAT

Equipped with a 14mm machine gun and a powerful anti-vehicle cannon, the formidable Odjur is the muscle of the Medician military.

IMPERATOR BAVARIUM TANK

SPEED	POWER	AGILITY	ARMOR	COMBAT

The Imperator assault tank is equipped with a heavy Bavarium shield that's capable of deflecting almost all explosive and ballistic weaponry.

URGA BKOLOS 2100

SPEED		
POWER		
AGILITY		
ARMOR		
COMBAT		

Urga's Bkolos 2100 light assault tank is the perfect complement to swift siege maneuvers or surprise flank attacks. It's equipped with a 76 mm turret.

SEA VEHICLES

Sea Vehicles aren't needed as often as terrestrial ones, but they're still very useful. When you're trying to go along the coast, take one of the speedier options, but look for the heavy craft (like the Custode 29, Powerrun, or Corvette) when combat is likely.

MINNOW FISHING BOAT

SPEED		
POWER		
AGILITY		
ARMOR		
COMBAT		

These small vessels are common to the waters of Medici, popular for a casual day at sea or chartered fishing excursion. At 20 knots, it does have a rather limited top speed.

WHALESHARK

SPEED		
POWER		
AGILITY		
ARMOR		
COMBAT		

Once a vibrant sector of the national economy, Medici's fishing fleet amounts to little more than these half-rusted hulks. They've been battered by decades of daily use.

BRISE 32

SPEED		
POWER		
AGILITY		
ARMOR		
COMBAT		

The world is your playground in the Brise 32, the sailboat of choice for Medici's sophisticates. It cruises at 20 knots when employing its motor.

DAME DE LA MER 99

SPEED			
POWER			
AGILITY			
ARMOR			
COMBAT			

The Dame de la Mer 99 brings luxury and sophistication to the high seas, with all hardwood decks, a king-sized cabin, and cruising speeds topping 40 knots.

PESCESPADA SS

SPEED			
POWER			
AGILITY			
ARMOR			
COMBAT			

Mugello's scintillating Pescespada SS racing boat cuts through whitecaps as though they were marshmallows. It easily achieves speeds of 70 knots in calm waters.

URGA HROCH

SPEED			
POWER			
AGILITY			
ARMOR			
COMBAT			

Designed with an armored front ramp for immediate beachhead deployment, the Urga Hroch is an essential tool when conducting island warfare.

CUSTODE 29

SPEED			
POWER			
AGILITY			
ARMOR			
COMBAT			

Topflight handling, superior pursuit speed, and a bow-mounted machine gun make the Custode 29 the perfect perimeter patrol unit.

CS POWERRUN 77

SPEED			
POWER			
AGILITY			
ARMOR			
COMBAT			

With first-response speed, tight maneuverability, and dual machine gun mounts, the Capstone Powerrun 77 is the enforcer unit of the high seas.

REBEL CORVETTE

SPEED			
POWER			
AGILITY			
ARMOR			
COMBAT			

The rebel seizure of these massive warships was a huge coup in the fight for naval supremacy. At a top speed of 40 knots, they can keep pace with any strike force.

STRIA PW 220 R-GT

SPEED			
POWER			
AGILITY			
ARMOR			
COMBAT			

The Stria PW 220 R-GT is the ultimate in nautical freedom. With speeds that spike at 60 knots, every well-struck wave is a first-class flight.

SQUALO X7

SPEED			
POWER			
AGILITY			
ARMOR			
COMBAT			

Wealthy Medicians only dare use Mugello's speedy and sexy Squalo X7 on secluded private lakes, where the risk of running afoul of trigger-happy soldiers is low.

HELICOPTERS

Helicopters are usually very well armed. The majority of these vehicles are your most aggressive option for firefights; they're delightful to use during Liberations, Story missions, or while causing general Chaos. These aircraft won't survive for too long under sustained enemy attacks, so watch out and dive for safety if your Helicopter is getting trashed.

EUBUS EAGLE

SPEED			
POWER			
AGILITY			
ARMOR			
COMBAT			

More than a helicopter, the Eubus Eagle is a status symbol among Medici's ultra-rich. Its utility is paramount in a nation composed of islands.

URGA POSTOLKA

SPEED		
POWER		
AGILITY		
ARMOR		
COMBAT		

This light assault helicopter is equally equipped to handle patrol detail, base sieges, or air-to-air firefights. It comes equipped with the Janus-45S minigun.

NEWS CHOPPER

SPEED		
POWER		
AGILITY		
ARMOR		
COMBAT		

Di Ravello's Ministry of Illumination and Stability has drafted these capable helis to report (inaccurately) on happenings around Medici's capital city.

CS NAVAJO

SPEED		
POWER		
AGILITY		
ARMOR		
COMBAT		

Capstone's assault chopper combines speed, power, and versatility. It offers two missile types: the rapid-strike 64 Volcanus and the punishing 99 Vindicator.

CS COMET

SPEED		
POWER		
AGILITY		
ARMOR		
COMBAT		

The CS Comet's highly armored chassis allows it to take risks when delivering reinforcements to the front lines. It is well protected, but has no weapons of its own.

URGA HROM D

SPEED		
POWER		
AGILITY		
ARMOR		
COMBAT		

The Urga Hrom D is pure mayhem with a rotor on top. With the Janus-88M minigun and 95 Volcanus missile pre-loaded, it can make entire bases disappear in seconds.

URGA RACEK

SPEED					
POWER					
AGILITY					
ARMOR					
COMBAT					

The Racek from Urga is a marine-focused helicopter specializing in ocean surveillance and rescue operations. Cruising speed is at 150 km/h.

URGA MSTITEL

SPEED					
POWER					
AGILITY					
ARMOR					
COMBAT					

The intimidating Urga Mstitel is equipped with four precision rocket launchers and a heavy machine gun. Soldiers scatter when this monster arrives at a skirmish.

GOLDEN URGA MSTITEL

SPEED					
POWER					
AGILITY					
ARMOR					
COMBAT					

Manufactured for Sebastiano Di Ravello's personal use, this fearsome chopper boasts four precision rocket launchers, a machine gun, and Bavarium shield technology.

PLANES

Planes get you from point A to point B better than anything else in the game. They have top-notch speed and don't have to worry about roads; you didn't pay for these, so ditching over any site and parachuting down is totally okay.

Though many are armed, they still can't take out ground targets as well as a Helicopter. On the flipside, your Planes survive longer, can get away from trouble in mere seconds, and are usually only endangered by other Planes and SAM sites.

URGA U17 AKROBAT

SPEED					
POWER					
AGILITY					
ARMOR					
COMBAT					

As Medici is an archipelago, chartered flights are common among those that can afford them. The Urga U17 Akrobat is the workhorse of the domestic flight circuit.

CS7 THUNDERHAWK

SPEED		
POWER		
AGILITY		
ARMOR		
COMBAT		

When it comes to aerial firefights, few top the CS7 Thunderhawk. It features the M98 machine gun, M-62 Mako repeating missiles, and M-78 Kaluga heat-seekers.

STRIA GHIBLI 3

SPEED		
POWER		
AGILITY		
ARMOR		
COMBAT		

It's not unusual to see the Stria Ghibli floating prop plane gliding over Medici. Its sea landing capabilities allow access to remote areas of the nation.

U-7 DRAVEC

SPEED		
POWER		
AGILITY		
ARMOR		
COMBAT		

Rain fire from the skies with the U-7 Dravec, equipped with both rockets and bombs for carpeting your enemies in chaos.

U41 PTAKOJESTER

SPEED		
POWER		
AGILITY		
ARMOR		
COMBAT		

The gargantuan U41 Ptakojester transport plane can hold an impressive 10 full-sized land vehicles in its cargo bay. A landing strip is definitely recommended.

CARMEN ALBATROSS

SPEED		
POWER		
AGILITY		
ARMOR		
COMBAT		

Developed by the Carmen brothers, the Albatross fighter plane was a staple during various sorties in the 1940s. It was abruptly phased out of service in favor of the land-based jets of the 1950s.

ENEMIES

THE MILITIA OF MEDICI

Medici's militia has been dramatically expanded during General Di Ravello's reign. As a military man himself, he looks to solve all of his problems with militaristic solutions. If you're going to free Medici, expect to encounter almost ceaseless resistance from these enemies. Know their strengths and weaknesses so that you can defeat them en masse!

PRIVATE

NAME	Private
HEALTH	60
WEAPON	U-39 Plechovka
NOTES	N/A
LOCATIONS	All regions

Privates are the rank and file troops for the Medici militia. You find them all over the island nation, and none of them is especially dangerous on their own. Sadly, they often in appear in squads that can pose a real threat to the rebels due to their numbers. Almost any weapon or attack is likely to be successful against a Private. They're easy to take down, have no armor, and aren't resistant to any form of attack. Lay waste to them, as needed.

ARMORED DRIVER

NAME	Armored Driver
HEALTH	60
WEAPON	U55 S Pozhar
NOTES	Tank and APC driver
LOCATIONS	All regions

Armored Drivers are found at the wheel of land-based military vehicles. If pulled out of their tanks or APCs, they're almost entirely worthless and cannot pose a major threat to you. Either shoot them with any of your weapons or get into their vehicles and turn the guns against their previous owners!

AIRPLANE PILOT

NAME	Airplane Pilot
HEALTH	60
WEAPON	U55 S Pozhar
NOTES	Airplane driver
LOCATIONS	All regions

Airplane Pilots aren't any better off than the Armored Drivers. Grapple onto their planes, pull the Pilots out of their cockpits, and throw them to their deaths. If you're on the ground, they can try to fight back, but will not threaten you for long.

HELICOPTER PILOT

NAME	Helicopter Pilot
HEALTH	60
WEAPON	U55 S Pozhar
NOTES	Helicopter driver
LOCATIONS	All regions

Yet another form of fodder for Rico's vehicular assaults. Use your weapons to kill any passengers before you go after the Pilots, and then commandeer their vehicles.

SCOUT

NAME	Scout
HEALTH	60
WEAPON	Prizarak 04
NOTES	Bike driver
LOCATIONS	All regions

Scouts are found most often in Story missions. They pursue you on motorcycles and can drive and shoot simultaneously. They're a dangerous distraction, but cannot survive much return fire. You can attack them directly, but for a flashy and effective counter, shoot out their front tires and watch the hapless bikers go tumbling.

MACHINEGUNNER

NAME	Machinegunner
HEALTH	500
WEAPON	Urga Vdova 89
NOTES	Only staggers from high caliber weapons such as sniper rifles, miniguns, revolvers.
LOCATIONS	All regions

Machinegunners have higher damage output than the troops we've covered so far. They're much tougher to kill, so you can't count on a few shots to put them in the dirt. Focus your heaviest weapons on them, including grenades, explosives, and whatever else you're carrying.

Heavy single-shot weapons are the best when you're attacking Machinegunners. Sniper rifles let you aim well, shoot for the head, and keep these enemies staggered. This prevents them from counterattacking effectively.

SNIPER

NAME	Sniper
HEALTH	60
WEAPON	USV 45 Sokol
NOTES	Switches to Pistol when at close range.
LOCATIONS	All regions

If you see the telltale laser from a Sniper, then either get to cover or attack immediately. These foes are weak when they take damage and die easily, and they're pathetic at close range. However, they do tremendous amounts of damage if you let them take pot shots at you.

Trace the line of their lasers back to the source to find the Snipers quickly. Either use your own long-range weapons to kill them before they get a proper bead on you, or grapple to short range and deal with the Snipers where they're weakest.

DEMOLITION

NAME	Demolition
HEALTH	250
WEAPON	UVK 13
NOTES	Only staggers from high caliber weapons such as sniper rifles, miniguns, revolvers. Switches to pistol when at close range.
LOCATIONS	All regions

Demolition troops are heavier and take many hits to bring down. Like Snipers, they're best eliminated at close range because they only have pistols to rely on. If you hold back and trade blows with them, you're likely to get beaten up. Stay behind cover and ensure that you have a place to retreat to if you start taking too much damage.

PARATROOPER

NAME	Paratrooper
HEALTH	175
WEAPON	CS Predator
NOTES	Doesn't stagger from fine caliber weapons such as pistols and SMGs.
LOCATIONS	All regions

Paratroopers are well-armored and have reliable amounts of health; they're a substantial threat and come in decent numbers if you see them at all. Try to kill these guys before they land because they cannot dodge while descending. This makes it easier to hit them and score kills quickly.

Once Paratroopers hit the ground, they spread out and act like Elites (high health, harder to stagger, etc.).

ELITE

NAME	Elite
HEALTH	175
WEAPON	CS Predator
NOTES	N/A
LOCATIONS	All regions

Elites have decent rifles, good health, and are deployed in any area where the fighting gets heavy. Keep them staggered with faster weaponry and thin their ranks without taking as much damage. If there are troops clustered around an Elite, use grenades or other explosives to bring the group down quickly instead of taking their hits while you deal with the Elite.

COMMANDER

NAME	Commander
HEALTH	300
WEAPON	Varies
NOTES	Spawns in some military bases.
LOCATIONS	Military bases, All regions

Commanders are found inside military bases, so you must defeat them when you're completing some of the harder Liberations. Vehicle attacks are excellent for killing them, but you always have alternatives. Lay explosives around a corner and detonate them when the Commander comes closer to attack you; snipe them, etc.

GUARD

NAME	Guard
HEALTH	60
WEAPON	Prizarak 04
NOTES	N/A
LOCATIONS	All regions

Guards have very little health and are weak at medium or long range. However, they can dish out reasonable damage if you get close to them because of their SMGs. Stay back and use weapons with superior range to kill them safely.

ASSAULT TROOPER

NAME	Assault Trooper
HEALTH	175
WEAPON	U96 Kladivo
NOTES	Their hits will "stun" you for a short while.
LOCATIONS	All regions

Assault Troopers are the bane of your existence if you get caught out by one of them. Their attacks stagger you, limiting your chance to respond as the damage begins to mount. As soon as you spot these guys, back off and find cover. The farther away you can engage them, the easier it is to avoid their staggering shots.

DRM PRIVATE

NAME	DRM Private
HEALTH	60
WEAPON	U55 S Pozhar
NOTES	N/A
LOCATIONS	Police stations

DRM Privates aren't any better than their regular militia equivalents. They're almost harmless and can easily be eliminated.

DRM SWAT

NAME	DRM Swat
HEALTH	350
WEAPON	CS Wraith 225R
NOTES	N/A
LOCATIONS	Police stations

DRM Swat troopers are much better than the Privates. They defend the police stations with high-damage SMGs, and their considerable health makes it difficult, dangerous, and foolish to trade blows with them. Use buildings/walls as cover, toss grenades, fire at long range, and keep away from SWAT troopers until they're badly wounded or killed outright.

DRM CAPTAIN

NAME	DRM Captain
HEALTH	250
WEAPON	Urga Vdova 89
NOTES	N/A
LOCATIONS	Police stations

DRM Captains guard their stations with LMGs. They provide heavy and continuous fire to support their allies. If you spot them, take out the Captains before worrying about the SWAT. Captains are slightly faster to kill, and they're effective at longer range (which makes them harder to flee from if you get into trouble).

BLACK HAND PRIVATE

NAME	Black Hand Private
HEALTH	410
WEAPON	CS Predator
NOTES	Doesn't stagger from fine caliber weapons such as pistols and SMGs.
LOCATIONS	Region 2 bases, region 3 bases and outposts

Black Hand Privates fight like Elites, but they have way more health. You see them in the late game, and it requires decent tactics and weaponry to defeat them unless they're isolated. Use heavy weapons to keep Black Hand Privates from firing back effectively.

BLACK HAND GHOST

NAME	Black Hand Ghost
HEALTH	500
WEAPON	CS Wraith 225R
NOTES	Only staggers from high caliber weapons such as sniper rifles, miniguns, revolvers.
LOCATIONS	Region 2 bases (rare) and region 3 bases.

Black Hand Ghosts have powerful SMGs, fire quickly, and can be a massive pain when you aren't ready for them. Back off and switch to long-range weaponry to ensure that you don't take too many hits and have more time to focus them down. Snipe these enemies with vehicle attacks, rifles, or explosives.

BLACK HAND TITAN

NAME	Black Hand Titan
HEALTH	1200
WEAPON	Urga Vulkan
NOTES	Doesn't stagger.
LOCATIONS	Region 2 bases (rare) and region 3 bases.

Nothing gets nastier than Titans. They have ungodly amounts of health, deal brutal damage, and won't stagger no matter what you're hitting them with. It's kill or be killed when you're facing them.

The good news is that Titans are not common targets and attack you only when you're going after high-level bases (in the later portions of the game). Once you start seeing them, use vehicles so that you get a bit of extra cover while you're fighting. Alternatively, back up and lure Titans to your position, and then use your most damaging weapons to ambush them and burst them down before they can beat you.

THE PATH TO FREEDOM

Rico Rodriguez is returning to his homeland. The people are under the boot of an oppressive regime headed by General Di Ravello, and you are going to change the way things are going. When soap, ballot, and jury boxes fail, Rico is ready to turn to the last box that he has: ammo.

He and Tom Sheldon start the game on an old prop plane. You're only moments away from the coastline, and Di Ravello's air defenses aren't going to wait very long. Watch the cutscene that begins everything, and then get ready as Rico climbs to the top of the plane. This is where the action begins!

WELCOME HOME

PROTECT THE PLANE

Your revolution won't last very long if the plane gets shot down, so the first priority is to defend the plane from surface-to-air-missiles. Rico has a rocket launcher, so he can do serious damage against anything on the ground below.

Look at the ground while scanning the area for missile batteries. These are highlighted by white boxes, and the word "Destroy" appears above them. You couldn't ask for a better invitation!

Fire at the batteries as soon as you have a good shot lined up. Ammo is not a problem, so you don't have to conserve anything. Just try not to miss, because reloading takes a few moments.

Infinite Ammo is a Rarity

Use your free rockets to destroy anything that looks fun to blow up. You won't get to have infinite rockets like this at other times, so enjoy the freedom while you have it! Shoot at bridges, enemies, buildings, etc.

Your flight isn't too dangerous as long as you keep detonating the batteries below. Look at the scenery and start getting a feel for the terrain. It's possible to pause the game by going into the menu, and that's where you can look at the map. Start getting your bearings now if you like.

The SAMs are going to be in front of the plane, so keep your eyes primarily focused on wherever the plane is turning.

After a couple of minutes, an enemy jet shows up. You can't do much about this, and the plane takes some major hits. Rico is thrown off into the night sky, and soon begins plummeting toward the ground.

LAND IN THE CAVE

A new goal appears underneath Rico. There's a cave down there that you should try to land in. Wait for a "Parachute" icon to pop up, and then press the button before you meet the ground in an unfriendly fashion. Direct Rico toward the cave, and float down toward your objective.

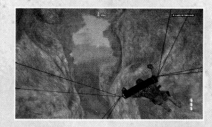

Settle onto the cave floor as safely as you can.

REACH MARIO

Your buddy Mario is close by. He calls for help, and you should head toward him soon. Look on the ground for a rocket launcher, and then pick one up when you find it.

Mario is higher up, and there isn't an easy way up the cave wall. At least, there wouldn't be for most people.

Try out your grappling hook. Pull Rico to the top of the cave, toward the yellow objective marker. Mario is up there, but enemy militia are all over the place. Help Mario take them out!

If you take too long to do this, Mario loses a ton of health. You can see his health in a yellow bar at the top of the screen, so that lets you know how aggressive to fight. If it starts getting too low, wade into the enemies with reckless abandon to make sure your buddy doesn't get killed.

MANY ROUTES TO VICTORY

There are multiple options for killing these enemies. You already have an assault rifle and a rocket launcher. You can also use your grappling hook to zip over toward enemies, throwing them around in the process. You don't have to get creative about this just yet, but thinking outside the box becomes a major way to survive and have fun as you progress through the game.

Rico and Mario are reunited. When a short cutscene finishes, get into the nearby truck and drive Mario to the rebels.

DRIVE THE TRUCK TO THE REBELS

The route to the next objective takes you south and then east. Practice your driving along the way. It's not too dangerous for now, so try out the brakes, turning with the hand brake, and just get used to everything.

A few minutes down the road, you come across a militia checkpoint. Drive right through it, and run over a few enemies while you're there. Keep barreling down the road. Mario covers you while riding shotgun, so that helps to fend off any of the militia that try to follow.

He also explains the changes that have taken place in Medici while you've been gone. When you get to the objective, it's time to fight.

DEFEAT THE SOLDIERS

Blazing through that checkpoint had one downside: the soldiers spotted you. This builds up Heat, and your enemies won't stop going after you if you have too much of it. Stop at the objective and kill all of the enemy militia troops.

One way to go about this is to hop into a disabled tank close by. Zip onto the top of the tank and use the indicated button to jump inside.

Use both the primary and secondary guns on the tank to clear the surrounding enemies. You're fairly safe inside the tank, because your opponents don't have too much heavy weaponry here.

A Tip About Tanks

Use the machine gun for killing soldiers that are off on their own, and save the heavy cannon for attacks against groups of enemies, or targets hiding behind vehicles. The cannon takes out the vehicles, the soldiers, and anything else that's nearby.

Take out all of the militia targets, and then watch a short cutscene. A helicopter lands, and Rico is asked to hop inside. Get to the chopper and fly toward your new objective. It's northeast of the Baia border, if you take a quick look at your map.

REACH DIMAH'S HIDEOUT AND DEFEAT THE SOLDIERS

Fly to the yellow marker and listen to a road report along the way. You can land the helicopter inside the rebel base, or simply parachute out once you're above it and float to the ground. Just try not to let the chopper land on you!

There are two groups of combatants at the site. You may have noticed the people in blue earlier; those are rebels. Don't attack them because they're on your side! The guys in red are loyal to the general. Kill them on sight, because that's exactly what they're trying to do to you and your allies.

You don't have any tanks this time, so be a bit more careful during the firefight. Aim for headshots against the enemy troops when you're using your assault rifle, and try out grenades to damage their jeeps or anything that they try to hide behind.

If you start taking too much damage, the screen becomes red around the edges. Back off from the fighting, take cover, and let Rico rest for a moment to get your health back.

There's a tower with a minigun in this compound. Grapple to the top (where an objective marker appears), and then use the indicated button to grab the weapon. Aim toward the dirt road that leads into the base, and vaporize anything that tries to drive toward the rebels.

Some of the targets are going to come from the side, so watch out for any movement. Keep your gun focused on vehicles until they explode, and enjoy the rising Chaos.

The most important target to take out quickly is a helicopter that flies into the area. Focus your full attention on that until it goes down, and then get back to the troops below.

Kill everything you can and relax once a cutscene starts.

The coast is clear for a moment. Dimah calls you on the radio, and again she mentions that your grappler could use a bit of an upgrade. Why not, right?

She's still close by. Follow the marker toward a building at the edge of the compound. Start your next story mission there.

NO ONE HAS A GUN TO YOUR HEAD

You don't have to follow the story immediately. Go ahead and explore if you'd like to have some fun and see what the world is like. Come back here when you're ready to progress!

TIME FOR AN UPGRADE

MISSION REWARD: Unlock Wingsuit, Dual Tether, and Planted Explosives

Dimah talks to you about your grapple, Bavarium, and the state of Medici. There's so much potential here, but you must get everything that Dimah needs before moving forward. It sounds like she's ready to take that step.

Try out the grapple under Dimah's instructions. She asks you to reel yourself toward things a couple of times, and try out your parachute partway through. This is a valuable skill for gaining altitude and control while using your grapple, so the practice is welcome.

The next step is to meet Dimah again. While traveling there, use grapple, reel in, parachute, and grapple a new target. This chain allows Rico to quickly traverse huge swaths of countryside. He can keep up with vehicles, escape enemies, and enjoy the lovely sites of Medici.

Grapple and fly to the marked objective to continue. Dimah works on your glove a bit more to reduce the chance of sudden detonations (a good thing, right?).

LIBERATE GUARDIA ALPHA

After another scene, you can mess with the new settings on your glove. Try out the tether functions. Once you feel comfortable, tether an explosive barrel to the fence ahead of Rico. The barrel is pulled into the fence and explodes, making the way into the next plant much easier for everyone.

For even more fun, tether the fuel containers ahead onto each other. This pulls them down, creating havoc. You can also keep tethering explosive barrels to the tanks around the compound.

MEET DIMAH AND THEN REACH THE BRIDGE

Follow your next objective and meet Dimah on the cliffs. She gives you an upgrade. Rico now has a wingsuit! Flying around was already quite doable, but now it's easy. Jump off of the cliff and try your new feature out. Glide to the bridge below the cliffs and land there.

You keep hearing about this Bavarium stuff, but now is the time to try out its more destructive properties. Dimah secretly stashed some GE-64 on you. This is a relatively stable compound that you use to destroy heavy emplacements.

Put two sets of GE-64 on the bridge, as marked by your objectives, and then get to a vantage point high above the bridge.

Wait up there for an enemy convoy to approach, and then take out the bridge when there are multiple vehicles near the middle of the structure. So much for those poor folks, but there is still more work to be done.

WHATEVER WORKS!

You still get credit and can continue the mission if you ambush and destroy the convoy manually. You don't need to use the bridge explosives to take them out.

Glide down the cliff to a SAM site. Hack the two batteries while killing or avoiding the enemy soldiers nearby. The sites are easy to hack; you only need to approach them and interact with the batteries. Once they're under your control, use them to ambush and destroy the approaching wave of helicopters.

WHY WASTE A GOOD CHOPPER?

If you want to try something fun, take out the helicopters on your own (without using the SAM). Commandeer one of them and then park it near the stunt area by Granmatre's place.

Use this gunship to clear Manaea later. You can even park the ship near the Di Ravello statue so that you can use the ship again in the next mission.

Talk to Dimah and Mario on the commlink after the choppers have been destroyed. Use your newfound powers of flight to pull Rico across the island, toward Mario's marker. Granmatre Frigo has prepared dinner, and you're invited!

You and Mario have a good conversation when you arrive. This is where the two of you solidify your plan of attack against the General.

After dinner, you hear from Alessia. She's in charge of the rebel's radio program. You can tell that she's in the know, because she has already heard that you're planning to go after the Vis Electra plant. This power plant is west of your current position. Another place that needs your help is northeast. It's the town of Manaea. Liberations are covered in another chapter; this section of the guide deals only with Story missions.

WHAT DO LIBERATIONS DO?

Before you move out, let's quickly discuss Liberations. These actions convert enemy settlements and place them back in the hands of the rebels. Doing so unlocks extra challenges, garages where you can save and retrieve vehicles, and the process breaks the hold that General Di Ravello has over the area. Fully Liberated provinces let you fast travel through them, which is certainly a nice perk.

Liberate Vis Electra and Manaea as you please, then look for a mission that starts near the docks on the southern end of Manaea. You can  even select this ahead of time while scrolling through your map. Make a waypoint to find the location easily and begin the mission as soon as you get there!

MARIO'S REBEL DROPS

MISSION REWARD: Unlock Frigo Garages and Rebel Drops

Now that you're starting to get some territory, it's good to do a mission that lets you look into the vehicles of Medici. Mario sends you on a quest to find something interesting!

REACH THE MYSTERY LOCATION

A waypoint is placed on your map. It's up to you how to get there. A scenic drive through the mountains is lovely and lets you get some fighting against the militia. Grappling and flying up there is a little bit faster, but you won't get to mess around with anyone.

Approach the waypoint and find the "special" vehicle that Mario has located. It's, well, probably not what you'd expect.

Now that you're there, use your map and mark a garage as your next waypoint. This is worth doing any time you find a vehicle that you want to save; the game shows you a good path to take to get the vehicle home, and this lights up the roads that you're meant to take, so you won't have to switch back and forth between the game and the map while you're driving.

Get this vehicle down to the garage. No one knows what you're doing, so there isn't likely to be any fighting unless you get yourself into serious trouble.

Park in a blue circle by the garage and you're good to go. This is how you save and unlock vehicles for future use. This one might not be suitable for heavy combat, but you're not limited to little ones like this.

After saving the scooter, look for a Beacon in a crate several feet away. Take it. Beacons let you call in rebels with the vehicles that you want. Go into the menu, select Rebel Drop, and then request weapons, vehicles, etc. Once done, throw your Beacon at a safe spot nearby and wait for your delivery.

Try this right now! Get some weapons and a vehicle to test this and finish the mission. Make sure to request things that you actually want to use so that this free Beacon does the most good for you!

With all of these basics mastered, you should finish your Liberation of Baia. As soon as that's done, you can continue on the path to victory.

Sheldon, your buddy from back in the plane, radios in when the province is fully Liberated. He talks to you about problems in Costa Del Porto. As usual, you can go directly there, or take some time to complete challenges, have fun, or explore the island.

THE MILITIA IS CARRION FOR THE VULTURES

Now that you can get vehicles, consider this: there's an airstrip up in Maestrale. Go up there and Liberate that base (Vulture). By doing this, you can access free bombers for the rest of the game, and there is no way that you won't be able to take advantage of that.

When you're ready, commandeer a helicopter or boat, and make your way to the province south of Baia. It's called Sirocco Nord. Not far onto that island, you reach a set of ruins. Walk onto your objective marker and start the next mission.

A TERRIBLE REACTION

After an exciting cutscene, you're returned to the area near Costa Del Porto.

DESTROY THE TANKS

Mario is heading into town while your job is to take out three tanks. Parachute down toward the town, but keep to the higher ground so that you have a great vantage point. You can destroy the tanks from long range with your rocket launcher (this is even doable while you're in the air above them, making it impossible for the tanks to use their heavy guns against you).

If you're really gutsy, an alternative is to parachute right onto the tanks and use your explosives to detonate them as you leap to safety. This one isn't for the faint of heart, but it's especially fun to try out.

Blast all three tanks and then head into the city proper.

PROTECT MARIO

Militia forces inside the city are attacking the rebels and civilians alike. Get to Mario quickly so that you can help the rebels push back.

Parachute and glide into the city and land on a rooftop near Mario's position. Militia troops are all over the roads, but none of them was clever enough to secure the rooftops. You gain a huge advantage by staying above them. Go to the edge of a roof, kill a few targets with your assault rifle, and retreat if you take any damage.

Make sure that Mario doesn't take too much damage. He has a health bar onscreen again, and you can jump down into the fray if you think Mario is in trouble. There's a cache of weapons in a green locker at ground level; restock if necessary, and keep the pressure on these jerks.

The militia troops get reinforcements as soon as their numbers begin to thin. Watch the skies, because many of them are parachuting down toward you. Snipe them out of the sky if you can. Or, destroy the large fuel container that they pass over to kill the entire group in one fell swoop. Very nice!

A gate drops to block the escape of the rebels. Tether the gate to the top of the structure that houses it to open the way. A truck drives through; jump into the back of it and provide cover as they evacuate the city.

Grappling Gets Stuff Done!

When you're on top of the truck, use your grapple to destroy or commandeer other vehicles. This is a quick way to take out important enemy targets. Shooting them works just fine, but your tethers are always a fast, valid, and sensible option.

A gunship flies overhead. Grapple up to the ship and pull the pilot out of his seat. That settles the matter immediately! Now that you have a helicopter at your disposal, follow it and destroy anything that tries to stop it.

You "only" have a minigun, but that's more than enough to stop the light vehicles pursuing your allies. Look for things to attack to thwart the enemies, like explosives on the side of the road, or on the bridge that the truck drives across afterward.

If you lose your chopper, zip to the vehicles that are close to the truck and kill their gunners and drivers. You can keep doing this to lower the pressure on Mario.

Get Mario far enough away from the city and he reaches a small airpad and escapes. This concludes the mission. Good job on your escort, Rico!

Costa Del Porto took serious damage, and many people are dead. But, you're alive, and it's time to regroup. Mario and Dimah are at the southern edge of Soros. When it's time to advance the story, meet them there! It's at the end of the island chain, so keep flying southwest to get there.

Before you leave, you can quickly complete a Liberation, so think about doing that!

Ways to Lose

If Mario's truck gets destroyed, you must try again. However, it's even easier to lose if you simply fall behind and don't catch up to Mario within 15 seconds. Always keep an eye on Mario's truck, and stay close to it with Rico and any vehicles that he commandeers.

Never be afraid to ditch a fight or vehicle and grapple your way toward Mario. It's more important to stay close to him than to kill everything in sight.

FRIENDS LIKE THESE

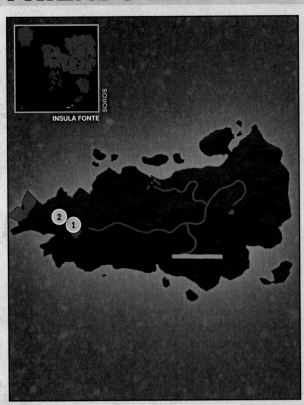

This mission starts in a rocky cove, at the edge of the island. Use your map to locate the starting point if you're having any trouble (the marker is visible from the land, air, or water, which makes things nice and easy).

As you trigger the mission, Sheldon and Mario are engaged in a conversation. Mario leaves, and Rico gets to talk to Sheldon. Being such a giver, he's agreed to help you and the rebels.

Approach Mario after this short meeting and talk to him, as well. This scene is perfect.

Rico meets Dimah afterward. She tells him to seek out a contact, but that can wait just a moment.

REACH MARIO'S FRIEND

With all of these scenes completed, you begin the actual mission. Cross a small river and meet Mario's buddy. He's standing beside a boat. Tether the boat to the sand bar ahead to pull the craft into the water.

You've done a good deed. Now it's time to test out something fun. Go to your map, select an icon up by Manaea, and then use the Fast Travel function that has been unlocked. This is your ticket to getting around Medici even faster than before!

Doing this completes the mission and unlocks Fast Travel for the rest of the game!

Dimah calls in and tells you where her contact is; this person is named Looch. He's at Vigilator Nord. That's to the north of Manaea, along the coastline. Travel there next.

FAST TRAVEL ISN'T JUST FOR THE BIRDS

Use Flares to jump to challenges and other important points around Medici. This saves tons of time and lets you focus on the goals that are most important during each play session. It's not that worthwhile if you're only 20 seconds away from a target area, but it's amazing when you're on entirely different islands or need to travel several provinces away.

CONFLICTING INTERESTS

This mission begins on the docks. Drive up the coast, fly, or even take a boat to get to it. Start the mission when you arrive, and talk to Looch. He's a decent sort, and points out the military base where a Bavarium Scanner is located. That's what Dimah wants you to find, so it's clearly your next target.

Who's Playing With Laser Pointers?

Be very careful about the snipers here. They have laser sights and would love to give you a friendly headshot. Stay behind cover while you get your bearings, and trace the angle of their lasers back to determine where the snipers are.

GET TO VIGILATOR NORD AND SEARCH FOR THE BAVARIUM SCANNER

Drive a motorboat around the coast and into Vigilator Nord, the nearby settlement. This place is well defended, so you can't search for the scanner immediately. Instead, take out the defenders before opening the marked containers.

Also watch out for patrol boats and regular militia troops. Approach this area cautiously and fight as you go. It's easy to get overwhelmed if you push right into the center of the settlement.

While you're here, take aim at the many destructible targets. Use rockets and your tether to destroy a variety of radar towers, fuel containers, and so forth. It's all health anarchy for you to spread.

Liberate the settlement to give yourself some breathing room, and then get the scanner from the shipping containers. This is a breeze once all of the defenders are down!

That said, you can get the scanner without Liberating Vigilator Nord. If you're trying to get through this quickly, go ahead and grapple to the marked containers. Blow them open (with any type of explosive), search each, and get out of there. It's efficient to clear this settlement right now, but not required.

Once you have the scanner in your possession, set a waypoint for Cima Leon. It's about 2.5km to the west. That area does have aerial defenses, so fly low and watch out if you're taking a chopper over there. It's easier to come by land because you can stay under cover and avoid a fair amount of trouble, but that's up to you!

REACH THE GRATE

The marked grate is on a large wall of the compound. Zip up to it and watch Rico place the scanner. A short scene follows.

The scanner has a minor malfunction, as it were. Go pick it up in the valley below, and talk to Sheldon. He's at Café Francesco in the town of Fortalessa, 1.6km to the south. Head to him right now.

MEET WITH SHELDON

Clear any Heat that you pick up along the way, because Sheldon isn't the type of guy who wants his business aired publically. If you run into too much fighting, you might have to simply Liberate the entire town. It's not nearly as heavy a battle as you had back in Vigilator Nord.

Sheldon is in the center of town. Find him when the fighting cools off. Give him the scanner and complete the mission.

Mario calls in and has very good news. There might be a defector from Di Ravello's researchers. To find out, meet Mario in Lantuina. It's in the province of Lavanda, which is northwest from where you are now.

Or, if you're willing to do more work for the cause, you can unlock another mission right now.

THE SECRET OF VIS ELECTRA

This mission requires you to complete a fair amount of Liberation throughout this area. Right now is about the time that you're likely to consider that mission, so we're going to cover it here and then get back to our defecting scientist afterward!

THE SECRET OF VIS ELECTRA

MISSION REWARD: Insula Fonte FOW disabled

Once you have enough territory Liberated, return to Vis Electra, and look for this mission to the northwest of the power plant. Start the mission when you arrive.

Dimah figured out one of the reasons why Di Ravello constructed the power plant; it supplies power to his FOW. You now are in a position to take out the hidden portion of Vis Electra and disable the FOW entirely.

FOLLOW THE PIPES

When the cutscene ends, start following the power conduits in front of Rico. They're glowing, which makes it fairly easy to spot where you need to go. If the conduits go into a rockface, continue directly forward over the rocks until you see the next run of the cables.

Scout From the Air

You can always use a helicopter or your parachute to get high over the area. This makes it a bit easier to scout, as long as you're comfortable flying over the site instead of walking along it.

The pipes take you up a cliff and to a small town. Go directly over the small settlement and rejoin the conduits on the other side of the area.

Grapple into the air and parachute down a long hill while watching the cables. The conduits drop into the water, but come out again on the other side. Stick to the coastline when the pipes disappear again, and land once you see a patrol boat ahead. There's a checkpoint to dispatch.

KILL THE GUARDS

Destroy two boats and a few small clusters of soldiers before looking for the entrance to the facility. The fight isn't hard, especially if you use rockets on the boats to take them out before the enemies know that you're there.

A marker appears to show you where the underground entrance is located. Swim through there and come out into a cavern. There's only one way forward, so follow the path. A few men are in the next room, but they aren't armed and it doesn't look like they're dangerous. Let them be, and search for the power node farther along.

Hack the controls by a heavy gate that blocks your way forward. This opens the gate and lets you into the power node. Destroy everything there. Use an automatic weapon to bring down the enemy soldiers first, and then fire rockets into the generators behind them.

Dimah unlocks a massive vault door to let you escape the power plant, and the mission ends as soon as you get outside. No more FOW for the General now!

WHAT DID THAT ACCOMPLISH?

You might be wondering why that FOW had to be taken down. This region's central command was heavily protected by the FOW system. With that down, you have the chance to take out the central command for this region once and for all. Very nice!

Turn to the northwest and set your waypoint for Turncoat, the next mission in our story.

TURNCOAT

Lantuina is in Lavanda. Fly or drive over there and Liberate the town to get easier access to this mission, then talk to Mario at the objective marker. He's dancing the day away there. Your mission is to help a scientist named Zeno defect from Di Revello's weapon program.

BRING MARIO A MILITARY VEHICLE

Mario wants to get a decent vehicle for your mission. Search around town for a heavy military transport. There are Urga Szturms here and there. You can find a couple of them within a block or so of Mario's dancing spot. They're heavily armored and have a turret, so it's a solid choice for this run. Bring one of them back to Mario as soon as you can.

DRIVE TO ZENO'S LOCATION AND DEFEAT THE SOLDIERS

Take the short drive to Zeno's location, but be ready for trouble. There are about half-a-dozen soldiers attacking the area around the marker. Use your turret to slice through them, or get out and engage in some close-range fighting.

The defector comes out as soon as the fighting ends. His full name is Dr. Zeno Antithikara. He gets into a chopper to start his escape, while Mario drives the transport that you brought in the first place. You must ensure that both of these men survive the trip, otherwise the mission is a bust!

ESCORT YOUR ALLIES TO THE SAFE HOUSE

Zip onto the top of Mario's vehicle to ensure that you have a great line of sight on anyone who comes after you. Watch the roads heavily, because that's where all of the early attackers come from. Rockets really help here, but automatic weapons are useful against the motorcyclists.

Both vehicles stop as you get close to a checkpoint. Leave your buddies, for a moment, and zip ahead on your grappling line to approach a missile battery (it's marked on your map). Hack this SAM site and then get back onto Mario's transport as soon as you can.

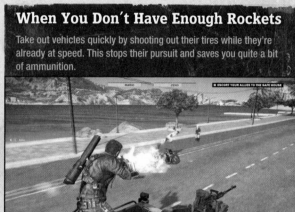

When You Don't Have Enough Rockets

Take out vehicles quickly by shooting out their tires while they're already at speed. This stops their pursuit and saves you quite a bit of ammunition.

Time is a Factor, Rico

A tank shows up if you take too long working on the SAMs. That could be disastrous for your buddies, so keep a quick pace as best you can!

Or, intentionally waste some time and wait specifically for that tank. If you hijack it quickly, your allies won't get killed. You now have a free tank to play with for the remainder of the mission. Oh, yeah!

Your group leaves the checkpoint and drives into a city a bit farther down the road. They stop in the middle of that section because there's another SAM site ahead. Disable it at maximum speed and grapple back onto Mario's vehicle as he barrels down the road toward you.

A gunship flies into the area as your people drive out of the city and into the hills. Grapple toward it to take out the pilot, or do some precision shooting to knock the chopper out of the sky.

Mario reaches the destination and tells you to destroy any remaining militia forces. Do so to make sure that the Doctor isn't followed. Zeno lands and goes off to see Dimah. With that, you've won the mission!

Your next task begins at the Cima Leon command base. If you've completed The Secret of Vis Electra, the only other requirement to begin this is to Liberate Cima Leon: CentCom. Take care of that now, and then proceed to Missile Cowboy, on the eastern side of the island.

MISSILE COWBOY

MISSION REWARD: Unlock Dionysus Airstrike FOW

The starting point for Missile Cowboy is in the middle of Cima Leon. Fly or grapple on top of a large building and look for the marker there. Rico meets Dimah again and steels himself for a major attack.

REACH THE TRANSMITTER

Jump off of the building and travel toward the new marker; it's only a bit over a km away, so the trip is fast if you just glide there.

You reach a military base. It doesn't have any worrisome defenses, but you still must fight through a mess of soldiers. Take out their fuel containers and electrical substation to build Chaos, and work your way to the marked transmitter.

Hack the marked computer system to raise the transmitter, and then attack it directly with your weapons. It blows up without a lot of protest, and Dimah can start working on her end to take care of a few problems.

Sadly, this isn't enough to win the day. General Di Ravello has started a huge attack all across the region. The rebels are hard pressed, and they even stand a chance of being wiped out entirely if you can't help them turn the tide.

A marker appears at the top of the screen. This shows the tug of war between the rebels of the soldiers. You can't afford to let the needle swing all the way to the left. To stop this, your goal is to attack enemy forces and defeat them quickly and with brutal force.

DESTROY THE ATTACKING VEHICLES

Battle waypoints pop up on the map. Rush to those. To the north you find a marker that isn't very far away. Grapple and glide over there to stop a group of three armored transports that are attacking a town. Hop directly into one of the transports, use it to destroy the other two, and then jump out to blast the one that you were using. Enemies have probably softened it for you already, but using your explosives should do the trick either way.

The next major battle is west from there. Use your grapple and parachute to get there quickly, and kill soldiers along the way to ensure that things are going well for the rebels.

EVERY LITTLE BIT HELPS

The major battles that you win turn the tide quite nicely, but all of the kills you earn contribute toward the total war effort. Destroy vehicles and kill soldiers to move the bar to the right.

It is 100% possible to win these massive battles just by killing enemies throughout the region! The battlefields that are shown as your objectives make this faster and easier, but they are optional.

DESTROY MILITARY TANKS

Watch the sky for heavy gunships that fly overhead. Commandeer one of them (preferably an HROM D, because of its minigun and missiles). Use one of these gunships to destroy the tanks to the west. They're driving close together, which is why missiles are especially effective. You can trash the entire convoy in just a few seconds.

REACH THE MISSILE

A short cutscene plays, and Rico gets into a helicopter. You're flown back toward the launch site where Di Ravello is about to deploy a missile. Glide toward the missile and don't give up too much height, too quickly. Your target is the lower section of the missile; get close enough to grapple onto it and reel yourself in. If you're off to the sides, you miss and the mission fails. If you lose too much height or go over the top of the missile, you're also doomed. Glide in a direct line toward the missile and let the grapple shot line itself up as the missile rises into position.

Another cutscene plays, and the mission concludes!

Mario radios in and says that he has to meet you immediately. He's north of Cima Leon. Fly down to him (you can do this as you're landing after the end of the previous mission). Going to this objective starts your next mission.

OF COWS AND WINE

You are treated to a wonderful intro video to begin this. Mario lets you know that he's down in the vineyard below the supposed meeting spot. Glide down to the objective marker. It's under 2km away. You don't need to hurry this time, but Mario seriously needs some payback.

BE ON THE LOOKOUT

When you're close to the water, look for a rebel ally who is standing at the edge of the land. Go over to him and see what happens. This is not an essential part of the mission.

Land in the marked vineyard and get into a red truck laden with wine.

REACH THE REBELS WITH AS MANY CASKS AS POSSIBLE

Okay, so this task isn't monumentally important compared to the last one, but Mario keeps things moving with his commentary! Drive the truck along the marked route, and try not to bump into anything. Cornering is the tricky part, because the barrels weren't tied down by anyone; you can lose some of the wine by turning too quickly, so drive like it's a calm Sunday morning.

If you're really trying to perfect this process, try tethering something to the top of the flatbed so that the barrels are held down the entire trip.

Take the truck to the delivery point and see what Mario has planned. After everything that happened earlier, this is actually a pretty darn good idea.

Finish the good times and wait for a call from Sheldon. He's looking for you at Pointe Laurino.

CONNECT THE DOTS

Start your mission with a friendly talk. See how Sheldon is doing. He seems nice and relaxed. That's great and all, but you can't afford to sit back; things are about to go down close by, and you have to be there.

DEFEAT THE REINFORCEMENTS

Jump into the nearby rebel chopper and fly toward your objective. You have both missiles and a minigun to work with, and your targets are a series of heavy military ships that are speeding toward your buddies.

Don't get too high in the air as it reduces the accuracy of your missiles if they have to travel really far. Get closer to the water and strafe the heck out of your victims. You want to drive those missiles right down their necks.

There are occasional helicopters patrolling to defend the navy. Make sure to attack the choppers as soon as you see them, because losing your own gunship makes this mission much more difficult.

REACH MARIO AND DIMAH

As soon as the third ship is destroyed, you can start to see Mario's position. Fly over there and take out a SAM site on the way (look for the red light over the missile battery so that you don't miss it). Once the SAM site is down, attack the ships that are going after Mario and Dimah.

Ditch your chopper when the coast is clear, and grapple your way into the rebel boat with your allies.

CHECK ON THE INFORMANTS

Pilot the boat around the coastline and check on some informants. There aren't any enemies at the first site, so continue on toward the next objective marker. You pass through a minefield on the way there. Either maneuver in between the mines, or try a turbo jump with your modified boat.

Check out the small island at the second site, and then turn the boat around to hit open water and go around to the final informant location. It's there that you meet Annika and Teo. They become part of the cause (for a buck or two).

Talk with them for a second, and then hurry back to the docks to repel enemy soldiers that attack.

PROTECT THE REBELS

Commandeer an enemy helicopter that comes in, and use its minigun on the ships and trucks that pull up.

The nastiest threat comes at the end of the mission; another heavy ship pulls toward the harbor. Its guns are mean, and the ship is likely to take out any aircraft or boats that you've been using to defend the rebels. Should you lose your craft, grapple onto the big vessel, deploy explosives from the rear of the ship, and blow the target up while you're safe. Never stand in front of the ship or to its sides. The gun can rip you open without missing a beat.

As soon as the big ship is destroyed, you're done. Watch the end scene of the mission.

AN ACT OF PIRACY

CAUDA

INSULA DRACON

Trigger the mission and watch a scene with Dimah and the smugglers. You guys can help each other out. You're going to steal a tank, and they're going to get you the supplies you need. Get into a plane as the scene ends.

REACH PONERE TO STEAL THE TANK

Take off and fly north, toward Ponere. When you get close to the objective, parachute out of the plane and drop toward the convoy below.

You can't directly land on the super tank and hijack it. The tank's designers thought of that and have given it a powerful Bavarium shield that prevents such attempts. However, this method of protection isn't perfect. Every few seconds, the shield goes down so that the coils powering it don't overheat. That's your big chance.

Use your parachute to fly over the convoy, and drop onto the super tank as soon as its shield falls. This is the only way to capture the vehicle. Once you're inside it, destroy any nearby enemy vehicles and start to make your escape.

You need to get better supplies and medical care for your allies. This mission starts in Grotta Contrabandero. Get onto the upper cliffs of the area, and look for the marker. It's very close to where Connect the Dots ends, so doing these back to back is very efficient.

DELIVER THE TANK TO THE DROP POINT

You have a minigun and a heavy cannon to work with. The super tank (labeled as the Imperator Bavarium Tank) also has very strong armor. Use your Bavarium shield to supplement this, and almost nothing is going to be able to touch you.

Cut through your opposition and drive along the route that Teo gives you that leads toward the drop-off point.

There are gates blocking your path out of the military base. Shoot the gate controls to open these barriers. When you pass the main gate, you're practically home free. Drive to the docks and continue destroying any enemy vehicles that pursue you so that the tank doesn't take much damage.

Load your sweet prize onto the transport at the end of the route, and the mission is done.

Free Carnage

If you want to risk things a little, stay near the military compound that the convoy was entering and destroy everything in sight. You have a great vehicle to work with, so the Chaos is fast and easy to achieve.

In fact, you're free to drive around Medici with the super tank, blowing apart everything that gets in your way. Go crazy on the militia; they have only their own engineers to blame!

THREE'S COMPANY

And again, your missions chain from one to the next. Three's Company starts only a few steps away from where you finish the last mission. Begin this as soon as you can.

REACH THE OVERLOOK

Talk to Dimah and Annika, then leave the rebel base. Get into a chopper that's waiting on the beach and head toward the marked objective; it's 3.5km to the northeast. You don't run into trouble on the way there, so it's a fast flight. Sheldon calls in, so you learn more about the political lay of the land while you're flying.

Ditch the chopper when you get to town and grapple onto the marked overlook. You find a sweet sniper rifle up there (thanks Annika)!

DRAW OUTSIDE THE LINES

You don't need to use the sniper rifle to do the following sections. We explain how to proceed normally, but you're able to use any weapons available to get this done. There's even a grenade launcher on one of the weapon racks. Don't let us hold you back from a good time.

Annika: He is just a big baby.

DEFEAT THE REINFORCEMENTS

The smugglers make a distraction to draw out your targets. As they do this, position yourself on the edge of the overlook. You should be watching the long stretch of road that leads away from your tower. This gives you a great sniping angle against the vehicles that drive past. A few shots in each and they go up in flames. Repeat this for the helicopters that fly toward the smuggler's distraction, as well; they're easier to hit than the fast-moving vehicles below, so save the choppers for last.

Grapple over to the site that the soldiers are reinforcing and take out any of the troops you missed during your sniping attacks.

REACH THE NEXT OVERLOOK

When the attack ends, you're asked to go to another overlook. It's close by, to the east. Grapple and glide over to it. Annika gets there by car, and arrives shortly after you do. Watch her come in, and shoot at the gate controls to ensure that she can drive into the shipping area below.

Provide overwatch and shoot at the soldiers that attack Annika and Teo. They need time to break through the system firewall. Direct sniping attacks on the soldiers are effective enough, but shooting at the barrels of fuel in the yard takes out more targets per shot!

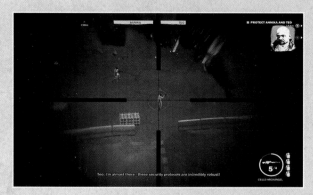

There are also tanks of compressed gas in the lower yard. Watch the groups of soldiers rush to attack, and always try to splatter entire groups when they pass by these explosive objects. It's much easier than taking them all out individually. This is very important because Teo and Annika fail the mission if they take too much damage.

You can get additional ammunition from the package on your overlook. Make sure to do that if you're running low.

Annika and Teo rush to a helicopter once they've gotten the data they needed. Continue to provide cover for them until they get over to the pit at the end of the yard. Jump off of your cliff and glide down to them.

Use an automatic weapon to engage the remaining soldiers by the chopper, and grapple onto the vehicle when Annika and Teo take off. While hanging off of the chopper, shoot the enemies below during your escape. There are guys with RPGs and patrol boats. Gun down the former and use rockets on the latter, if at all possible. This keeps the helicopter from taking much damage. The RPG soldiers are near explosive barrels again, so they're easy to punish.

Save some firepower for the enemy gunship that attacks later on. You can grapple onto that, commandeer it, and use the gunship to defend your allies from additional attacks (from above and below). Alternatively, you should aim for the pilots and shoot them to quickly bring down the gunships. This is also quite effective.

Escort the helicopter a tad bit farther and finish any remaining nearby soldiers. This ends the mission with another glorious success.

Your next mission is north from there, near Capite Est. This is a good time to take a break and run Challenges and Liberations. Do some fun stuff around Medici before you get back to the dangerous business at hand!

A LONG AND DANGEROUS ROAD

Take the road up through Capite Est and stop at the marker. This begins A Long and Dangerous Road. You have a meeting between Rico, Teo, Dimah, and Annika, and everyone debates how to test the new hardware that you've all been working on. It's time to see how this stuff performs in the field!

Teo: Look. Your friend Sheldon showed-up at the cove. That's a dangerous man.

PROTECT THE EMP AND YOUR ALLIES

As the scene ends, you can grapple onto one of the vehicles in a rebel convoy. Get toward the front so that you can defend everyone if there's an ambush—and you know darn well that there will be! Soldiers attack from a bridge above the road, and from the area ahead. Grapple up to the high ground, defeat the soldiers on the bridge, and attack the group below once you've secured the bridge.

The convoy starts up again, but you don't get to ride for long before there's another blockade in the road. Kill the soldiers that pop up with a grenade toss or two, and then turn left to shoot explosive barrels as more enemies hide behind cover up there.

Commandeer a gunship at the end of this skirmish so that you have superior firepower for the remainder of the escort.

The convoy goes through a couple of tunnels, but you still have a great angle of fire most of the time to ensure that no one is overwhelmed. Bust the team through a gate, and continue mowing down everything that moves around them.

Another barricade then stops you. After a small fight there, you must fight several vehicles. Remember that shooting out tires is a great tactic during these chases. It's a fast way to get rid of your enemies without wasting ammo!

The team passes a military base (which probably wasn't the best idea when you were planning a route), and another gunship descends. Don't give it any time to fire on your allies; that thing can do massive damage. Commandeer it immediately, or destroy the gunship with your best firepower!

There are a couple more choppers on their way. Give them the same treatment.

Soon, the convoy stops as you finally reach the enemy tank yard. Snipers are above, on your right. Jump into a tank and kill the soldiers nearby and above you without mercy. On the other side of the convoy, more troops are deploying. Drive over to obliterate them, and make sure that you don't hit your buddies' vehicles with any explosions.

Use the EMP weapon that you guys brought when the battle ends, and watch the mission complete. Di Ravello won't be happy to hear about any of this!

ABANDON SHIP

INSULA DRACON

CAUDA

Your next task begins in the southwest, by Cauda. Return to Contrabandero to speak with Sheldon about everything that has happened. After hearing his warning, you need to get everyone ready to go—quickly!

It's really nice to have a Fire Leech for this mission, so make sure that you get that if you use any Rebel Drops.

PROTECT MARIO AND THE EMP

Combat is joined as soon as the cutscene ends. Militia forces are heading in. You have to kill them while protecting Mario and EMP.

Plow through the soldiers in front of the rebel base, and push out toward a mounted gun that gets marked early in the fighting. Use that to defend the area. Another tactic is to commandeer one of the enemy vehicles and use the machine guns on that to help thin the enemies while avoiding some of the damage coming at you.

Whatever heavy gun you want to use, it's essential that you keep the pressure on the enemies throughout these waves. The first group is primarily infantry, but more landing vessels come in, and waves of ground transports arrive, as well (coming from deeper in the cave complex).

You get word after these encounters that helicopters are inbound. Grapple up to them to take out the pilots quickly, or zip over to an AA Gun on the other side of the river. Both of these methods allow you to bring down the gunships quickly.

Could You Move That a Bit to the Left?

If you like using the heavy gun emplacements but can't get a great angle, remember that your tether works on them. Pull the guns closer to the edge of the platform to get a superior vantage point.

As the EMP finishes charging, keep your eyes on the skies. Paratroopers drop into the cavern, and another wave of vehicles drives in at the same time. Hold them off as best you can, and start moving back toward the EMP device. It finishes its charge, and you can take out the remaining vehicles by activating it.

Do this and quickly restock your supplies while there's a lull in the action. Get into a vehicle when you're done, or take a minigun from a weapon emplacement so that you can strike hard when the paratroopers return.

Shoot as many of the paratroopers as you can before they land and get to better cover, then steel yourself for a huge rush of helicopters and battleships. They bombard you from range, so stay mobile to avoid their heavy (but slow) attacks. Look for red circles on the ground and make sure to stay out of them by grappling to reposition if you're being targeted.

Get back to the EMP and use it a second time. This takes out all of the remaining vehicles. Clear any final stragglers. A tank might be able to survive the blast if it's at the end of the cavern, so track down any red markers. Commandeer the tank, if it's available, and use that as your primary weapon in the next wave.

Teo and Annika return for this portion of the fight, so it's mostly cleanup. Finish this, and end the mission.

ELECTROMAGNETIC PULSE

MISSION REWARD: Insula Dracon FOW disabled

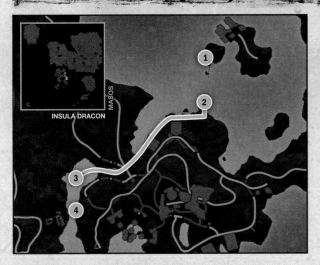

The next mission is up north in Massos, past Corda Dracon. Liberate settlements in Insula Dracon to unlock this mission before you head over there. The mission starts on a small island, so it's useful to grab a helicopter before taking the trip.

Talk to Dimah and then start your task. This is similar to The Secret of Vis Electra in that you must follow a series of pipes to uncover a militia compound. Take that out so that the FOW for this region goes down. Once that happens, you can Liberate the people.

FOLLOW THE PIPES

Grapple and glide over to land, where the marker is glowing. Trace the route of the pipes as they lead under the hills and through a rocky tunnel. Soldiers are ahead, in a lower cavern. Watch out for them and for several boats, as well. You have to kill these guards before you proceed.

Use a rocket launcher to destroy the boat quickly, so that you don't take much damage. If you see any gunships above, commandeer them and use the choppers' guns to destroy the enemies below.

Dimah hacks a security gate as you return to the pipes. Swim through another small tunnel, and you soon arrive at the underground site. Their main door is sealed tight, but a tunnel underneath this base lets you slip through anyway, after another swim. You come up the other side and are very close to your destination.

THAT LOOKS INTERESTING

When you reach the scientists part of the base, stop for a second. Grapple to the catwalks above, and then look down at the insignia in the center of the room. Hmmm…

DESTROY THE COMMAND NODE

Use an automatic weapon to eat through the small detachment of guards by the transformers, then detonate those machines. The FOW is disabled, and you're free to leave the cave. A tunnel straight up lets you grapple out of the cavern quickly and efficiently! And with that, you're done.

TANGLED UP IN BLUE

MISSION REWARD: Unlock Thunderbird EMP FOW

INSULA DRACON — CORDA DRACON

Dimah: ... Would obliterate entire base

The main assault on this region's command center is imminent. Go immediately over to Dimah's location and talk to her. You won't lose any momentum, and it's a short trip. She's by Corda Dracon, less than 1km away.

Beginning Tangled Up In Blue starts another battle scenario. The rebels and the militia are now engaged in a bitter struggle for survival. You can turn this tide by engaging and eliminating enemy troops throughout the province.

Look to the northwest, at the first marked battle site. That's your goal right now.

HELP THE REBEL AIRCRAFT TAKE OFF

REBEL PLANE — PROTECT REBEL PLANE — Rebel Plane

It's a few kilometers to the airstrip where you can do the most good. Fly over there as soon as possible, and help a rebel plane take off without getting destroyed. Shoot the soldiers trying to seize the airstrip, and wait for your buddies to leave. As soon as it does, the objective changes and you're asked to go to the next site.

DELIVER A REBEL BOAT

Commandeer one of the fighter jets at the airport, and then fly that to your next objective. The target is a rebel boat, out on the water already. Destroy any aircraft or boat as you approach your destination, and then take charge of the marked craft when you arrive.

Pilot that ship over to the beach and leave it there.

BRING DOWN A MILITIA BASE

There's one more battlefield to the east. The objective marker takes you to a small boat outside of a water gate. When Dimah gets the gate open, take the boat inside, then dock it and look for a cooling generator at the back of the first room. Shoot that until it blows up.

Search for a tunnel back in the water, then swim through it. You can't make the entire swim in one go, so watch for a pocket of air just as you're beginning to drown. Rest there for a second and then finish your swim.

Grapple out of the water and open the heavy door into the generator room. There's a post with a bright, red button that you have to press to get inside. Shoot the generator and kill any soldiers that investigate.

Look up to find the other two generators. They're on higher levels inside the room. Grapple up to them and repeat this process (expose the generator and blow it up).

Evacuate the cave quickly after the third generator goes down. Things are going to explode soon, and you probably enjoy having all of your bits intact. Look for a tunnel at the top of the chamber, then grapple up through it to escape.

And with that, you've won again. The base is destroyed, and another bastion of Di Ravello's power has fallen! You've earned some relaxation time. Go for a swim or do some fishing.

RICO AND THE ROSE

INSULA DRACON

CAUDA

The action resumes in the southwest. Rose Manuela, the leader of the people, is returning to the country. She's flying in and Rico is going down there to make sure that everything is safe enough for her return.

Go to Grotta Contrabandero once again, and start this mission whenever it feels right.

Get into the jet fighter that's parked nearby. Fly several kilometers to rendezvous with President Manuela's plane, and make contact with her pilot when you get close. It's a surprise to no one at all that you aren't the only craft inbound. Enemy fighters are already closing in!

Use your homing missiles to take out the enemy fighters as quickly as you can. Even if you're perfect, President Manuela's plane is going to take damage and start going down. Finish the enemy targets and get close enough to the other plane to grapple onto it. This is a very tricky maneuver, and the game reloads you into a much more advantageous position if you fail this the first time, so don't stress out about it.

To make your attempt, fly close to Rosa's plane and drop some of your airspeed. Try to match the speed of her craft so that this is as easy as possible. Use the Stunt button to get onto the roof of your airplane, and then grapple onto hers. Once again, this is easy the second time because they load you in a perfect spot to do it automatically.

Take over for the pilot, who has had some medical complications, and land the craft at the airstrip marked on your map. Don't dive too aggressively into the runway or else you might crash the plane. Take it easy!

The mission ends after you land.

DERAILED EXTRACTION

Your next goal is to meet with President Manuela in the northeast. Go to Refugio Umbra, and start the mission. Everyone meets and plans a way to stop Di Ravello from getting his Bavarium out of the nation.

Rosa: Well, that settles it, then. Good luck, Rico.

FLY OVER AND PROTECT THE TRAIN

Grapple onto Teo's chopper as the briefing ends. He flies you over to a train. Grapple onto the train as it passes. Get out a heavy weapon and prepare to fight off an enemy helicopter as you leave a tunnel.

This is by no means the last of the gunships that attack the train. Take all of them out, preferably while staying on the train so that you don't get ditched during the fighting.

Start making your way toward the rear of the train while you beat back the aircraft. At the end of that fight, Di Ravello sends a train to try and crash into the back of your cars. You need to shoot a coupler toward the back of the train to prevent this from happening.

Try Not to Fall Off

If you do fall off or get left behind by the train, grapple back toward it as quickly as possible. You can pull yourself back into the mission if you're quick about this!

Another train comes from behind and needs to be destroyed. Take care of that, and then return to the front of your own train. You're almost where you need to be!

DERAIL THE ONCOMING TRAIN ENGINE

Grapple onto the inbound train and place explosives on the lead car. Use them to derail the train and prevent the extraction of Bavarium. There aren't any defenders to worry about, so you only have to dodge fire from surviving helicopters.

Alternatively, you can destroy the other train with just about anything creative in your arsenal. Experiment with anything that you'd like to try out, because many different strategies work.

The mission ends as soon as the train is put out of action!

THE GREAT ESCAPE

Annika calls you after the end of Derailed Extraction. She asks for a meeting, over in Maestrale. Travel there and see what she's planning. It sounds like a prison break!

GO INTO UNDERGROUND PRISON AND ACTIVATE TWO SWITCHES

Glide down the hill toward the prison entrance. It's super easy to break in there. And no one is in your way as you head down. That's, well, actually rather alarming.

Things go pear shaped very quickly. Soldiers pop out in an ambush. Use close quarters weaponry to fight through the corridors. Search for the two switches as you go; they are on opposite sides of the floor. Both are against the far walls and are surrounded by electrical paneling.

Hack the terminal by the large, lower door after you've pushed both switches.

MOVE DEEPER INTO THE PRISON

You must do the same thing on the lower level; find two switches. However, this area has snipers all over the place. Don't try for the high ground this time. Stay in the area between the buildings to block the line of sight between Rico and the snipers. This lets you fight groups of enemies here and there rather than getting shot by everyone at once.

If enemies pile up in one particular area, use grenades or a rocket to blow them apart. Otherwise, stick with your guns to eliminate targets that are somewhat isolated.

One of the switches is closer to the center of the room compared to last time; it's not on the outer wall. Push both buttons and then hack the terminal that unlocks. You gain access to the generator level.

DESTROY BOTH GENERATORS

The enemies in the next room have a great angle of fire against you. Use the depression where you enter the room as cover, and return there to regain health if anything goes wrong. Blast everyone down before you explore too much, because their damage output is quite decent if you simply ignore them and try to run through.

Use the switches in this room to expose each generator, and attack the machines directly to blow them apart. As soon as you finish, hurry to the surface via a vertical tunnel here.

DEFEAT THE SOLDIERS

Grapple out of the tunnel and back into fresh air. Glide to the next waypoint, and help the escaping prisoners fight off Di Ravello's men.

Focus on the snipers in the guard towers first; they're some of the deadliest targets, but they die quickly if attacked.

The mission ends after you save your allies and kill off all of the militia forces in the area.

BAVARIUM ON A PLANE

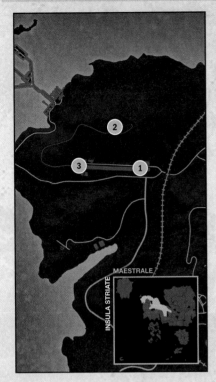

Sheldon warns you about a new threat and asks that you travel up to the northwest. Do this when you have time, and begin Bavarium on a Plane.

DRIVE THE CAR TO THE AIRPORT

Resupply before you get in the nearby vehicle; there are tons of goodies lying around. Hop into the Weimaraner and drive to the airport. Pick up speed as you descend the hill, and break right through the airport gates. Stay in your vehicle and maintain your velocity all the way across the tarmac. Approach a huge cargo plane that's trying to take off, and drive onto its loading door (which is luckily still in a lowered position).

GET ONTO THE ROOF AND PROTECT THE PLANE

Kill the two soldiers in the cargo bay, then climb into a red hatch to get onto the roof of the airplane. As soon as the enemy jet fighters get close, commandeer one of them and drop your speed so that the cargo plane and your enemies pass by. You can also do a loop-de-loop to let the enemies get in front of you.

From behind, you get a great targeting solution against them and start taking out these fighters one after the other.

Destroy their reinforcements as they arrive to ensure that the cargo plane doesn't take much damage while your friends are inside trying to get things figured out.

Eventually, you're told to get back into the plane. Grapple back onto the roof, and use the red hatch to get back inside. Hop into the rigged truck and drive out of the cargo bay as quickly as you can.

This completes the mission.

THE WATCHER ON THE WALL

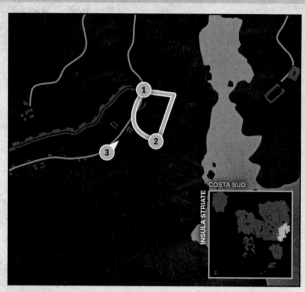

Travel east of Costa Sud to start Watcher on the Wall; that's your next goal. Get over there and meet Mario and the president. Afterward, deploy and look over the area. The rebels have cargo that needs protection, and you're just the person to do it.

Mario of vigilance they built this thing, I say, "earned by Mario Frigo is going to

Second Time Around

Our walkthrough offers one way to get through the large battle that's coming up. It works, and it's fun too. However, there's an easier way to beat this if you're not afraid of being really unfair to your opponents.

Use your tethers to pull the heavy AA gun on the tower forward so that it can hit aircraft and ground forces alike. Now, get it and use that for the entire mission to rip apart everyone and everything.

And yes, this also works to kill the special helicopter at the end of the mission. Get off of your bike when the cutscene ends, zip back to your AA gun, and start firing before the chopper escapes.

Deeply unfair. Very fun.

PROTECT THE REBEL CARGO

Militia vehicles are already inbound, on the road. Grapple over to the towers near the cargo and start attacking the enemies. Use higher ground for a slight defensive advantage, and see if you can commandeer an enemy gunship during the battle. That gives you even more firepower and protection.

Watch the yellow health bars for both sets of cargo. If one of them is dropping even faster than the other, you need to reposition yourself and make sure that the weaker area gets more protection.

There's a minigun by some sandbags at the base of your towers. Use that if you're on ground level and need to put the pain onto your enemies. This comes in handy during the second big wave, when even more gunships attack.

The third wave begins when jet fighters come in. Use the AA gun at the top of the main structure to fight them off before they destroy your cargo. It's MUCH more effective at taking out the jets compared to the minigun, or even a chopper.

From that position, you can even attack a number of distant ground targets. Hit a few of those after the jets are all destroyed, and then get back to ground level to deal with more soldiers.

DESTROY THE HELICOPTER

Once the last wave ends, a single enemy helicopter tries to escape the scene. This one is worth going after, so Rico gets onto a motorcycle and gives chase. When you get close enough to the helicopter, grapple onto it and hang from the bottom of the aircraft. Plant some explosives onto the chassis, shoot the chopper with your guns, and detonate everything as you drop off of the craft.

Repeat this, as needed, to destroy the helicopter and complete the mission.

Before starting the next mission, think about catching up on your Liberations and Challenges. Things proceed quickly during the next few missions, and you're getting somewhat close to the ending. Take a few moments to smell the roses!

BAVARIUM BLACKOUT

MISSION REWARD: Insula Striate FOW disabled

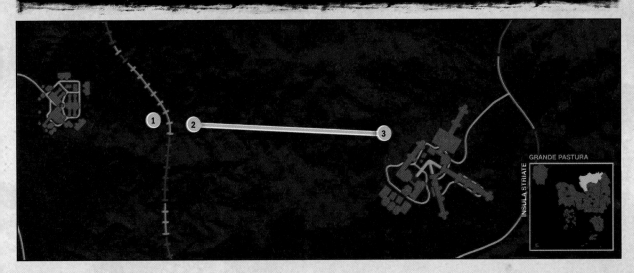

When you're ready to do this, go to Grande Pastura. Di Ravello has another buried bunker you must infiltrate and destroy. As before, follow the cables through the wilderness to get wherever it leads.

FOLLOW THE PIPES

At first, the trek involves fairly simple climbs up the hills. The pipes are easy to see, and the way is clear. It's up to you whether to grapple your way up or to use the chopper near the starting point.

Get to the top of the mountain and look for a large hatch in the ground. Dimah hacks it open for you. Drop into the base below and start killing guards. There are a decent number of them in here, but you can grapple onto a balcony above the first room if you need a place to hide and rest during the skirmish.

DESTROY THE COMMAND NODE

Kill the guards, from higher ground if needed, and go into the next room. There are only scientists inside. Look for a panel to open the next gate, and use that to continue.

The soldiers in the Command Node are very heavily armored. They take plenty of shots, even to the head, before they go down. Hang back and hit them at range so that you don't expose yourself too early in the fight.

Use the miniguns that the enemies were carrying to destroy the transformers in that room.

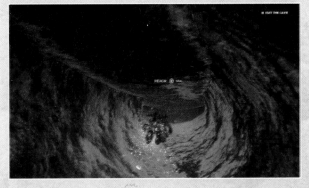

Swim out through a submerged tunnel on the side of the command node. There's a merciful air pocket halfway through the exit tunnel, and after that you hit open air once again.

That was way easier than expected. Should that make us nervous? Hmmmm…

THE SHATTERER OF WORLDS

MISSION REWARD: Unlock M488 Bavarium Nuke FOW

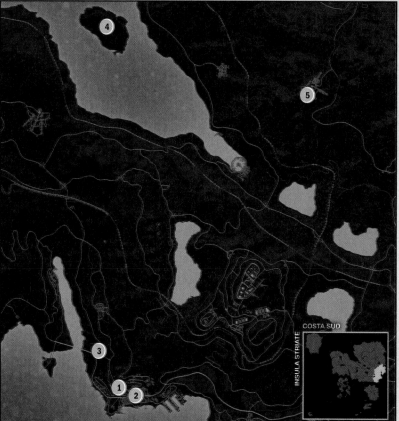

COSTA SUD

INSULA STRIATE

Go to Regno for a strike at the very core of Di Ravello's power and his knowledge of Bavarium. Starting this mission begins a battle in the center of the nation. As before, you must hurry to the various battlefields and destroy your targets to ensure that the rebels win!

DEFEAT THE SNIPERS

Your first target is on top of a skyscraper downtown. Glide onto that building and eliminate a few snipers to ensure they cannot control the streets below. The snipers can't resist for long in a close quarters battle, so they're pretty much doomed from the get go.

DEFEAT THE MILITARY PLATOON

Take the chopper on the roof that the snipers were using, and fly northwest. A rebel contingent is locked down by a platoon of militia troopers with armored support. They need assistance right now!

Land by one of the tanks in the open field and commandeer it. Use your heavy cannon to destroy several of the militia's vehicles in short order.

Gun down any survivors, using your minigun, and then leave the field when the fighting dies down.

REACH THE REBEL ENCAMPMENT AND DESTROY ATTACKING JETS

Search for a jet on the northern side of the battlefield, and take off in that direction. Your next battle site is over 7km away, so something fast really helps you get there without wasting precious time.

When you arrive, use your homing missiles to blow through Di Ravello's aircraft. It's a short engagement.

ATTACK THE MILITARY TO FINISH THE BATTLE

You are close to victory, but may still need to finish off a number of targets around the area to complete the mission. Destroy naval craft with your jet fighter, or fly back toward the city and search for targets there (it's a much easier place to find enemies).

Dimah calls for you when the battle finally turns fully in the rebel's favor.

REACH THE FALCO MAXIME CENTCOM TOWER

Commandeer an aircraft if you can, and make the flight over to Centcom Tower, as marked. The mission ends when you arrive.

THERE ISN'T A POINT OF NO RETURN

There's only one mission remaining, but don't let that deter you. It's possible to play the game after things are over with the main story, so there's no reason to avoid completing the story.

SON OF MEDICI

MISSION REWARD: Unlock Bavarium-Shielded rebel chopper

Fly to Maestrale and begin the last mission. You talk to the full team and then set off after General Di Ravello.

REACH THE VOLCANO AND DEFEAT DI RAVELLO

Take a jet fighter from the rebel position and fly northwest, toward the big volcano that sets on the border of Medici. A cutscene plays when you arrive, and soon Rico must face off against Di Ravello's helicopter in the middle of a fiery basin.

There are plenty of Beacons at the top of the volcano. Grab these and make sure that you have some heavy weapons before starting things off.

A Few Helpful Tips

The Thunderbird and M488 can obliterate Di Ravello's chopper (as long as its shield is down, of course). That's one of the most evil weapons to bring for this final fight.

Heavy automatic weapons are also very helpful. The URGA VDOVA 89 and CS Predator are both excellent choices.

Beacons work during the battle, so call down additional supplies if you run out of anything.

THE FALL OF DI RAVELLO

The enemy chopper has powerful missiles, and its Bavarium shield protects it from damage most of the time. You must time your shots so that you attack when the glowing shield is down.

Use the stone pillars around the basin for cover if you need a few moments to regenerate health while on the ground. Don't stand still out in the open, or you're pretty much guaranteed to take major damage.

It's easiest to dodge his missiles when you're airborne. Parachute above the helicopter to get a good view and stay safe while waiting out the Bavarium shield. If you want another cue to know when the Bavarium shield is up, look at the General's health bar; it crackles with energy when the Bavarium shield is active!

It takes four hits with your rockets to bring the helicopter out of the sky.

And with that, you enter the final scene. Decide how you want to handle everything, and then watch the credits. Sandbox Mode is unlocked afterward. This allows you to go back through the world and complete anything that isn't done quite yet.

Also, you can re-Oppress settlements and Liberate them again, if you're in the mood to relive some of the most incredible moments from the game!

You've really done your part, son of Medici. Vaya con Dios!

LIBERATION

You must liberate settlements to progress through Rico's story. Many Story missions have a set number of settlements that must be liberated before you can start those missions. The concept of liberating a settlement is easy, but the execution difficulty varies greatly, depending on the size and defenses of a settlement.

To liberate any settlement, you must destroy all military assets within it. Certain towns also require you to deactivate monitoring systems and overtake the police station. Some police stations have multiple tasks you must accomplished, such as raising a Havoc Meter to 100%, freeing prisoners, and raising gates to call in Rebel reinforcements.

This section of the guide reveals all the military assets and challenges in every settlement. Military assets are not marked on the in-game map—at least not until there are only a few remaining and you're struggling to find them. Check our map before entering an area so you know exactly where the SAM sites are located and can figure out the settlement's weakness and find weapon caches. And, of course, if there's a military asset you cannot find, our maps become priceless.

SETTLEMENT PROGRESS TRACKING

Your liberation progress is tracked in the Progress menu, which provides a breakdown of discovered and liberated settlement totals by region and settlement type.

REGION SETTLEMENT TOTALS

- ■ Insula Fonte: 9 Provinces, 39 Settlements
- ■ Insula Dracon: 7 Provinces, 33 Settlements
- ■ Insula Striate: 13 Provinces, 58 Settlements

SETTLEMENT TYPES

- ■ Village (6)
- ■ Town (28)
- ■ Capital (1)
- ■ Outpost (51)
- ■ Base (20)
- ■ Airbase (2)
- ■ Radar (3)
- ■ Region Central Command (3)

130 SETTLEMENTS? IT'S NOT ADDING UP!

Once you discover you need to liberate 130 settlements and want to check your progress, you naturally go to the map or simply look farther down in the Progress menu. When you add up the Settlement Type amounts, you quickly realize that there's a discrepancy in the totals. Don't fret. The named ruins and tourist attractions, such as Sancte Malco in Insula Striate, become liberated when that region or nearby settlement is liberated. These areas cannot be liberated on their own—they have no military assets. There are 16 of these settlements, which are added to the 114 settlements (with military assets) for the grand total of 130.

Capital & Villages & Towns

The capital, villages, and towns are the residential areas of Medici. They have very similar military assets. Most have statues of Di Ravello, speakers, and Di Ravello billboards. Towns are bigger than villages and have those assets and more, such as monitoring systems, propaganda vans, projectors, and captains. The biggest difference is that towns (and the capital) have a police station.

The police stations have internal challenges of their own. Once you've beaten the police station challenge and the monitoring system challenge and have destroyed all military assets, you must then raise the Rebel flag to call it liberated. Many towns have garages that are unlocked once liberated. These always have resupply points where you can find Beacons and Flares.

After liberating the capital, villages, or towns, you are sometimes rewarded with a garage, a challenge, and maybe a Rebel Drop vehicle or weapon unlock.

Outposts

Outposts are smaller than bases and primarily service Di Ravello's campaign in the fields of communications, power production, refueling, oil drilling, and air support. Outposts come in all sizes and varying amounts of defensive power. There are more outposts than any other type of settlement.

Airbases

There are only two airbases in Medici and they're extremely fortified with tremendous air support. If you take out their surface-to-air defenses early in the battle, you can easily turn their air force against them. Airbase liberation awards you the same type of unlockables as do the bases, towns, and villages.

Bases

Bases vary in their size and the amount of their defensive capabilities. Expect to battle airdropped reinforcements and a base commander in some. Much like liberating a village or town, base liberation comes with rewards, such as a Rebel Drop weapon or vehicle unlock and/or challenges such as a wingsuit course, Land and Sea races, a Demolition Frenzy, or a Crash Bomb challenge. Many bases reward you with multiple challenge unlocks.

Radars

There are three radar bases in Medici: two are located in Insula Fonte (Vigilator Nord, Vigilator Sud), one is located in Insula Dracon (Puncta Sud). These are very large compounds that specialize in spying, information collection, and communications. They are heavily fortified and offer the same liberation rewards as bases, towns, and villages.

Region Central Commands

Known as Centcom for short, these region central command centers are Di Ravello's theater-level combatant command fortresses. There are three Centcoms in Medici. They all hold vital information to Di Ravello's army, such as Bavarium research, and are the strongholds from which Di Ravello regional commanders keep Medici under dictatorial control.

LIBERATION CHALLENGES

POLICE STATIONS

Towns contain police stations, and taking control of one is a challenge within itself. Before you can completely liberate a town, you must first flatten the police station. This requires the completion of at least two objectives. In all police stations you must raise a Havoc Meter to 100% and open a gate (or gates) to allow the Rebel resistance to enter, assist, and take control.

CALLING IN REBELS

To call in Rebels, open each gate in a police station (some police stations have multiple entrance gates). Raising the gate is typically done by pushing the gate button near the gate. Or you can tether the lowered gate to the top gate frame and reel in to force the gate open. Even if you release the tether afterward, the gate remains open. The button is often quicker, but if there are heavy forces around the gate, it might be safer to tether the gate open from the safety of a nearby rooftop or anywhere the enemy is not.

FILLING THE HAVOC METER

The other challenge involved in liberating a police station is to cause so much havoc that you fill the Havoc Meter. These challenges do not activate until you fly over or are on the police station grounds. Havoc caused outside the police station does not fill the Havoc Meter. In order to cause havoc, you must blow stuff up. Blowing up the military assets inside the police station is a great first step. But this alone never fills the meter to 100%. Look for other things to blow up, such as vehicles parked inside, explosive barrels, and the actual walls in and around the police station.

RELEASING PRISONERS

Not all police stations are the same, and not all have prisoners. But for those that do, you must hack open their jail cells and let them out. This is best done once the Rebels have been called in so that the militia inside the police station have something else to shoot at besides you. What happens to the prisoners after they're released is not your concern, just as long as they have been freed.

POLICE STATION LIBERATION TIPS

As with any base, town, or outpost, it's always a good idea to assault the destructibles while piloting an attack helicopter. Towns and police stations are not protected by SAM sites, but you must contend with enemy air support. If the heat comes on strong, then attack the police station first. That way, if you lose the helicopter in battle, then the timeliest challenge—raising the Havoc Meter—has already been accomplished. If you lose your copter during or after the attack, simply hijack one of the enemy helicopters out of the sky using your grapple, then enter vehicle command.

DISABLE MONITORING SYSTEM

Some towns have a certain number of monitors to disable in an allotted amount of time. You must push the button on each monitor to disable it. The fastest way to reach each one is to grapple, parachute, or wingsuit it—and sometimes a combination of all three. Grappling is the fastest, but it won't always reach from one monitor to the next. Aim for the actual monitor pole or the rooftop just below the pole to be pulled directly toward the monitor. Grapple out of a parachute glide to quickly reach your destination. Whenever possible, disable the monitors from highest to lowest (falling is faster than climbing). Use our numbered monitors on our maps for the quickest route to all of the monitors.

BAVARIUM EXCAVATORS

There are many Bavarium Excavators in the Bavarium mining fields. These monstrous mining machines weigh tons and are heavily defended, but you must destroy them. An Excavator has two main components: the body and the drilling arm. You must destroy both to completely wreck the Excavator.

EXCAVATOR BODY

To raze an Excavator, you must destroy its eight generators on the top platform. There are four on each side. Some Excavators are equipped with Capstone FH155s on each side, which allows you to finish them off pretty quickly. Just be aware that the main platform explodes when you destroy the final generator, so clear out once you eliminate it.

EXCAVATOR DRILLING ARM

If destroying the eight generators does not finish off the Excavator, then make sure you destroy the excavation arm, as well. It's good practice to attack the arm first. There are seven main target points on the arm: the extension arm joints (colored red) and then the motor at the fulcrum of the arm. However, the two weakest points are the joints on the extension closest to the platform itself. Target these with explosives or rockets to blow them up quickly. Usually destroying these two is enough to eliminate the drill; however, sometimes you must also hit another target farther up the arm.

FINDING THE HELP YOU NEED, FAST!

The details on every settlement in Medici are arranged alphabetically, first by region name and then by the province name within that region.

LIBERATION TABLE OF CONTENTS

The settlements in this table of contents are arranged by Region alphabetically and then within the Region, by Province alphabetically. The numbers associated with settlement represent their location on our map on the next page.

There are 114 settlements to liberate. Three of these are liberated from the beginning of the game (82, 116, 24). These are labeled "Neutral Rebel Base" in this TOC. Since they are liberated already, you will not find details or tips on these settlements in our Liberation guide.

INSULA DRACON

INSULA FONTE

INSULA STRIATE

CALLOUT LEGEND

#	Numbered Location Activity
	Antenna Tower
H	Attack Helicopter
	Bavarium Dump Trailor
	Bavarium Refinery Station
	Billboard
C	Capstone FH155
	Captain
	Cell Block

	Circuit Breaker
	Core Electrical Unit
	Distillation Tower
	Doppler Radar
	Excavator
	Flag
	Fuel Tank
	Generator
	Long Range Radar
	Monitoring System

	Police Station
	Projector
	Propaganda Van
	Radar Spire
R	Resupply Point
S	SAM - Surface to Air Missle
	Satcom Dish
	Satellite Dish
	Speaker
	Sphere Tank

	Statue
	Substation Controls
T	Tank
	Transformer
	Transponder
	Turbine Block
V	Urga Vukan
	Water Tower
W	Weapons

MEDICI SETTLEMENTS

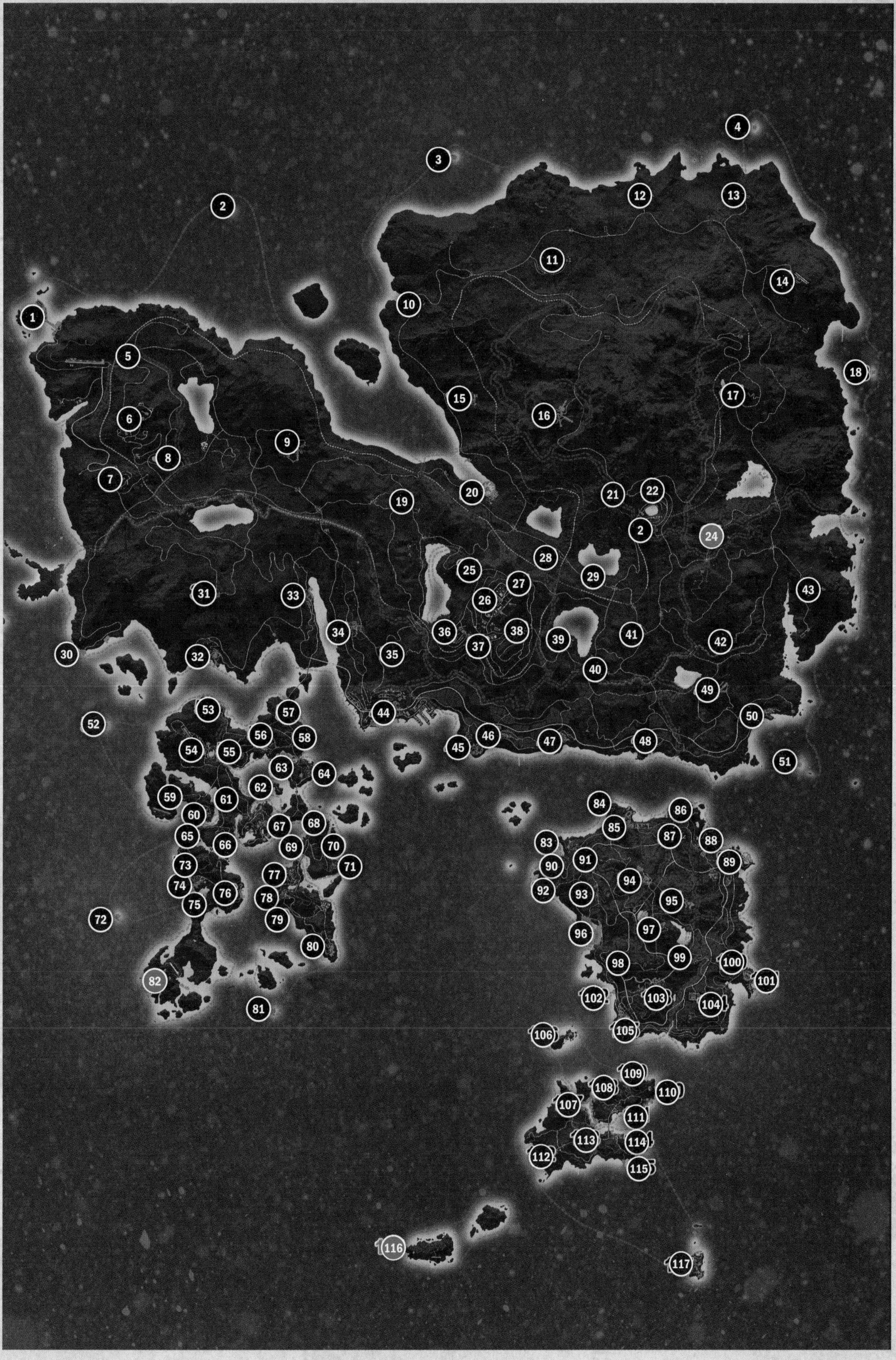

REGION: INSULA DRACON

PROVINCE: CAPITE EST

ESPIA ALTA

MILITARY ASSETS:
- Generator (3)
- Circuit Breaker (2)
- Core Electrical Unit (1)
- Doppler Radar (7)
- Fuel Tank (9)
- Satcom Dish (1)
- Transponder (1)
- Transformer (6)
- Water Tower (1)
- Commander

LIBERATION REWARDS
- Rebel Drop: CS110 Archangel
- Wingsuit Course: Undertown Tour
- Demolition Frenzy: Sniper Rifle Frenzy II

SETTLEMENT TYPE: BASE

Sister base to Espia Bassa, Alta's location was long known as a hot spot for unexplained aerial sightings before the General decided to establish a military facility there. Could there be a link between the area's mysterious history and its giant Satcom dish?

Tips

Since this base is deep in a canyon, we suggest first striking with rockets from high on a surrounding cliff. It's difficult to get a helicopter inside without first taking out the SAM sites. Move in and hack the SAMS, then hijack a helicopter to attack large targets like the Satcom dish.

Reinforcements

Enemy reinforcements arrive early. It comes in the form of some military vehicles, most notably a tank. Hijack the tank and destroy the others in the convoy, including any other tanks. Then turn the cannons on the military assets. You can take out the Satcom dish quickly with the tank's munitions—just get in a good position to point the cannon that high.

Generators

The three generators are in the buildings under Doppler radars surrounding the Satcom dish. When you approach a switch to reveal the generators, the word "activate" appears on-screen to mark the location. Press the button, like the one on the helipad ①, to open the doors to the hidden generator on the ground level of the same structure. Send a grenade or rocket inside to quickly destroy the generator. Repeat this for switches ② and ③.

Commander

The base commander appears near the end of the battle. He arrives in an attack helicopter through the natural tunnel that opens to the ocean. If you have hacked most of the SAM sites, then this guy may not ever see you. Otherwise, hijack his helicopter, throw him out, and kill him (if the fall didn't do the job). Turn his own flying weapon on him.

Transponder

If you haven't dealt with one yet, it's likely your missing military asset is the transponder. It's in a sealed underground silo on the ledge with the SAM site and guard tower near the ocean. Hack the terminal by the silo and start shooting the transponder as it rises from the silo.

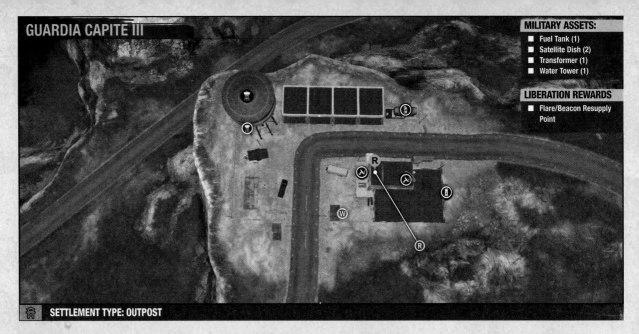

GUARDIA CAPITE III

MILITARY ASSETS:
- ■ Fuel Tank (1)
- ■ Satellite Dish (2)
- ■ Transformer (1)
- ■ Water Tower (1)

LIBERATION REWARDS
- ■ Flare/Beacon Resupply Point

SETTLEMENT TYPE: OUTPOST

Medicians are fond of saying, "You can't drive two minutes without seeing a soldier." The roads of Capite stay full of rambling convoys and patrols thanks to Guardia Capite III.

Tips

There are no anti-aircraft defenses here, so taking this outpost from the skies is quick and easy. If you're on foot or flying in, hijack the tank inside the shelter and demolish the outpost. If you are into gunning targets, try knocking the feet out from under the water tower to make it fall. This uses fewer bullets than shooting the container itself.

VICO SPIGOLA

MILITARY ASSETS:
- ■ Speaker (2)
- ■ Statue (1)
- ■ Raise the Flag

LIBERATION REWARDS
- ■ Sea Race: Regata Ponte

SETTLEMENT TYPE: VILLAGE

Every year Vico Spigola hosts the nation's oldest fishing contest, the Medici Sea Bass Classic. Last year's winning fish was caught by General Sebastiano Di Ravello, extending his winning streak to a remarkable 22 years.

Tips

With no billboards or monitor challenge and only a couple speakers and a statue, you can own this town as quickly as Di Ravello wins the local fishing tournament. Shoot the statue with a rocket or grenade, or take it down with a placed explosive. It requires only two bullets to take out a speaker, so use one to knock the cover off the box between the speakers atop the pole, and then another to shoot the innards. Raise the flag near one of the destroyed speakers to put the final touches on this town. Notice the Beacon/Resupply point marked on our map just outside the town, near the only road in and out.

VICO THUNNO

SETTLEMENT TYPE: VILLAGE

MILITARY ASSETS:
- ☐ Billboard (1)
- ☐ Speaker (1)
- ☐ Statue (1)
- ☐ Raise the Flag

LIBERATION REWARDS
- ☐ Wingsuit Course: Monte Dracon Tour

Vico Thunno is truly the forgotten village of Insula Dracon's fishing community. Locals contend that the last piece of mail the community received was in 1988, and that was meant for Angelo's cousin, Andres, in Cinta.

Tips

This one-speaker-one-billboard town is a pushover for any well-armed skydiver. Bomb the statue, shoot the speaker where it counts, and blow up the billboard to trigger the flag-raising event.

VINIALETTA

SETTLEMENT TYPE: TOWN

MILITARY ASSETS:
- ☐ Billboard (2)
- ☐ Police Station
- ☐ Fuel Tank (1)
- ☐ Generator (1)
- ☐ Satellite Dish (1)
- ☐ Speaker (2)
- ☐ Statue (1)
- ☐ Raise the Flag

LIBERATION REWARDS
- ☐ Vinialetta Garage

Vinialetta is home to the nation's most creative vintners, both in the variety of wines produced there and the yield gained from its rocky, unforgiving soil. It's not uncommon to see a Vinialetta wine on the General's dinner table.

Tips: Police Station

If you are piloting an attack helicopter, target the police station first. Raise the Havoc Meter to 100% while taking out all the targets inside. If you lose the helicopter, then you've accomplished the most time-consuming part of this liberation. You can always hijack an enemy chopper if you want to continue in this fashion.

There are two prison control panels on the police station building ① (one on the ground level and one on the second level). Hack the prison doors to free both prisoners. It's easier to do this after you call in the Rebels (by pressing the gate switch ②) or by tethering it open. They'll keep the enemies somewhat distracted while you hack.

PROVINCE: CAPITE WEST

ARCO SPERANTIA

MILITARY ASSETS:
- Billboard (2)
- Police Station
- Fuel Tank (2)
- Projector (1)
- Speaker (3)
- Statue (1)
- Substation Controls (1)
- Transformer (2)
- Raise the Flag

LIBERATION REWARDS
- Arco Sperantia Garage
- Sea Race: Regata Curvare
- Air Race: Volo Dracon

SETTLEMENT TYPE: TOWN

Arco Sperantia's origins date back to Medici's antiquity, when it served as a military garrison for Insula Dracon's western flank. Its name means "Arch of Hope," a reference to the town's imposing front entrance. As the centuries passed, locals began to settle within the massive fort, first for protection and later to capitalize on the streams of tourists that flowed through the ruins.

Tips: Police Station

If you are not attacking the police station in a helicopter, then disarm the militia with the Urga Vulkan (minigun) near the fuel tanks. Use this weapon to clear the area of riffraff, take out the military assets, and destroy everything that is destructible, raising the Havoc Meter to 100%.

From a rooftop vantage point near the Urga Vulkan, you can destroy most of the targets in the police station and tether the gate ➊ open to call the Rebels in. With that done, hack the prison control panel ➋ on the second level of the structure with the two transformers underneath.

GUARDIA CAPITE I

MILITARY ASSETS:
- ☐ Antenna Tower (1)
- ☐ Doppler Radar (3)
- ☐ Satellite Dish (1)
- ☐ Transformer (1)

LIBERATION REWARDS
- ☐ Flare/Beacon Resupply Point

🏠 **SETTLEMENT TYPE: OUTPOST**

Along with discipline, the secret to Di Ravello's constant victories over the Rebellion is constant, uninterrupted communication. Guardia Capite I helps connect forces throughout Capite West.

Tips

Try to destroy the legs of the antenna on the side closest to the Doppler radar array; you may be able to kill four birds with one stone—if the tower falls on those birds. There's no air defense at this outpost, so you can flatten it in seconds with an attack helicopter.

GUARDIA CAPITE II

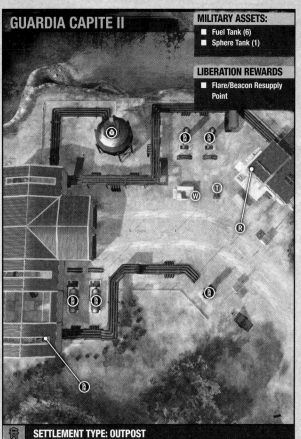

MILITARY ASSETS:
- ☐ Fuel Tank (6)
- ☐ Sphere Tank (1)

LIBERATION REWARDS
- ☐ Flare/Beacon Resupply Point

🏠 **SETTLEMENT TYPE: OUTPOST**

The sheer size of Medici's ever-expanding military spurred demand for storage and refueling facilities like Guardia Capite II.

Tips

If you aren't attacking in a flying machine, then hijack the tank parked near the weapons cache inside the outpost and just annihilate everything with it. Don't forget to destroy the fuel tank tucked away in a corner inside the large shelter.

PLATTEFORMA CAPITE I

MILITARY ASSETS:
- Circuit Breaker (1)
- Doppler Radar (4)
- Fuel Tank (10)
- Generator (2)
- Satellite Dish (1)
- Transformer (5)

LIBERATION REWARDS
- Flare/Beacon Resupply Point

SETTLEMENT TYPE: OVUTPOST

Di Ravello's twin obsessions—maintaining order through military might and strip-mining Medici of all its precious Bavarium deposits—require thousands of barrels of petrol a year. Plattforma Capite I works around the clock to provide fuel for the Medician war machine.

Tips

This platform is brutal. Your helicopter won't last long even if you attack from afar, as you must deal with naval forces. Try reaching the platform's top level and grab the Urga Vulkan. Use it to destroy all the enemies, helicopters, and military assets on the top level. Put it down and hack the two SAMs on the top level to ward off those machines buzzing overhead. Walk the edges of the upper-level catwalks and aim at everything red below.

Some of the trickier military assets to find are the fuel tanks on the support columns at water level and the satellite dish on the arm jutting off the oil rig's first and second levels.

PORTO CAVO

SETTLEMENT TYPE: BASE

Tips: Airfield

This is a very large base with some serious surface-to-air defenses. We suggest taking over the airfield first. It's difficult to jack a jet fighter from the end of the runway; they probably won't survive the takeoff with all the heavy shelling you'll encounter. Concentrate on hacking the two SAMS on the runway's opposite end. Soon a tank will be dispatched. Hijack this and destroy everyone and everything around the airfield. Drive the tank to the cliff's edge and start destroying all the assets possible, starting with the radio spires. Next start taking out military assets in the base in the caves below.

Capstones

Parachute down into the cave, destroying what you can with rockets as you head to the many Capstone FH155s along the pier weapon platforms. Use these to destroy aerial and naval enemies, and then start on all the military assets in range. Move from Capstone to Capstone, using these weapons to destroy the base.

Rebel Support: Bridge Controls

Activate the bridge controls on the drawbridge ① to allow Rebel naval forces to assist you. At least they can distract the enemy while you do the real work. Continue using Capstones, Urga Vulkans, tanks, and our mapped asset locations to liberate the base. The base is large, but we have revealed all the targets so you can locate everything quickly.

PROVINCE: CORDA DRACON

CORDA DRACON: CENTCOM

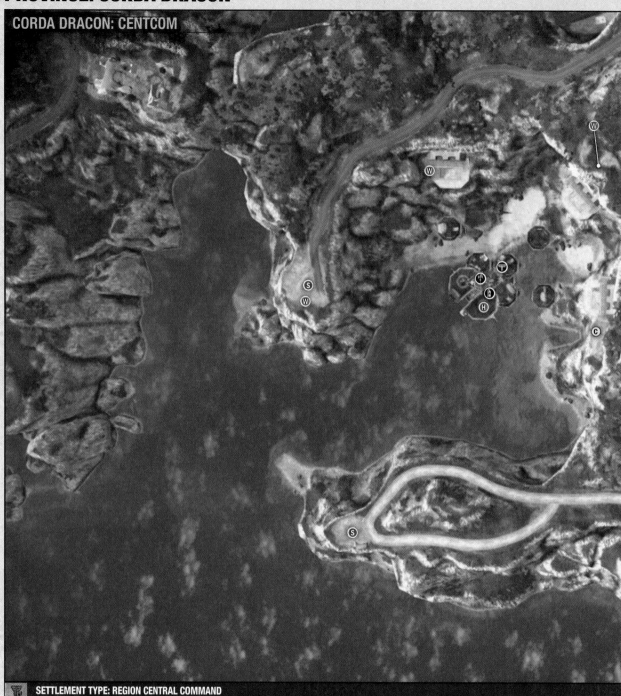

SETTLEMENT TYPE: REGION CENTRAL COMMAND

Corda Dracon translates to "Heart of the Dragon." Its central location and elevated vantage have long made it the key to controlling the region. The base's construction was the forerunner for the General's grand experiment of marrying classical and contemporary military installations, a theme later reproduced across Medici.

Tips: EMP Cannons

Corda Dracon is very difficult to attack while flying or driving any kind of machine; the many EMP cannons stop you quickly even if you make it past the SAM sites. Do what damage you can from a distance if you are flying. Otherwise, parachute into the base, looking for high ground from which to start your attack. We like to start atop the large tower in the middle of the central base structure. From here, you can rocket the military assets below from the edge of the rooftop.

Transponders

There are three transponders to destroy, if you have not dealt with them yet. They are inside closed silos (see our map). Raise each transponder by hacking one of the three switches ①, ②, and ③ near the silo sites. Clear the enemies from the area and then hack the switch. Shoot the transponder as it rises from the silo.

MILITARY ASSETS:

- Antenna Tower (4)
- Doppler Radar (1)
- Fuel Tank (5)
- Long-Range Radar (2)
- Radar Spire (1)
- Transponder (3)
- Transformer (1)

LIBERATION REWARDS

- Rebel Drop Boat: Urga Hroch
- Demolition Frenzy: Helicopter Frenzy II

Hack the SAM sites near the transponders (the middle platform). Since the EMP cannon makes it hard to drive heavy military vehicles, use a rocket launcher on the legs of the antenna towers to bring them down quickly.

Radar Spire

Use the Capstone on the mountainside ledge to destroy all the targets in the bay, namely the radio spire and the other military assets on this platform. Behind this gun, there is an open cave with militia inside, so turn around periodically to blow up the attacking soldiers behind you.

PROVINCE: MASSOS

CINTA

 SETTLEMENT TYPE: TOWN

Insula Dracon's easternmost settlement has long since been the landing site of invading forces looking to gain a foothold in the region. Consequently, it is a patchwork of defensive structures razed and rebuilt over a millennium of warfare. The locals are known for their jaded outlook on Medician politics, regardless of the figure in charge.

Tips: Hidden Billboard

Di Ravello has not yet erected a statue of himself in this small town, but he has certainly made his presence known with his three billboards. The tough one to find is inside the tunnel. The only road into town passes through here.

Police Station

Hijack a helicopter or use a Rebel Drop to annihilate the targets in the police station and raise the Havoc Meter. There are three poisoners to free from jail cells here. Two of the prisoners are on the police station's top level, above the generator.

Hack the two door switches ① and ②; the third cell ③ is on the ground level. Open the one gate Ⓐ in the police station to call in the Rebels.

Disable Monitoring System
Time Limit: 1:19

There are only three monitors to disable in this town. You must push the button on each monitor to disable it. The fastest way to get to each is to grapple, parachute, or wingsuit it (and sometimes a combination of all three). Work in the order we've mapped or use the opposite order. See monitors ④, ⑤, and ⑥ on our map.

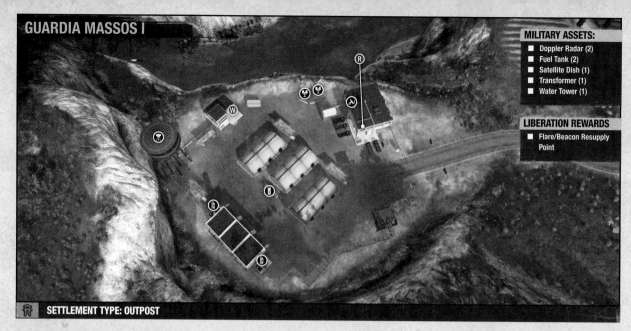

GUARDIA MASSOS I

MILITARY ASSETS:
- ☐ Doppler Radar (2)
- ☐ Fuel Tank (2)
- ☐ Satellite Dish (1)
- ☐ Transformer (1)
- ☐ Water Tower (1)

LIBERATION REWARDS
- ☐ Flare/Beacon Resupply Point

SETTLEMENT TYPE: OUTPOST

Housing is cheap and easy to find in Medici, mostly thanks to outposts like Guardia Massos I, which houses the large percentage of young Medicians lured by endless propaganda to serve in General Di Ravello's army.

Tips

Everything is out in the open (nothing hidden inside a shelter), and there are no SAMs. You can flatten it in seconds with an attack helicopter or glide in on a parachute and finish off all the targets with six rockets.

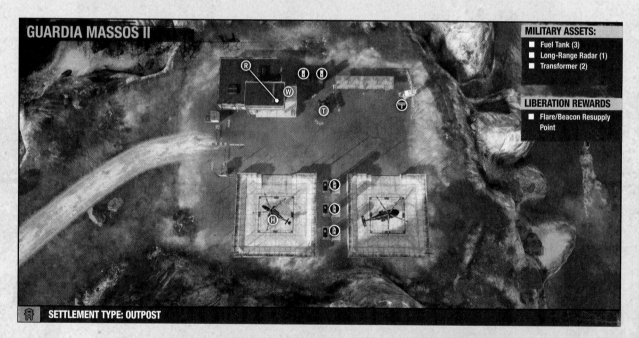

GUARDIA MASSOS II

MILITARY ASSETS:
- ☐ Fuel Tank (3)
- ☐ Long-Range Radar (1)
- ☐ Transformer (2)

LIBERATION REWARDS
- ☐ Flare/Beacon Resupply Point

SETTLEMENT TYPE: OUTPOST

Medici's skies are among the safest in the world, due largely to airfields like Guardia Massos II, which launches routine patrols and scrambles choppers to assist in frequent uprisings throughout Massos.

Tips

If you didn't arrive with an attack helicopter, there is one parked on the helipad nearest the gates. You can also flatten the outpost in seconds by hijacking the tank, which is also on the grounds.

GUARDIA MASSOS III

MILITARY ASSETS:
- Fuel Tank (1)
- Satellite Dish (2)
- Transformer (1)
- Water Tower (1)

LIBERATION REWARDS
- Flare/Beacon Resupply Point

SETTLEMENT TYPE: OUTPOST

The people of Medici are fond of saying, "You can't drive two minutes without seeing a soldier." The roads of Massos stay full of rambling convoys and patrols thanks to Guardia Massos III.

Tips

No SAMs in sight. Confidently fly in overhead in an attack chopper and lay waste to this small outpost. Send a rocket into the water tower just to see water spray everywhere. The small bridge outpost nearby is not part of the base, even though there's a Doppler radar there. If you are without aircraft, use the minigun from this guard post to infiltrate the outpost.

GUARDIA MASSOS IV

MILITARY ASSETS:
- Circuit Breaker (2)
- Core Electrical Unit (1)
- Transformer (4)

LIBERATION REWARDS
- Flare/Beacon Resupply Point

SETTLEMENT TYPE: OUTPOST

Reliable energy is hard to come by for the Medician people, but not for the Medician military. Larger power plants serve smaller outposts like Guardia Massos IV to keep the lights on for monitoring devices, propaganda, and the military.

Tips

Even with the outpost's SAM site, you can attack this location from a helicopter flying low beside the cliff side. From just out of range, you can send a volley of rockets or bullets into the transformers and core electrical unit; a chain reaction should do the rest.

GUARDIA MASSOS V

MILITARY ASSETS:
- Doppler Radar (2)
- Fuel Tank (1)
- Satellite Dish (2)
- Transformer (2)

LIBERATION REWARDS
- Flare/Beacon Resupply Point

SETTLEMENT TYPE: OUTPOST

Medici possesses the largest military harbors in the Mediterranean, but smaller ports like Guardia Massos V serve as waystations for small flotillas during patrols and tactical exercises.

Tips

First, destroy or hack the SAM site and sink the military boat. If you're attacking from the ground, you could miss the second satellite dish at the top of the control tower. If you're attacking from above, you may miss the satellite dish mounted to the side of the control tower. Destroy both and then take out the ground targets.

SOLIANA

MILITARY ASSETS:
- Billboard (3)
- Police Station
- Fuel Tank (2)
- Propaganda Van (1)
- Speaker (2)
- Statue (1)
- Transformer (2)
- Raise the Flag

LIBERATION REWARDS
- Soliana Garage
- Crash Bomb: Massos Bridge Blast
- Air Race: Volo Stretto Di Ravello

SETTLEMENT TYPE: TOWN

Soliana locals claim their town to be the oldest established settlement in Insula Dracon. Its hilltop temple dates back to Roman occupation and honors the sun god, Apollo. Early birds can catch magnificent sunrises from the ruins.

Tips

For such a big town, there are not a lot of targets. After knocking out a couple speakers, a propaganda van on the move, and three billboards, you just have the statue and the police station to deal with.

Police Station

This police station has four military assets to destroy, and you can find the weapons cache on the second level under the tallest building. Hack or tether the two gates ① and ② to call in the Rebels. Now go raise the Havoc Meter and the flag to liberate this town.

PROVINCE: PETRA

ESPIA BASSA

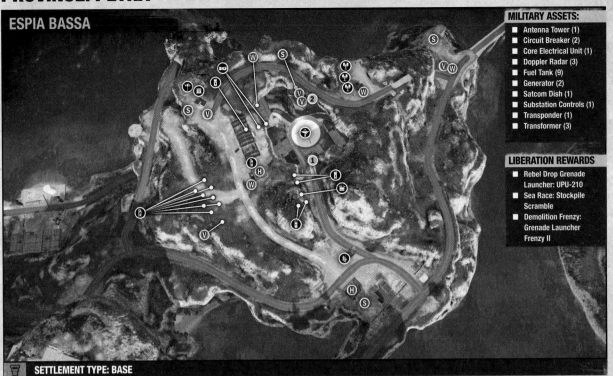

MILITARY ASSETS:

- Antenna Tower (1)
- Circuit Breaker (2)
- Core Electrical Unit (1)
- Doppler Radar (3)
- Fuel Tank (9)
- Generator (2)
- Satcom Dish (1)
- Substation Controls (1)
- Transponder (1)
- Transformer (3)

LIBERATION REWARDS

- Rebel Drop Grenade Launcher: UPU-210
- Sea Race: Stockpile Scramble
- Demolition Frenzy: Grenade Launcher Frenzy II

SETTLEMENT TYPE: BASE

This is the sister base to Espia Alta. Little is known about the brand of information gathered by Alta's massive satellite dish. Leaked recordings reveal simple, low-frequency radio patterns, suggesting a monitoring of deep space.

Tips: Surface Attack

One half of this base has its military targets exposed on the mountaintop and the other half is inside the large cavern inside the mountain. Hit the outposts on the outer edges of the exterior base first. Start by commandeering the Vulkan guns nearby, clearing the enemy and aerial attacks, and then hack the SAMs. When above ground, keep grappling to move around to avoid the airstrikes.

Transponder

There's also a mounted Urga Vulkan next to the road and building in the transponder area. Use the Vulkan to clear the riffraff. If things get hairy, use the transponder silo as a foxhole or just parachute around a bit. Hack the transponder controls to raise the device, and then destroy it. Hack the nearby SAM.

Vehicle Ramp

A good way to start your attack on the interior base is to drive a heavy vehicle off the ramp ①, parachute out, and allow the vehicle to explode when it hits the Satcom dish below.

Ledge of Death

There's a ledge below ground level, but high above most of the cave's military assets. Defeat the Black Hand Titan (the well-armored soldier holding the Urga Vulkan) and steal his weapon. Turn it on the nearby enemies and vehicles. Put it down for a second to hack the SAM on the same ledge. Pick it back up, walk to the edge of the ledge, and begin decimating all the targets you see in the base below.

Cavern of Fuel Tanks

It's easy to miss, but there's a cave a little farther away from the rest of the base, inside the cavern that contains eight very large fuel tanks. A Black Hand Titan (among other soldiers) guards the entrance to this cave. Defeat him (rockets, grenades, and grappling attacks are some suggestions) and steal his weapon. Turn it on the remaining enemies, and then destroy the eight fuel tanks.

Commander Battle

The base commander appears near the end of the battle, tucked safely inside his tank. Meet him face-to-face with your own tank or simply hijack his, and then blast him with his own cannon.

OLIVO MORO

MILITARY ASSETS:
- Billboard (2)
- Police Station
- Generator (1)
- Monitoring System (4)
- Speaker (3)
- Statue (1)
- Raise the Flag

LIBERATION REWARDS
- Olivo Moro Garage
- Wingsuit Course: Olivo Bassa Tour
- Crash Bomb: Mountain Bend Blast
- Sea Race: Regata Precipito

 SETTLEMENT TYPE: TOWN

There was a time when Olivo Moro was known throughout the Mediterranean for its high-quality olive oil, but it has slowly deteriorated under the constant strain of civil unrest. The town today consists of rubble, graffiti, and abandoned buildings.

Tips

You can hang on the underside of a helicopter and use a rocket launcher on the statue, switch weapons, and then annihilate many of the targets before re-entering the helicopter. Attack the police station and other targets that were out of range from your previous location.

Police Station

Use a helicopter to eliminate the military targets and raise the Havoc Meter. There's only one gate Ⓐ to open in this police station. Use the gate button or tether it open from a safe distance.

Disable Monitoring System
Time Limit: 1:29

There are four monitoring systems to disable in this town. We suggest starting with the one on the highest structure first ① and moving on from there using the numbered route on our map. You should complete the course easily with 30 seconds remaining by parachuting, then grappling as soon as you have a lock-on just below the monitor or on the monitor itself.

PLATTEFORMA PETRA I

MILITARY ASSETS:
- Fuel Tank (11)
- Generator (2)
- Substation Controls (1)
- Transformer (3)

LIBERATION REWARDS
- Flare/Beacon Resupply Point

SETTLEMENT TYPE: OVUTPOST

Di Ravello's twin obsessions—maintaining order through military might and strip-mining Medici of all its precious Bavarium deposits—require thousands of barrels of petrol a year. Plattforma Petra I works around the clock to provide fuel for the Medician war machine.

Tips

This is one of the easier oil-rig platforms to liberate. If you lose your helicopter, attack from the bottom, down. Hack the SAM site on the top level and work your way around the top deck, destroying targets on the lower decks. Continue this way until you reach the bottom. Parachute around the rig, shooting targets while making yourself a harder target to hit. You can actually fire a weapon while wading in water. This is an easy way to take out the two fuel tanks on the support legs.

PUNCTA SUD

SETTLEMENT TYPE: RADAR

Occupying the southernmost tip of Insula Dracon's Petra province, Puncta Sud is a major telecommunications hub for the General's regime. All decoding, encryption, and black market brokering between Medici and other rogue nations flow through its many antennas.

Tips

Flying an aircraft near this facility is short-lived; there are SAM sites all over the place. Start by crashing a helicopter into the Satcom dish, shooting rockets the entire way and bailing out at the last minute; this will do some damage, if not take it out completely. Next, parachute down to one of the few tanks on the ground and keep moving and shooting large targets (antennas) while avoiding the aerial bombardments.

MILITARY ASSETS:

- ■ Antenna Tower (7)
- ■ Circuit Breaker (2)
- ■ Core Electrical Unit (1)
- ■ Fuel Tank (5)
- ■ Long-Range Radar (1)
- ■ Satcom Dish (1)
- ■ Substation Controls (2)
- ■ Transformer (5)
- ■ Water Tower (1)
- ■ Commander

LIBERATION REWARDS

- ■ Rebel Drop Helicopter: CS Navajo
- ■ Wingsuit Course: Puncta Tour
- ■ Demolition Frenzy: Mortar Frenzy

Follow the roads in the tank and destroy all targets you can spot. You can also position yourself up a hill and get the turret high enough to shoot the Satcom dish. If you lose the tank, jack another and keep going.

There are several military assets under the Satcom dish on the radar tower. Parachute around the radar tower and finish off any targets the dish didn't take out when it fell. The Capstone Fh155s on the helipad jutting off the radar tower are also very handy for taking out the antennas.

Commander Battle

Near the end of the battle, the base commander appears (during an enemy paratrooper drop) on one of the higher levels of the radar tower. He's out in the open or in one of the radar tower hallways. Parachute around the facility with a rocket launcher in hand, and then punish him with explosive rounds when spotted.

VICO TRUCTA

MILITARY ASSETS:
- ☐ Speaker (1)
- ☐ Statue (1)
- ☐ Raise the Flag

LIBERATION REWARDS
- ☐ Land Race: Espia Sprint

SETTLEMENT TYPE: VILLAGE

Despite a deep-seated hatred for each other that goes back centuries, recent DNA testing suggests all seven of Insula Dracon's major fishing villages share common genetic ancestry.

Tips

Budget offense: use an explosive and two bullets, and pull a flag rope to free this oppressed village.

PROVINCE: TRIO

GUARDIA TRIO I

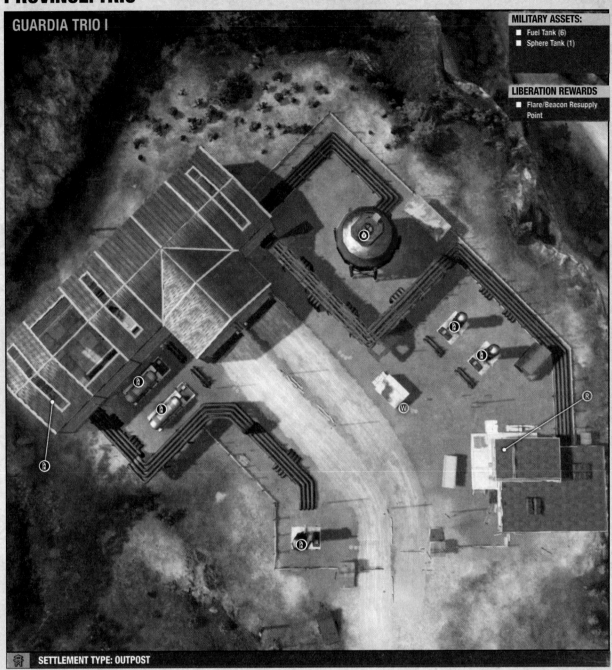

MILITARY ASSETS:
- Fuel Tank (6)
- Sphere Tank (1)

LIBERATION REWARDS
- Flare/Beacon Resupply Point

SETTLEMENT TYPE: OUTPOST

The sheer size of Medici's ever-expanding military spurred demand for storage and refueling facilities like Guardia Trio I.

Tips

There are no surface-to-air defenses and very little ground forces in this outpost. Run through on foot with a loaded grenade launcher (the fun option) or take advantage of this outpost from the air. Don't forget to destroy the single fuel tank inside the warehouse.

PLATTEFORMA TRIO I

MILITARY ASSETS:
- ☐ Doppler Radar (1)
- ☐ Fuel Tank (7)
- ☐ Satellite Dish (2)
- ☐ Transformer (4)

LIBERATION REWARDS
- ☐ Flare/Beacon Resupply Point

SETTLEMENT TYPE: OVUTPOST

Di Ravello's twin obsessions—maintaining order through military might and strip-mining Medici of all its precious Bavarium deposits—require thousands of barrels of petrol a year. Plattforma Trio I works around the clock to provide fuel for the Medician war machine.

Tips

This oil rig is light on the military assets, which may explain why they didn't include the added expense for a SAM site. With no surface-to-air defense (except the naval forces), this outpost can be liberated quickly with a helicopter's weapons. If you lose yours, there's a nice one for the taking on the helipad. Half the targets are on the support legs, including the odd placement of two satellite dishes— seems reception would be better up higher.

PONERA

MILITARY ASSETS:
- Billboard (2)
- Police Station
- Fuel Tank (2)
- Projector (1)
- Satellite Dish (1)
- Speaker (2)
- Statue (1)
- Substation Controls (1)
- Transformer (2)
- Raise the Flag

LIBERATION REWARDS
- Air Race: Volo Burrone

SETTLEMENT TYPE: TOWN

This settlement is based entirely upon the foundation of a defensive stronghold dating back to the Punic Wars. Myths persist of haunted figures still patrolling the war-scarred battlements. Adventurous visitors may find relics of a forgotten era hidden within its walls.

Tips: Police Station

Rip through this town in an attack helicopter and destroy all targets. Raise the Havoc Meter before aerial support arrives. When you drop into the police station, you must take care of matters on foot. Open the two gates ① and ② before opening the two jail cells ③ to free the prisoners. The jail cells are stacked on top of each other in the middle of the police station. Call the Rebels in before you open the cells so the militia will be distracted while you hack the doors.

PORTO DARSENA

MILITARY ASSETS:

- ■ Circuit Breaker (2)
- ■ Core Electrical Unit (1)
- ■ Distillation Tower (6)
- ■ Fuel Tank (8)
- ■ Sphere Tank (1)
- ■ Transformer (8)

LIBERATION REWARDS

- ■ Rebel Drop Boat: CS Powerrun 77
- ■ Wingsuit Course: Hilltop Tour
- ■ Wingsuit Course: Darsena Dive Tour
- ■ Demolition Frenzy: Boat Frenzy II

SETTLEMENT TYPE: BASE

Hidden within a subterranean cave complex, Porto Darsena is known to few outside the Medician military. It serves as a refinery for local hydraulic fracturing operations, where the government has successfully tapped a 110 trillion cubic foot reservoir of natural gas known as the Ponere Shale Shelf.

Tips

This base is completely hidden from the air, tucked inside a mountain cave complex. However, you can still assault the base with an attack helicopter—there's plenty of clearance to enter the tunnel entrance. There are also two attack copters available on helipads inside.

There's sufficient headroom inside the cave to fly freely, but beware of a few SAM sites. Hack these before hijacking any enemy choppers. You can also fly below the SAM's attack reach, as shown in this picture.

There's a cave away from the larger cavern (not far from a subterranean drawbridge structure) that should not be overlooked. Here you will find two transformers, a fuel tank, and a weapon cache.

VICO GAMBA

MILITARY ASSETS:
- ☐ Billboard (1)
- ☐ Speaker (2)
- ☐ Raise the Flag

🏠 **SETTLEMENT TYPE: VILLAGE**

Vico Gamba is historically the butt of jokes throughout Medici; its name is shorthand for stupid, ugly, or lazy. Every summer, the neighborhood cliff town of Ponere holds a feast that concludes with the townspeople shelling Vico Gamba with fireworks. The General is a noted fan of the event.

VICO MARQUERELLO

MILITARY ASSETS:
- ☐ Billboard (1)
- ☐ Speaker (1)
- ☐ Statue (1)
- ☐ Raise the Flag

🏠 **SETTLEMENT TYPE: VILLAGE**

Every year, anglers from around the world pilgrimage to this small fishing community to view the Marquerello Sancte, a miraculous fish caught in 1973 that, although deceased, has never exhibited signs of decay or decomposition. Rubbing its scales is thought to bring good fortune, though the practice is strictly forbidden.

VICO PLATESSA

MILITARY ASSETS:
- ■ Billboard (1)
- ■ Speaker (2)
- ■ Raise the Flag

⌂ SETTLEMENT TYPE: VILLAGE

Vico Platessa is home to Medici's oldest lighthouse keeper, Luis Berillos. At 98 years old, Berillos credits his longevity to regular physical activity, a diet rich in flounder, and an all-consuming hatred for those bastardos in Vico Maquerello.

SPEAKER

CHAOS 191255

REGION: INSULA FONTE

PROVINCE: ASPERA

CIMA LEON: CENTCOM

MILITARY ASSETS:
- ☐ Circuit Breaker (2)
- ☐ Core Electrical Unit (1)
- ☐ Doppler Radar (3)
- ☐ Fuel Tank (3)
- ☐ Long-Range Radar (2)
- ☐ Satellite Dish (5)
- ☐ Substation Controls (3)
- ☐ Transformer (9)

LIBERATION REWARDS
- ☐ Rebel Drop Helicopter: CS Comet
- ☐ Land Race: Ridgeline Sprint
- ☐ Demolition Frenzy: Grapple Frenzy

SETTLEMENT TYPE: REGION CENTRAL COMMAND

Built on the ruins of an ancient Salirosan fortress, Cima Leon's Centcom Tower is the bastion from which Di Ravello's regional commanders keep Insula Fonte under strict control.

Tips: FOW Airstrike Avoidance

You can liberate this Region Central Command base without completing the mission "The Secret of Vis Electra" to get rid of the FOW airstrikes. Easily avoid airstrikes by gliding around in your parachute or wingsuiting. You can also avoid airstrikes by taking cover under rooftops, such as the different levels of the Centcom Tower.

ASPERA
CIMA LEON: CENTCOM

WARNING
CIMA LEON: DEFENSES ACTIVE! AVOID THE AIRSTRIKE FOW!

COMBAT ZONE

Tips: Speed Grappling

Fly into the area with an attack chopper and do what damage you can before it's destroyed; then parachute to the top of the Centcom Tower. Destroy the rooftop targets while continuously grappling from one location to the next to avoid being caught in the airstrike's red target zone.

As long as your feet don't touch the ground, the airstrikes won't target you. When you do touch down, speed grapple from one location to the next. Make it to the weapon cache on the ruin wall near the Doppler radar closest to the tower, then arm yourself and get to gliding and rocketing targets again. Repeat until the base is liberated.

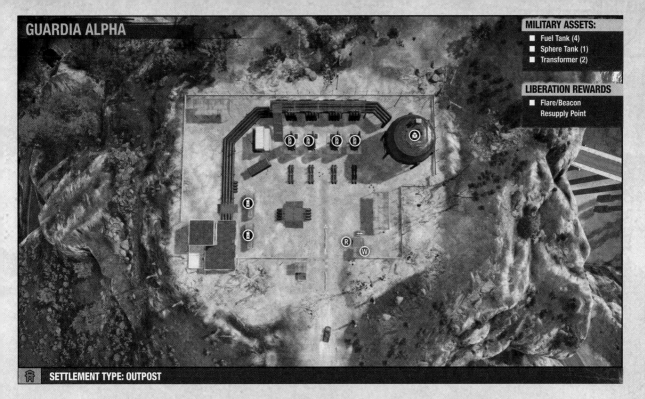

GUARDIA ALPHA

SETTLEMENT TYPE: OUTPOST

The sheer size of Medici's ever-expanding military spurred demand for storage and refueling facilities like Guardia Alpha.

Tips

As the name suggests, Guardia Alpha is the first outpost you must liberate. You reach this outpost during the "Time for an Upgrade" mission, near the beginning of the game. You must liberate this outpost in that mission using only your tether. To destroy the four fuel tanks in one shot, attach the first and last tanks in the line and pull them into each other. This takes out all four.

As for the sphere tank, simply tether a nearby fuel drum into the tank and retract it. This explodes, causing the sphere tank to explode and spin in the air. Fascinating to watch. Do the same thing for the two transformers: Pull an explosive barrel into them and watch the mesmerizing electrical explosions.

MANAEA

MILITARY ASSETS:
- Billboard (1)
- Police Station
- Fuel Tank (1)
- Speaker (3)
- Statue (1)
- Transformer (1)
- Raise the Flag

LIBERATION REWARDS
- Manaea Garage
- Wingsuit Course:
  Manaea Tour
- Land Race:
  Hillside Sprint

SETTLEMENT TYPE: TOWN

Manaea was the original capital of Medici, back when the island's name was first formally established by Roman-Hunnic occupants, following the Barbarian Invasions of the fifth century. This cliff-side gem sports some of Medici's best views; its downtown area, which winds through a bustling residential apartment district, was recently renovated and offers plenty of places to kick back and relax.

Tip: Alessia's Home Town

This is the first town you must liberate in the game to progress the story. It's also the town where Alessia grew up. Since you likely won't have access to an attack helicopter this early (unless you hijack one in the air during a high heat level), you'll have to take down the statue in the middle of town with explosives or a rocket launcher; bullets will not bring it down. A well-placed tether will also do the trick. Attach the tether at the top of the head and then across to a nearby building. Retract and drop the statue.

If this is your first town liberation, you should know that it takes only a few bullets to destroy a speaker. Aim and shoot at the box atop the speaker pole to remove the cover, and then shoot the innards to destroy the speaker. Once again, it requires just a couple bullets to do this.

Tip: Police Stations

Police stations are their own little project within towns that have them. There's always a process: destroy the military assets inside while defeating the constantly reinforced militia, hack gates to call in Rebels, raise the Havoc Meter, and free prisoners from cells when necessary.

You can safely open police gates 1 and 2 to let in Rebels by tethering the doors open (attach a tether to the door and the frame above the door and retract), instead of hacking the gate controls where sometimes the militia are heavily concentrated. Do this safely from atop a nearby structure.

Raise the Havoc Meter to 100% to complete the police station challenge. Defeating militia; destroying all military assets, walls, and other destructible; and exploding objects (such as fuel barrels and vehicles) raises the Havoc Meter. The last objective in a town or village is always to raise the flag. The flag is located near the statue. Raise it and liberate the town.

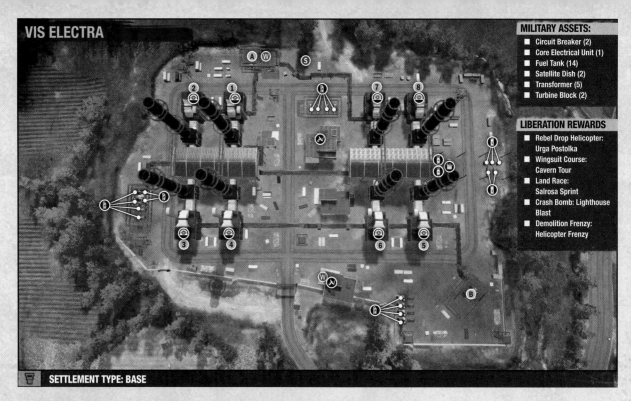

VIS ELECTRA

MILITARY ASSETS:
- Circuit Breaker (2)
- Core Electrical Unit (1)
- Fuel Tank (14)
- Satellite Dish (2)
- Transformer (5)
- Turbine Block (2)

LIBERATION REWARDS
- Rebel Drop Helicopter: Urga Postolka
- Wingsuit Course: Cavern Tour
- Land Race: Salrosa Sprint
- Crash Bomb: Lighthouse Blast
- Demolition Frenzy: Helicopter Frenzy

SETTLEMENT TYPE: BASE

A 600-year-old vineyard was flattened, and the military power plant of Vis Rlectra was built in two months by prison labor. To this day, no one knows where its power goes or how many political prisoners are entombed within its foundation.

Tips

We suggest dropping in via parachute and landing on top of one of the large smoke stacks. From this high perch, begin rocketing the many targets below. There's a weapon cache at a building model, near the front gate, that is known for having weapon caches. Replenish your rockets and ammo when low.

Many of the military targets in this base are grouped tightly together, which make them extremely easy to take out with a single rocket to the middle unit.

Turbine Blocks

Press the two heat exchanger buttons on the multileveled catwalk Ⓐ to give yourself 1:29 to destroy four turbines in the nearby turbine block. Destroying all four turbines destroys one block. After 1:29, the doors shut; if you have not destroyed them in that time, you must push the buttons again to open the doors. There's a button on the ground level of the catwalk and a second one on the second level.

Use the nearby weapon cache on the catwalk platform to make sure you have full ammo for your rocket launcher, then push the buttons and destroy the turbines in the order marked on our map ① and ②. After destroying the second one, grapple and glide to the other side quickly while you still have time to destroy the second two ③ and ④.

Replenish your ammo, clear some enemies, and replenish your ammo again to start on the second turbine block. Push the two heat exchanger buttons on the different levels of the platform Ⓑ and repeat the same process you did for the previous turbine block using the order we've marked on the map for turbines: ⑤, ⑥, ⑦, and ⑧. This time, try grappling away and gliding over the middle of the building between turbines to reach the second two quickly.

PROVINCE: FENO

ALBETO PERO

MILITARY ASSETS:
- ☐ Billboard (2)
- ☐ Police Station
- ☐ Fuel Tank (2)
- ☐ Generator (1)
- ☐ Satellite Dish (2)
- ☐ Speaker (2)
- ☐ Statue (1)
- ☐ Transformer (1)
- ☐ Raise the Flag

LIBERATION REWARDS
- ☐ Albeto Pero Garage
- ☐ Land Race:
  Side Street Sprint

SETTLEMENT TYPE: TOWN

The town of Albeto Pero came into being following a brutal navel siege on the ancient fort that once stood in its place. Ironically enough, the only surviving portion of its once-proud walls is the very same that was front and center to the most violent bombardments. Guided tours often stop atop the lighthouse at nearby Point Laurino, where tour guides badly botch their retelling of the conflict that took place around them.

Tips: Police Station

At the police station, you can safely raise gate ① by tethering it open while standing on the rooftop of the nearby house. Call in the Rebels and then start destroying the many targets inside. You can find the weapon cache next to the first gate. Raise the second gate ② to complete that objective and raise the Havoc Meter by blowing up everything in sight.

BABICA

MILITARY ASSETS:
- Billboard (3)
- Police Station
- Generator (1)
- Monitoring System (3)
- Speaker (4)
- Sphere Tank (1)
- Statue (1)
- Raise the Flag

LIBERATION REWARDS
- Bebica Garage
- Sea Race: Regata Petra

SETTLEMENT TYPE: TOWN

The boot-shaped port town of Babica has been growing rapidly; recent additions include a modern high-rise community and a cocker field that already looks as though it's seen better days. Those looking to enjoy a coastal drive will be delighted to find various stretches of road running right up against the sea and sand.

Tips: Police Station

 The police station in this town is one of the largest in the game, yet there are so few military assets inside. Just hitting the sphere tank and generator raises your Havoc Meter more than halfway. Use an attack helicopter to shred the police station. Land and open the two gates Ⓐ and Ⓑ and call in the Rebels. Hack the jail cell doors Ⓒ, Ⓓ, and Ⓔ to free the prisoners.

Disable Monitoring System
Time Limit: 1:59

Leave town or stay out of sight for a bit to get rid of the heat level. Now find the monitor on the rooftop of the house near the beach billboard. Push the button on this monitor ① to give you almost two minutes to push two more monitor buttons. This is a lot of time. Grapple and glide to the next rooftop monitor ②, press the button, and grapple and glide to the final one ③ on the ruins near the ocean. Raise the flag near the crumbled statue to completely liberate the town.

CIMA LEON: TRANSMITTER

MILITARY ASSETS:

- Antenna Tower (1)
- Circuit Breaker (4)
- Core Electrical Unit (2)
- Doppler Radar (2)
- Fuel Tank (1)
- Satellite Dish (1)
- Sphere Tank (1)
- Substation Controls (3)
- Transformer (9)

LIBERATION REWARDS

- Rebel Drop Tank:
  Urga Bkolos 2100
- Crash Bomb:
  Hayfield Blast
- Demolition Frenzy:
  Tank Frenzy I

SETTLEMENT TYPE: BASE

A peaceful mountain village was leveled to construct Cima Leon's expansive transmitter complex. The purpose of its heavily guarded transponder is shrouded in mystery.

Tips

For this base liberation, drop in high over the base (jumping from a plane or helicopter) and volley rockets down onto your targets, starting with the sphere tank. Glide over the transponder side of the base (near the Capstone FH155s) and shoot rockets into the middle of the groups of military assets like the core electrical unit.

If the FOV airstrikes are still active when you attack this base, then you want to grapple quickly from point to point without letting your feet hit the ground for long. If the FOV is down, then hack the SAM site and use the Capstones to take out the remaining targets, including the antenna tower and other assets around that area. Resupply your weapons at the cache, and then move to the next location. If you use the helicopter near the Capstones and SAM site, be aware there are a couple more SAMs on the other side of the base itching to knock you out of the sky.

GUARDIA FENO I

MILITARY ASSETS:
- ☐ Fuel Tank (3)
- ☐ Long-Range Radar (1)
- ☐ Transformer (2)

LIBERATION REWARDS
- ☐ Flare/Beacon Resupply Point

SETTLEMENT TYPE: OUTPOST

Medici's skies are among the safest in the world, due in large part to airfields like Guardia Feno I, which launches routine patrols and scrambles choppers to assist in frequent uprisings throughout Feno.

Tips

There's a SAM site at this small outpost. Be wary when attacking in a helicopter. Approach in the direction shown in this picture so the weapons cache/resupply building blocks the SAM's attack. From here you can destroy all the targets in seconds without being hit by the air defense system. A nice Rebel attack helicopter spawns on the helipad when liberated.

GUARDIA FENO II

MILITARY ASSETS:
- ☐ Doppler Radar (2)
- ☐ Fuel Tank (1)
- ☐ Satellite Dish (1)
- ☐ Transformer (1)
- ☐ Water Tower (1)

LIBERATION REWARDS
- ☐ Flare/Beacon Resupply Point

SETTLEMENT TYPE: OUTPOST

Housing is cheap and easy to find in Medici, mostly thanks to outposts like Guardia Feno II, which houses the large percentage of young Medicians lured by endless propaganda to serve in General Di Ravello's army.

Tips

If attacking this outpost in a helicopter, then do so from the position shown in our screen shot. This allows you to rise just far enough above sea level to get the SAM site in your sights. Shoot a few rockets at it to take it out, then safely annihilate the military assets. If you do not have a helicopter, hijack the tank parked under the shelter in the back corner of the base near the Doppler radars.

PROVINCE: LACOS

ALBA

MILITARY ASSETS:
- Billboard (2)
- Police Station
- Fuel Tank (1)
- Generator (1)
- Satellite Dish (1)
- Speaker (3)
- Statue (1)
- Raise the Flag

LIBERATION REWARDS
- Alba Garage ???

SETTLEMENT TYPE: TOWN

The hilly, relatively quiet town of Alba is one of Medici's top wine producers. Alba was lucky enough to avoid "major restructuring" by Di Ravello, in that its vineyards weren't immediately razed to make way for some military support structure.

Tips: Police Station

Use a helicopter equipped with rockets to flatten the town's military assets and the targets inside the police station. Raise the Havoc Meter to 100% by unloading missiles inside the police station, and then park the helicopter somewhere safe to return to it later. Enter the police station, open the gate Ⓐ to call in the Rebels, and then hack the two jail cell doors Ⓑ (on two different floors of the police station structure) behind the generator. Raise the flag and liberate the town.

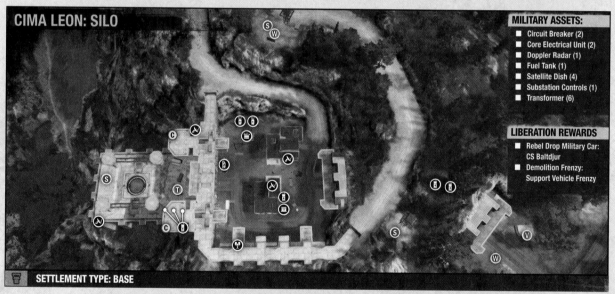

CIMA LEON: SILO

MILITARY ASSETS:
- Circuit Breaker (2)
- Core Electrical Unit (2)
- Doppler Radar (1)
- Fuel Tank (1)
- Satellite Dish (4)
- Substation Controls (1)
- Transformer (6)

LIBERATION REWARDS
- Rebel Drop Military Car: CS Baltdjur
- Demolition Frenzy: Support Vehicle Frenzy

SETTLEMENT TYPE: BASE

Built into the craggy rocks atop Lacos, the Silo of Cima Leon is a remnant of Medici's early nuclear ICBM tests during the Cold War. Locals mutter that the military presence there is too large to simply be protecting radioactive waste.

Tips

Parachute into the base and hack the SAMs to keep the air enemy support busy. Use the Capstones to take out enemy helicopters and pull them to the edge of the nearby ledges. Tether them where you want and reel them in. This will allow you to hit targets on the lower level.

Hijack the tank near the three transformers and eliminate the targets in the area where you found it; then drive it into the main base area and take out all the military assets there. Drive into the tunnel toward the front entrance to take out the two transformers there.

COLLE SALROSA

MILITARY ASSETS:
- Police Station
- Captain (1)
- Fuel Tank (1)
- Generator (1)
- Monitoring System (4)
- Satellite Dish (1)
- Speaker (4)
- Statue (1)
- Raise the Flag

LIBERATION REWARDS
- Colle Salrosa Garage
- Wingsuit Course: Tunnel Tour!

SETTLEMENT TYPE: TOWN

Centuries ago, the gentle leader Cirillo Salroso founded this city-state as a venue for trade. Today, Colle Salrosa is one of the top tourist destinations in Medici, thanks to its brand-new hotels and beautiful ocean views. Just about every world traveler is clamoring to get a selfie atop its tallest cliff, standing against the sparkling backdrop of the sea. This has led to an unfortunate string of fatal falls and the birth of the local nickname "Selfie Crag."

Tips

Don't look too hard for those billboards to blow up… because this town ain't got 'em. However, you can find a captain in this town. He is on foot and usually around the commons area where the flag is located. Simply glide overhead and drop explosives to get rid of him quickly.

Police Station

 Open the single gate Ⓐ to call in the Rebels, destroy all the police station's military assets, raise the Havoc Meter, and then free the prisoners by hacking the door locks on building Ⓑ. The jail cells are stacked on top of each other.

 Disable Monitoring System
Time Limit: 00:59

There are four monitor systems to shut down. Start with the monitor on the rooftop near the pier ① and then grapple to the second one near the pier ②. The third monitor ③ is on a small crosswalk rooftop between buildings. This one's a little tougher to grapple to from a distance, so glide and then grapple downward as you are floating over. Finally, grapple up to the rooftop and parachute to the final one near the flag ④. Shut it down to complete the challenge. Raise the flag after all assets are destroyed and the monitor challenge is complete.

FORTALESSA

SETTLEMENT TYPE: TOWN

Fortalessa is set atop a plateau in one of Lacro's most coveted stretches of land; to the west, a glimmering lake weaves through cliff sides and into a secluded, water-worn ravine. You can see Vis Electra's rising smokestacks from the southern vista, while Di Ravello's CentCom Tower looms on the mountain to the northwest. This gives the people of Fortalessa a lot to look at.

Tips

Annihilate the town with a helicopter equipped with rockets. This will allow you to easily take out the Propaganda Van (instead of chasing it around town) and make quick work of the Captain, who appears on foot near the end of the battle.

Police Station

The police station is small in this town, but has two gates to open (1) and (2) to call in the Rebels. Destroy the single military asset inside: the fuel tank. Raise the Havoc Meter by blowing up its walls and destroying any vehicles around the police station.

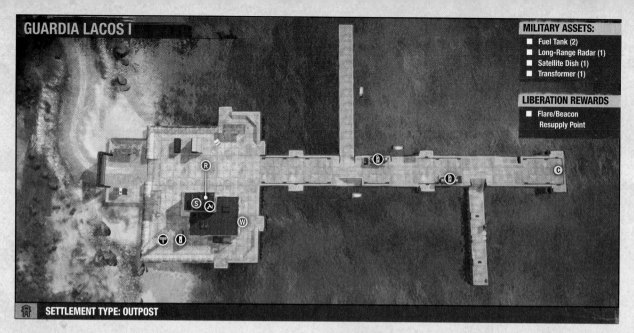

GUARDIA LACOS I

MILITARY ASSETS:
- Fuel Tank (2)
- Long-Range Radar (1)
- Satellite Dish (1)
- Transformer (1)

LIBERATION REWARDS
- Flare/Beacon Resupply Point

🏠 **SETTLEMENT TYPE: OUTPOST**

Medici possesses the largest military harbors in the Mediterranean, but smaller ports like Guardia Lacos I serve as waystations for small flotillas during patrols and tactical exercises.

Tips

It's painfully obvious what you must do when you look at the objects called out on our map. That Capstone FH155 is screaming at you to mount and point at the outpost. The transformer on the opposite side of the building is difficult to hit, so you'll have to grapple over there and take it out the old-fashioned way.

GUARDIA LACOS II

MILITARY ASSETS:
- Fuel Tank (4)
- Sphere Tank (1)
- Transformer (2)

LIBERATION REWARDS
- Flare/Beacon Resupply Point

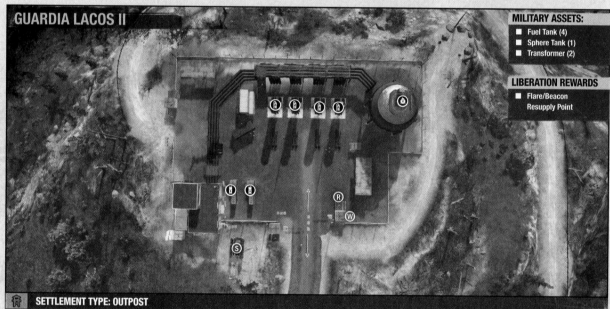

🏠 **SETTLEMENT TYPE: OUTPOST**

The sheer size of Medici's ever-expanding military spurred demand for storage and refueling facilities like Guardia Lacos II.

Tips

To avoid the SAM site at the land entrance to this outpost, approach at low altitude from the seaside. All the targets are exposed on this side. Just shoot and sweep to wipe out the outpost in seconds.

PROVINCE: LAVANDA

GUARDIA LAVANDA I

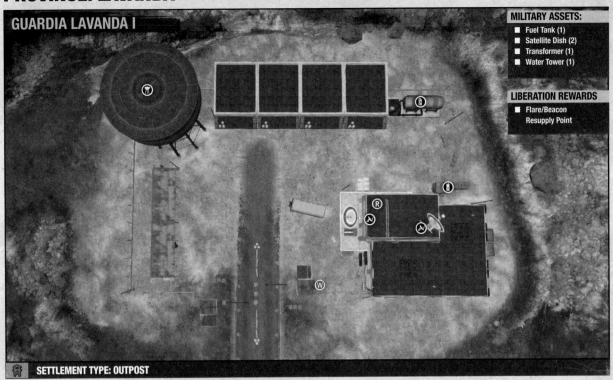

MILITARY ASSETS:
- Fuel Tank (1)
- Satellite Dish (2)
- Transformer (1)
- Water Tower (1)

LIBERATION REWARDS
- Flare/Beacon
  Resupply Point

SETTLEMENT TYPE: OUTPOST

Medicians are fond of saying, "You can't drive two minutes without seeing a soldier." The roads of Lavanda stay full of rambling convoys and patrols thanks to Guardia Lavanda.

62m

LANTUINA

MILITARY ASSETS:

- Billboard (2)
- Police Station
- Captain (1)
- Fuel Tank (2)
- Propaganda Van (1)
- Speaker (3)
- Statue (1)
- Transformer (2)
- Raise the Flag

LIBERATION REWARDS

- Lantuina Garage
- Wingsuit Course: Via Campania Tour
- Land Race: Latuina Sprint

SETTLEMENT TYPE: TOWN

Lantuina is nestled within an intersection of roads that form a triangle around the town, with most of its residential plots spidering out along its outer fringes. This is mainly because Lantuina was born of a trade boom, providing respite for weary traders and travelers heading along the route with their goods. It wasn't until this trade hub was well established that people started settling here in earnest.

Tips

The Propaganda Van normally begins its route on the outskirts of town near the police station. Be on the lookout for the large van that looks like a moving Di Ravello billboard and blast it! Captains normally hang out around the main attractions, like the militant flag or a statue in a town commons. When you get close, a prompt will appear on-screen suggesting you "defeat" the target.

Police Station

There are two gates (A) and (B) in this police station to open to call in the Rebels. Between these doors are two jail cells (1) and (2) to hack open to free two prisoners. You must do these tasks and raise the Havoc Meter to beat the police station challenge.

Gas Station Resupply Crates

Did you know that most towns that have a gas station also have a Beacon/Flare Resupply crate near the front entrance? Case in point. This town's gas station also has a Resupply point.

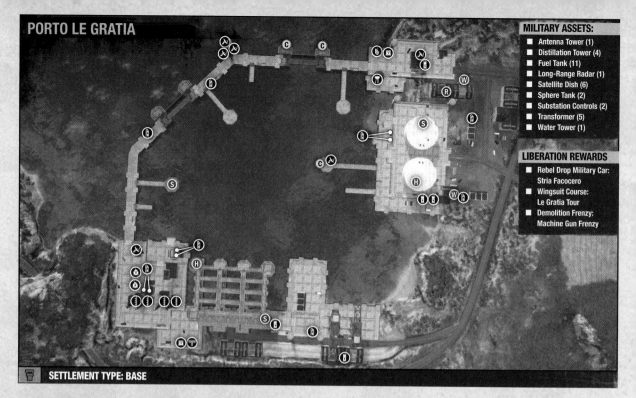

PORTO LE GRATIA

MILITARY ASSETS:
- Antenna Tower (1)
- Distillation Tower (4)
- Fuel Tank (11)
- Long-Range Radar (1)
- Satellite Dish (6)
- Sphere Tank (2)
- Substation Controls (2)
- Transformer (5)
- Water Tower (1)

LIBERATION REWARDS
- Rebel Drop Military Car: Stria Facocero
- Wingsuit Course: Le Gratia Tour
- Demolition Frenzy: Machine Gun Frenzy

SETTLEMENT TYPE: BASE

Razed during the second World War and rebuilt during tenure of the late President Dante, Porto Le Gratia processes the great bulk of Medici's inbound shipments of tanks and artillery and facilitates their distribution across the island.

Tips

This is a large base with military targets spread throughout, so it's going to take some time to liberate. The enemies aren't of the highest caliber, but there are a few tough ones guarding the SAMs. Defeat these guards at the SAM sites while taking out snipers from guard towers. After you hack all the SAM sites, you can hijack and safely fly the enemy choppers parked in the locations marked on our map.

Capstone FH155s are spread throughout the base. Each of them can easily reach the large targets that would otherwise take time to bring down, such as the distillation towers. Use the tether if you need to move the Capstone into a better position. If railings are in your way, tether them out of the way.

Base Commander

The base commander appears near the blue cargo cranes (by the building with the transformer inside). He is in a utility vehicle and is an easy kill if you wield a rocket launcher. Glide over his vehicle and let him have it!

RONDELLA

MILITARY ASSETS:
- Billboard (2)
- Police Station
- Captain (1)
- Fuel Tank (2)
- Generator (1)
- Monitoring System (4)
- Satellite Dish (1)
- Speaker (4)
- Statue (1)
- Raise the Flag

LIBERATION REWARDS
- Rondella Garage
- Wingsuit Course: Rondella Tour

SETTLEMENT TYPE: TOWN

Rondella was built hundreds of years ago, right into the cliffs beneath Sancte Esteban. For generations its denizens have been visiting Esteban for guidance (or escape) regarding the hardships of their lives.

Tips

This small town is laid out with a high concentration of military assets in close proximity to each other. It is also tiered on the mountainside, making attacking from a helicopter a no-brainer.

The Captain is near the church on the bridge side of town. He's on foot and an easy target. Parachute over him and toss grenades, or hit him with a rocket for a quick kill.

Police Station

 Raise the one gate Ⓐ to call in the Rebels, then hack the two jail cell doors Ⓑ to free the prisoners. Destroy the military assets inside the police station and raise the Havoc Meter to 100% to complete the police station challenge.

Disable Monitoring System
Time Limit: 1:29

You have 1:29 to disable the four monitoring systems in Rondella. This is more than enough time, especially if you use the route we marked on our map with monitor numbers ① through ④.

PROVINCE: PLAGIA

GUARDIA PLAGIA I

MILITARY ASSETS:
- ☐ Fuel Tank (3)
- ☐ Long-Range Radar (1)
- ☐ Transformer (2)

LIBERATION REWARDS
- ☐ Flare/Beacon Resupply Point

SETTLEMENT TYPE: OUTPOST

GUARDIA PLAGIA II

MILITARY ASSETS:
- ☐ Antenna Tower (1)
- ☐ Doppler Radar (3)
- ☐ Satellite Dish (1)
- ☐ Transformer (1)

LIBERATION REWARDS
- ☐ Flare/Beacon Resupply Point
- ☐ Shooting Gallery: Handgun Training Course
- ☐ Air Race: Volo Infra Ponte

SETTLEMENT TYPE: OUTPOST

Medici's skies are among the safest in the world, due in large part to outposts like Guardia Plagia I, which launches routine patrols and scrambles choppers to assist in frequent uprisings throughout Plagia.

Along with discipline, the secret to Di Ravello's constant victories over the Rebellion is constant, uninterrupted communication. Guardia Plagia II helps connect forces throughout Plagia.

Tips

Here's a different way to take out an outpost with a SAM site present: With a raised heat level, attach to the bottom of an attacking enemy helicopter and rocket all the military assets below! The SAM will not attack the enemy chopper.

Tips

It's crazy that Di Ravello didn't fork out the cash to have a SAM site at this outpost. And this close to an airport. What was he thinking? Take advantage of this failure to defend and flatten the outpost in seconds with rockets from your helicopter.

SURPICCO

MILITARY ASSETS:

- ☐ Billboard (3)
- ☐ Police Station
- ☐ Captain (1)
- ☐ Fuel Tank (2)
- ☐ Monitoring System (?)
- ☐ Projector (1)
- ☐ Speaker (4)
- ☐ Statue (1)
- ☐ Substation Controls (2)
- ☐ Transformer (2)
- ☐ Raise the Flag

LIBERATION REWARDS

- ☐ Surpicco Garage
- ☐ Land Race:
  Surpicco Sprint
- ☐ Land Race:
  Daredevil Sprint

SETTLEMENT TYPE: TOWN

Of what little global media coverage has been given the plight of Medici, most has mentioned Surpicco in particular—a fact that was hastily parlayed into making it a tourist hot spot. How this "hot spot" status stuck is uncertain, but it's widely believed—by romantic individuals, anyway—that visitors can feel the "heart" of the island's struggle beneath the battle scars of this very settlement.

Tips

Fly into town in an attack helicopter and surgically remove the billboards, speakers, statue, and Captain quickly, then attack the police station. Next, find the targets you missed in town, like the projector and remaining billboards; then park the helicopter and enter the police station on foot.

Police Station

 Blow the police station all to hell with the CS Navajo's rockets and missiles combination. Watch for attacking enemy aircraft and take them out by climbing altitude quickly and rocketing them when they climb to reach you. If your helicopter survives, park it and get to the station on foot to open the gate Ⓐ and call the Rebels in. Hijack a tank at Heat Level 4 and fill the Havoc Meter (if you haven't done so already) by demolishing everything in the police station.

🄿 Disable Monitoring System
Time Limit: 1:29

You have 1:29 to disable the five monitoring systems in Surpicco. This is more than enough time if you use the route we marked on our map with monitor numbers ① through ⑤.

VIGILATOR NORD

MILITARY ASSETS:
- Circuit Breaker (2)
- Core Electrical Unit (1)
- Doppler Radar (3)
- Fuel Tank (13)
- Radar Spire (4)
- Satcom Dish (1)
- Satellite Dish (3)
- Substation Controls (2)
- Transformer (8)

LIBERATION REWARDS
- Rebel Drop Sniper Rifle: USV 45 Sokol
- Demolition Frenzy: Sniper Rifle Frenzy I

SETTLEMENT TYPE: RADAR

The inefficacy of the rebellion in Insula Fonte is mainly because of Vigilator Nord's diligent eavesdropping. The massive dish and spires maintain watch over the entire northern island of Insula Fonte.

Tips

Vigilator Nord is a huge radar facility and lots of fun to destroy. If you plan on using a helicopter, then first take out or hack the many SAM sites around the base. An easier approach would be using the many Capstone FH155s all around the base to destroy, well... pretty much everything. There are so many Capstones that you will be able to get in one that will reach your target.

There are many military assets on the large Satcom dish tower. Circle it a few times while gliding to make sure you got everything.

PROVINCE: SIROCCO NORD

COSTA DEL PORTO

MILITARY ASSETS:
- Billboard (3)
- Police Station
- Fuel Tank (1)
- Speaker (3)
- Statue (1)
- Raise the Flag

LIBERATION REWARDS
- Costa Del Porto Garage

SETTLEMENT TYPE: TOWN

Costa Del Porto translates into "costal port"—a name that eloquently captures the town's quaint, no-frills history. Many make their living here fishing and selling their catch, though some are content to simply laze about Cliffside and soak up the sun as waves crash against the rocks below. It's a town that's never done wrong by anyone and if you lived there, you'd be content to do no wrong yourself.

Tips: Police Station

This simple little town can be liberated in a couple minutes. You can hit most of the targets in one helicopter pass or when hanging underneath one near the coastline. The police station has two gates (1 and 2) that you must raise to call in the Rebels, and you must raise the Havoc Meter by blowing up everything destructible inside.

COSTA DI RAVELLO

MILITARY ASSETS:
- Billboard (2)
- Police Station
- Fuel Tank (3)
- Speaker (2)
- Statue (1)
- Raise the Flag

LIBERATION REWARDS
- Costa Di Ravello Garage

SETTLEMENT TYPE: TOWN

This is a very small town; you can count the number of homes on your hands. No one remembers what Costa Di Ravello was called before it was renamed—or is it that no one's allowed to remember? Either way, the General's presence lingers here, even with his regime shooed away.

Tips: Police Station

This small town and small police station are a pushover, but bring your own ammo because you won't find a weapons cache at this police station! The Havoc Meter is raised to 90% when you take out the three large fuel tanks inside. Do a little more damage and open gates 1 and 2 to call in the Rebels. Raise the flag and call this town liberated.

GUARDIA SIROCCO II

MILITARY ASSETS:
- [ ] Circuit Breaker (2)
- [ ] Core Electrical Unit (1)
- [ ] Transformer (4)

LIBERATION REWARDS
- [ ] Flare/Beacon Resupply Point

SETTLEMENT TYPE: OUTPOST

GUARDIA SIROCCO III

MILITARY ASSETS:
- [ ] Antenna Tower (1)
- [ ] Doppler Radar (3)
- [ ] Satellite Dish (1)
- [ ] Transformer (1)

LIBERATION REWARDS
- [ ] Flare/Beacon Resup

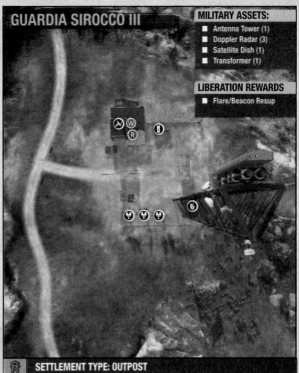

SETTLEMENT TYPE: OUTPOST

Reliable energy is hard to come by for the Medician people, but not for the Medician military. Larger power plants route through smaller outposts like Guardia Sirocco II to keep the lights on for monitoring devices, propaganda, and the military.

Along with discipline, the secret to Di Ravello's constant victories over the Rebellion is constant, uninterrupted communication. Guardia Sirocco III helps connect forces throughout Libeccio.

Tips

Try to get the large antenna tower to fall on the three Doppler radars and kill four birds with one stone… or rocket.

LE TUTOR

SETTLEMENT TYPE: BASE

Mysterious Le Tutor stands guard atop a tiny, weathered island. The giant dish here intercepts radio signals from as far away as Libya and Croatia, ensuring Di Ravello's security by providing him with valuable insight into the political turmoil of the region.

Tips

It's convenient to arrive at this island base in an attack helicopter, but don't expect to get too close; every inch of the island is protracted by multiple SAM sites. We suggest attacking the Satcom dish before you lose your helicopter, and then parachute around rocketing the big targets, like the antenna tower.

As you glide around the base, drop down and hack SAM sites you encounter to help keep the enemy air support at bay.

Don't forget to destroy the transformer and substation control inside the tunnel road that runs under the Satcom dish.

Base Commander

Use the Capstone FH155s located on the radar spire's top platform to destroy pretty much everything in the outpost at the end of the road (opposite the Satcom dish). Destroy the electrical assets, fuel tanks, and satellite dish atop the weapons cache building. The base commander will arrive via attack helicopter about this time. Use a few shells from the Capstone to bring down him and his chopper.

PORTO VENA

MILITARY ASSETS:
- Antenna Tower (1)
- Circuit Breaker (4)
- Core Electrical Unit (2)
- Doppler Radar (2)
- Distillation Tower (2)
- Fuel Tank (13)
- Long-Range Radar (1)
- Satellite Dish (7)
- Sphere Tank (1)
- Substation Controls (2)
- Transformer (12)
- Water Tower (2)
- Commander

LIBERATION REWARDS
- Rebel Drop Boat: Custode 29
- Sea Race: Seaport Scramble
- Demolition Frenzy: Boat Frenzy I

SETTLEMENT TYPE: BASE

Once a bustling, exotic market, the sprawling harbor of Porto Vena is now the largest military port in the Mediterranean.

Tips

Glide in and hack the SAM sites and then use the helicopters on the base to destroy military assets. There are also Capstones positioned in enough areas to hit many key assets. Weapon caches are scarce for such a large base, but you can find them near the second power array (see our map). The CS Navajo attack helicopter (equipped with heavy missiles and regular missiles) is on a helipad not far from the weapon cache. Hack the nearby SAM site and use this chopper to eliminate several targets very quickly.

Base Commander

The base commander arrives in an Urga Hrom D attack helicopter. Hijack it in midair and throw him out. If he lands in the water, make sure he is dead by sending him some missiles from his own aircraft.

PROVINCE: SIROCCO SUD

CIRILLA

MILITARY ASSETS:
- Billboard (2)
- Police Station
- Speaker (2)
- Raise the Flag

LIBERATION REWARDS
- Cirilla Garage
- Air Race: Volo Eagle

SETTLEMENT TYPE: TOWN

The quaint town of Cirilla is named after Cirillo Salroso, patriarch of the ancient Salirosan people. On the third Sunday of every month, those who still uphold the "Way of Cirillo" meet privately to share bottles of wine and good food, hoping the spirit of their once-beloved leader will look down upon them and their families favorably.

Tips: Police Station

You don't need much more than a Ruga Postolka (light helicopter) to take this town in minutes. However, having some rockets and missiles will make raising the Havoc Meter at the police station easier. There's one gate ① to open in the police station to call in the Rebels.

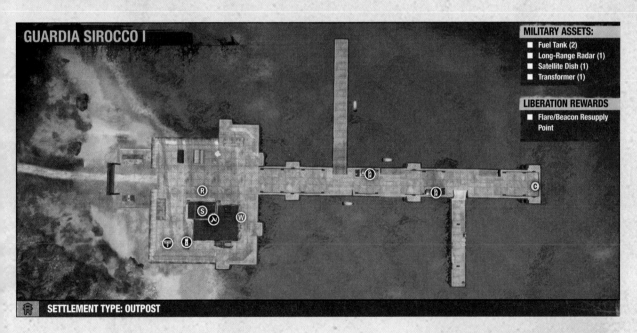

GUARDIA SIROCCO I

MILITARY ASSETS:
- Fuel Tank (2)
- Long-Range Radar (1)
- Satellite Dish (1)
- Transformer (1)

LIBERATION REWARDS
- Flare/Beacon Resupply Point

SETTLEMENT TYPE: OUTPOST

Medici possesses the largest military harbors in the Mediterranean, but smaller ports like Guardia Sirocco I serve as waystations for small flotillas during patrols and tactical exercises.

Tips

Use the Capstone at the end of the pier to take out all the targets. You will likely have to move to reach the transformer on the other side of the resupply building.

LAGUNA DEL SOL

MILITARY ASSETS:
- Billboard (2)
- Police Station
- Fuel Tank (1)
- Speaker (2)
- Statue (1)
- Raise the Flag

LIBERATION REWARDS
- Laguna Del Sol Garage
- Crash Bomb: Laguna Blast

SETTLEMENT TYPE: TOWN

Meaning "lagoon of the sun," Laguna Del Sol's unique location affords it calm waters year-round, as well as a nice view of Costa Di Ravello—the latter being an unfortunate feature for those who are not a fan of his iron reign of Medici.

Tips: Police Station

It's quick and easy to raise the Havoc Meter in the police station using an attack helicopter's missiles. But you need boots on the ground to raise the gates (1) and (2) to call in the Rebels (unless you hover low, stand on the bottom of the aircraft, and tether the gates open).

LE GALERA

MILITARY ASSETS:

- ☐ Cell Block (3)
- ☐ Circuit Breaker (2)
- ☐ Core Electrical Unit (1)
- ☐ Doppler Radar (1)
- ☐ Fuel Tank (5)
- ☐ Long-Range Radar (1)
- ☐ Satellite Dish (5)
- ☐ Sphere Tank (1)
- ☐ Substation Controls (1)
- ☐ Transformer (13)

LIBERATION REWARDS

- ☐ Rebel Drop Grenade Launcher: CS Negotiator
- ☐ Demolition Frenzy: Grenade Launcher Frenzy I

SETTLEMENT TYPE: BASE

The prison of Le Galera has existed, in one form or another, since the days of Nero. Christians were persecuted here until Constantine, and native Salirosans for centuries after. Pirates, fascists, and terrorists have called these halls home till the ends of their days. Now its primary demographic is the Medician revolutionary.

Tips

Begin your assault on this base in a CS Navajo, rocketing everything you can on the piers. Hold on to the chopper as long as possible before one of the SAMs' missiles ends your fun. Glide down to the platform with the two Capstones and use them to finish off all the targets on this side of the base.

LE GALERA

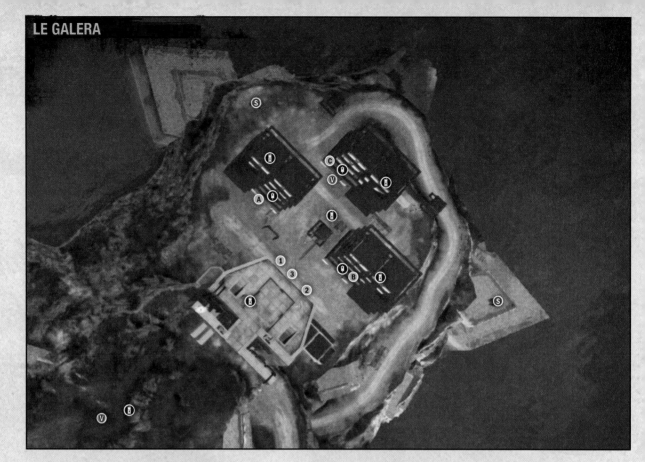

Glide slowly over the central base and rocket the military assets. Finish off all the targets on this side of the base, making sure to enter the tunnel between the central base and the cell block section to get the hidden transmitter on the side of the road.

Cell Blocks

Open each cell block door by using one of the switches on the two different levels of the control tower. So, switch ① opens cell block Ⓐ, ② opens Ⓑ, and the switch ③ on the lower platform opens cell block Ⓒ. Have a rocket launcher ready to blast the cell block while the door is briefly open. Also make sure you find and destroy all the transformers under the cell block structures.

VIGILATOR SUD

MILITARY ASSETS:
- ■ Circuit Breaker (2)
- ■ Core Electrical Unit (1)
- ■ Doppler Radar (2)
- ■ Fuel Tank (7)
- ■ Radar Spire (5)
- ■ Satcom Dish (1)
- ■ Satellite Dish (5)
- ■ Substation Controls (1)
- ■ Transformer (1)

LIBERATION REWARDS
- ■ Rebel Drop RPG: UVK-13
- ■ Wingsuit Course: Sirocco Skies Tour
- ■ Demolition Frenzy: RPG Frenzy I

SETTLEMENT TYPE: RADAR

Nestled in the otherwise tranquil pine forests of Sirocco Sud, this massive listening station gathers and processes hundreds of millions of telecommunication signals every day. The "Southern Overseer" is primarily tasked with intercepting revolutionary communiqués.

Tips

Get to the top platform of the Satcom dish tower and commandeer the Capstones to shoot the radar towers and the Satcom dish. Annihilate the substation controls and the transformer on this platform, as well. Use the tether to move the Capstones into better positions for more targeting.

Jump off the platform and glide around it, destroying all the fuel tanks, the satellite dishes, and the Doppler radar. Find the two fuel tanks attached below the platforms. Finish off the ground targets and clean up the outpost with the helipad.

REGION: INSULA STRIATE

PROVINCE: COSTA SUD

GRIPHON

MILITARY ASSETS:
- Antenna Tower (1)
- Doppler Radar (5)
- Fuel Tank (13)
- Long-Range Radar (2)
- Substation Controls (3)
- Transformer (5)

LIBERATION REWARDS
- Rebel Drop Plane: CS7 Thunderhawk
- Wingsuit Course: Griphon Tour
- Crash Bomb: Montana Bluff Blast
- Demolition Frenzy: Jet Frenzy II

SETTLEMENT TYPE: AIRBASE

The lofty fortress of Griphon is one of Medici's largest military airfields. During the Cold War, Di Ravello reluctantly loaned out Griphon to his Western allies, and a contingent of NATO aircraft called the base home during the days of the Cuban Missile Crisis.

Tips

Take out the four SAMs first if you enter battle in an attack helicopter. If you're not flying, then make hacking the SAMs your first priority to clear the skies of military reinforcements.

Defeat the heavily armored soldier toting the Urga Vulkan gun V near the southernmost SAM site. Defeat him and use his weapon to destroy all the enemies and targets nearby.

Hijack a CS Odjur tank near the antenna tower. Use this to take out the nearby enemies, the antenna tower, and the substation controls.

About halfway through your progression, enemy reinforcements arrive via transport plane. Man a Capstone FH155 on one of the raised runways to pick the paratroopers out of the sky before they land. You can also use the gun turrets to shoot planes as they leave the hangars.

Commander Battle

Near the end of the liberation process, the commander arrives in an Urga MSTitel Bavarium shielded attack helicopter. Stay close but covered to avoid its attack. As soon as the shields go down, grapple to the helicopter, throw the commander out, and then shoot him with his own chopper if the fall doesn't kill him. Once liberated, enjoy the Rebel fighter jets found in the hangars.

GUARDIA COSTA SUD I

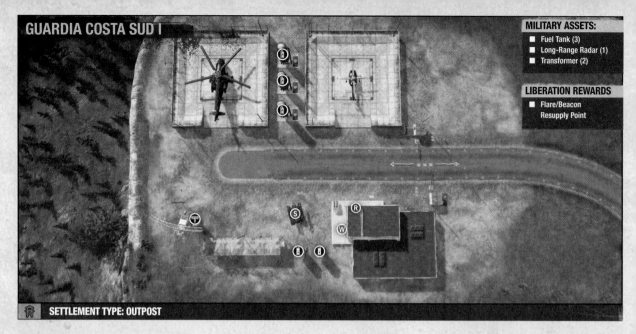

SETTLEMENT TYPE: OUTPOST

MILITARY ASSETS:
- Fuel Tank (3)
- Long-Range Radar (1)
- Transformer (2)

LIBERATION REWARDS
- Flare/Beacon Resupply Point

Medici's skies are among the safest in the world, due in large part to airfields like Guardia Costa Sud I, which launches routine patrols and scrambles choppers to assist in frequent uprisings throughout Costa Sud.

Tips

Use an attack helicopter to quickly decimate this small outpost, taking out the single SAM site first. If you are not in a vehicle, hack the SAM and hijack the weaponized helicopter on one of the two helipads; then turn the guns on the military assets.

GUARDIA COSTA SUD II

SETTLEMENT TYPE: OUTPOST

MILITARY ASSETS:
- Doppler Radar (2)
- Fuel Tank (2)
- Satellite Dish (1)
- Transformer (1)
- Water Tower (1)

LIBERATION REWARDS
- Flare/Beacon Resupply Point

Housing is cheap and easy to find in Medici, mostly thanks to outposts like Guardia Costa Sud II, which houses the large percentage of young Medicians lured by endless propaganda to serve in General Di Ravello's army.

Tips

Attack or hack the single SAM site near the front gate first. If in a helicopter, use the hill to stay below the SAM's detection range until you're ready to rise up and shoot it. Using an attack helicopter allows you to flatten this small outpost in seconds.

PERLA EST

SETTLEMENT TYPE: TOWN

Ancient art and architecture stand proudly in the shadow of apartment complexes. Luxury auto advertisements adorn tenements, and sadistic soldiers debase once-venerated churches. The oil rig of Platteforma Cost Sud and the monastery of Sanche Galile can be seen at the same time. The small city of Perla Est is a quiet chaos of conflicting influences.

Tips: Police Station

It's always a good idea to target the police station first if you have an attack helicopter. This allows you to volley missiles down into the compound, destroying all the military assets while raising the Havoc Meter. If you lose your copter during or after, simply hijack another using your grapple; your Heat level will surely be high enough that air support has been called.

Before you can liberate this police station, you must raise two gates, A and B. Use the gate switches or tether the doors open using the frame above the door for leverage.

There are six monitors to disable in this town. You must push the button on each monitor to disable it. The fastest way to reach each is to grapple, parachute, or wingsuit it (sometimes a combination of all three). Grappling is the fastest route, but it won't always reach from one monitor to the next. Always aim for the monitor pole or the rooftop just below the pole to be pulled directly toward the monitor. In general, approach the poles in an order where the buttons are facing you. Use our numbered monitors on the map for the quickest route to all six.

Disable Monitoring System
Time Limit: 1:19

Captain

The Captain (boss) appears in the streets after you complete all liberation tasks, except for raising the flag in Perla Est. Find him by spotting the "Defeat" prompt and the red triangle icon accompanied by a distance meter. Parachute above him and shoot him with an RPG or drop a grenade on him to finish him off quickly.

PLATTEFORMA COSTA SUD 1

MILITARY ASSETS:
- ☐ Fuel Tank (10)
- ☐ Generator (2)
- ☐ Substation Controls (1)
- ☐ Transformer (2)

LIBERATION REWARDS
- ☐ Flare/Beacon Resupply Point

SETTLEMENT TYPE: OUTPOST

Tips

You are likely approaching by air or via boat to reach this oil rig. Take out the air defense (helicopters and SAM site) first. If you're in an attack helicopter, keep flying sideways while circling the oil rig and sending a nonstop serving of rockets.

If you lose your aircraft and are getting beaten up by air and sea assaults, parachute and keep moving or grapple up underneath the oil rig to escape detection. Once the heat has cooled down, return to the decks and continue taking out assets. Hack the SAM (if you have not destroyed it) to help with the assaults from above.

Perch atop the tall spire on the highest level and shoot the soldiers and military assets below. If you start taking fire, jump and parachute around the oil rig, continuing your assault.

PROVINCE: FALCO

FALCO MAXIME: CENTCOM

MILITARY ASSETS:
- Antenna Tower (2)
- Circuit Breaker (2)
- Core Electrical Unit (1)
- Doppler Radar (2)
- Fuel Tank (12)
- Long-Range Radar (2)
- Satcom Dish (1)
- Sphere Tank (1)
- Substation Controls (2)
- Transformer (6)

LIBERATION REWARDS
- Rebel Drop Plane: U41 Ptakojester
- Wingsuit Course: Maxime Tour
- Land Race: Strip Mine Sprint
- Demolition Frenzy: FOW Frenzy

SETTLEMENT TYPE: REGION CENTRAL COMMAND

Perched high in the mountains and guarded by powerful Bavarium warheads, Falco Maxime is Di Ravello's grandest fortress. The CentCom Tower's computer network houses the largest and most comprehensive repository of Bavarium knowledge in the world.

Tips: Cap 'Em with Capstones!

This is a big airbase, but don't let that scare you. Drop in from above and destroy what you can by air before you lose your aircraft. Concentrate on taking out the four SAMs first. Do not destroy the Capstone FH155s—these are very useful when their barrels are aimed at the enemy. Get to the end of the runways where these guns are positioned. Defeat the enemy user and jump into the seat. Turn the large guns on the many targets around the base, especially the antenna towers and the Satcom dish. Scan the distance for as many targets as you can hit from the many different Capstone locations.

Golden Urga MSTitel

Throughout this base assault, multiple Golden Urga MSTitels respond with force. It is suicide to try to stop them with the Capstone FH155s, as their Bavarium-powered shields are not down long enough to do them sufficient harm. Instead, take cover and when the aircraft's shield goes down, hijack it using the grappling hook. Turn the powerful aircraft on the others and on whatever nearby targets remain.

PROVINCE: GRANDE PASTURA

ALTE POTENTIA

SETTLEMENT TYPE: BASE

The military plant of Alte Potentia, nestled on a remote mountainside in the far north, provides power to many of Di Ravello's bases throughout Insula Striate. The smog generated here has a direct effect on the air quality of towns as far away as Perla Est and Vista Fonte.

Tips

This military base is surrounded by mountains, making it terribly difficult to defend. To compensate for this weakness, multiple SAM sites are scattered throughout the base, making approach by helicopter very difficult. We suggest parachuting into the base, landing atop one of the large smokestacks, and starting your assault from there. Grapple from smokestack to smokestack, finding large targets to hit with explosives.

MILITARY ASSETS:

- Circuit Breaker (4)
- Core Electrical Unit (2)
- Doppler Radar (2)
- Fuel Tank (5)
- Satellite Dish (1)
- Transformer (8)
- Turbine Block (2)
- Water Tower (1)

LIBERATION REWARDS

- Rebel Drop Tank: CS Odjur
- Demolition Frenzy: Tank Frenzy II

Consider hacking all five of the SAM sites and then hijacking and attacking enemy helicopter. Expect paratrooper reinforcements early in the base attack. Try to pick them off before they land.

Heat Exchanger Switches and Turbine Blocks

Push the buttons on two paired heat exchangers: Ⓐ and Ⓑ or pair Ⓒ and Ⓓ. This opens the four large doors on the nearby turbine blocks ①–④ or ⑤–⑧. You have 39 seconds to press the second Heat Exchange button. This button combo opens the turbine doors, giving you 1:29 to destroy the turbines before the doors shut again. If they do shut without the group of four turbines being destroyed, simply press the button combos again and continue your assault on the large engines.

We suggest opening the turbine doors and then hijacking the Urga Szturm 63A from the garage near the weapons cache. Use the attached machine gun to quickly destroy the turbines and nearby enemies. Otherwise, visit the weapon caches often and use rockets and grenades for quick demolition.

GUARDIA GRANDE PASTURA I

MILITARY ASSETS:
- Bavarium Dump Trailer (2)
- Bavarium Refinery Station (1)
- Substation Controls (2)
- Transformer (1)

LIBERATION REWARDS
- Flare/Beacon Resupply Point

SETTLEMENT TYPE: OUTPOST

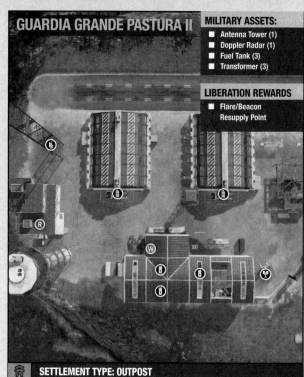

GUARDIA GRANDE PASTURA II

MILITARY ASSETS:
- Antenna Tower (1)
- Doppler Radar (1)
- Fuel Tank (3)
- Transformer (3)

LIBERATION REWARDS
- Flare/Beacon Resupply Point

SETTLEMENT TYPE: OUTPOST

The mines of Insula Striate produce roughly 80% of Medici's Bavarium stockpile, most of which goes to military use. Smaller operations like Guardia Grande Pastura I send their resources to scientists like Dimah, who toil under threat of torture to create weapons and military equipment.

Tips

This outpost has no SAM defense, making it extremely quick and easy to take out all the targets using an attack helicopter with rockets. You can even shoot some rockets through the building's skylights to destroy the transformer and Bavarium dump trailer inside.

Medici's skies are among the safest in the world, due largely to airfields like Guardia Grande Pastura II, which launches fighter jets, paratrooper carriers, and bombers to assist in frequent uprisings throughout Grande Pastura.

Tips

This outpost has no surface-to-air defense, but you may encounter a patrolling attack helicopter. Take out this target first and then begin eliminating the military assets. Using a weaponized helicopter is the quickest way to flatten this outpost. Once liberated, you can enjoy the free attack helicopter that is spawned on this outpost's helipad.

GUARDIA GRANDE PASTURA III

MILITARY ASSETS:
- Fuel Tank (6)
- Sphere Tank (1)

LIBERATION REWARDS
- Flare/Beacon
  Resupply Point

SETTLEMENT TYPE: OUTPOST

The sheer size of Medici's ever-expanding military spurred demand for storage and refueling facilities like Guardia Grande Pastura III.

Tips

This outpost has no air defense, making it extremely vulnerable to an air attack. If you're not in an aircraft, hijack the outpost's light tank to destroy the targets. Don't forget the fuel tank inside the warehouse.

PLATTEFORMA GRANDE PASTURA I

SETTLEMENT TYPE: OUTPOST

Di Ravello's twin obsessions—maintaining order through military might and strip-mining Medici of all its precious Bavarium deposits—require thousands of barrels of petrol a year. Plattforma Grande Pastura works around the clock to provide fuel for the Medician war machine.

MILITARY ASSETS:
■ Circuit Breaker (1)
■ Fuel Tank (7)
■ Generator (1)
■ Transformer (7)

LIBERATION REWARDS
■ Flare/Beacon
Resupply Point

Tips

As with any oil-rig outpost, you should arrive in an attack helicopter and approach slowly, looking for the red glowing light of a SAM site and for aerial and sea defenses. Destroy these targets first and then circle the rig sideways, throwing missiles into its multiple levels. Keep an eye out for naval and aerial reinforcements. This rig has two fuel tanks on opposite support legs. Once the outpost is liberated, you can use the Urga Postolka helicopter that spawns on the helipad to head back to shore—if you lost the one you arrived in.

PROVINCE: LIBECCIO

BURGOLETTO

MILITARY ASSETS:
- Billboard (3)
- Police Station
- Fuel Tank (2)
- Projector (1)
- Speaker (3)
- Statue (1)
- Substation Controls (2)
- Transformer (1)
- Water Tower (1)
- Raise the Flag

LIBERATION REWARDS
- Air Race: Volo Metropole

SETTLEMENT TYPE: TOWN

The town of Burgoletto petitioned fervently to prevent the installation of wind turbines. Di Ravello ignored their pleas, and now the locals enjoy the power they provide; some have even called them "belle." Parents in Burgoletto remind their children, "Even the General does good once in a while."

Tips

Almost all the military assets can be taken out from various positions on the yellow crane ① that towers over the police station. Raise the Havoc Meter while in the police station by blowing up everything possible, then open the gate ② to let the Rebels in for support.

CELATA

MILITARY ASSETS:
- Billboard (4)
- Police Station
- Fuel Tank (1)
- Monitoring System (6)
- Speaker (5)
- Statue (1)
- Raise the Flag

LIBERATION REWARDS
- Celata Garage
- Land Race: Railway Sprint
- Crash Bomb: Celata Seaside Blast

SETTLEMENT TYPE: TOWN

The cozy inlet of Celata was once home to a rowdy tribe of Salirosan fisherman. Urbanization and the march of progress have reduced Celata's population in size; now it is the sort of town that youngsters leave and the elderly retire to.

Tips

Statues don't crumble from bullets. Use rockets, missiles, grenades, explosives, or a strong tether to bring them down.

Hijack a helicopter when aerial support is called, and use its weapons to destroy everything possible in the police station to quickly raise the Havoc Meter. Open both gates Ⓐ and Ⓑ to allow the Rebels access.

 Disable Monitoring System
Time Limit: 1:19

Lose the Heat level and then activate one of the six rooftop monitoring systems to start the timed challenge. Check out the convenient monitor path we've marked on our map. Follow the monitor order ①–⑥ for a time-saving route.

Celata Garage

Once the town is liberated, you can deliver boats to the Celata Garage Ⓒ by docking them in the blue zone. You can also find a resupply crate near the vehicle garage on the pier.

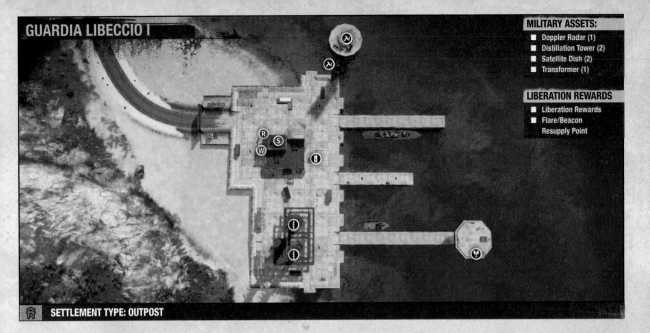

GUARDIA LIBECCIO I

MILITARY ASSETS:
- Doppler Radar (1)
- Distillation Tower (2)
- Satellite Dish (2)
- Transformer (1)

LIBERATION REWARDS
- Liberation Rewards
- Flare/Beacon Resupply Point

SETTLEMENT TYPE: OUTPOST

Medici possesses the largest military harbors in the Mediterranean, but smaller ports like Guardia Libeccio I serve as waystations for small flotillas during patrols and tactical exercises.

Tips

Take out the SAM on top of the weapons and resupply building. Next, rocket the distillation towers since these are the hardest targets to take out without heavy artillery. Defeat the enemy that calls for reinforcements to keep air support away. This buys you more time to finish off the remaining targets with minimal distractions.

GUARDIA LIBECCIO II

MILITARY ASSETS:
- Antenna Tower (1)
- Doppler Radar (3)
- Satellite Dish (1)
- Transformer (1)

LIBERATION REWARDS
- Flare/Beacon Resupply Point

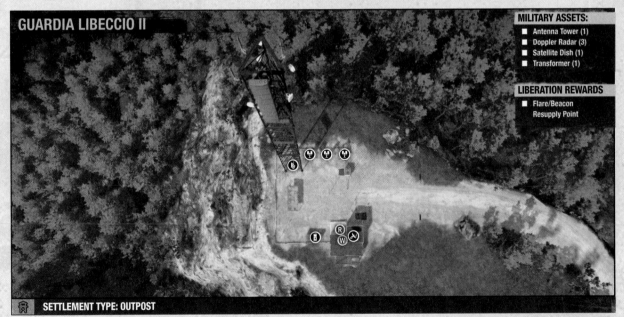

SETTLEMENT TYPE: OUTPOST

Along with discipline, the secret to Di Ravello's constant victories over the Rebellion is constant, uninterrupted communication. Guardia Lebecco II helps connect forces throughout Libeccio.

Tips

This settlement can be flattened in seconds with an aircraft equipped with rockets. Expect no surface-to-air defense. A soldier will attempt to call in for reinforcements. Take him out.

NACRE

MILITARY ASSETS:
- Billboard (4)
- Police Station
- Fuel Tank (3)
- Monitoring System
- Projector (1)
- Propaganda Van (1)
- Satellite Dish (2)
- Speaker (6)
- Statue (1)
- Substation Controls (1)
- Water Tower
- Raise the Flag

LIBERATION REWARDS
- Nacre Garage
- Wingsuit Course: Canyon Tour

SETTLEMENT TYPE: TOWN

The history of Nacre is told by its idiots. Venus was worshiped in the offshore ruins. But Venus was torn down by the Christians, who worshiped in the church they built at the center of town. But Di Ravello filled in the churchyard to erect a statue in his own image. Who will tear down the statue of Di Ravello?

Tips: Police Station

Destroy the six military targets within the police station and open the gates A and B to call in the Rebels. Find weapons near the central gate B.

Propaganda Van

 The Propaganda Van cannot be mapped since it moves around town. Look for the red, white, and green box truck with Di Ravello's image on it. The image is similar to the billboards you've been targeting. Blow it up.

Disable Monitoring System
Time Limit: 1:19

Lose the heat and disable the monitoring systems in any order. For a quick and convenient route, shut down the monitors in the order we've marked on the map ① – ⑥.

VISTA DRACON

SETTLEMENT TYPE: TOWN

MILITARY ASSETS:
- ☐ Billboard (2)
- ☐ Police Station
- ☐ Fuel Tank (1)
- ☐ Satellite Dish (2)
- ☐ Speaker (4)
- ☐ Statue (1)
- ☐ Raise the Flag

LIBERATION REWARDS
- ☐ Vista Dracon Garage ®
- ☐ Wingsuit Course: Vista Plunge Tour
- ☐ Air Race: Volo Montania

The children of Vista Dracon develop a healthy respect for heights at a young age. No gallows was ever built here; the condemned merely stepped off the cliffs into the clouds below.

Tips: Police Station

Use the Urga Vulkan ⓥ or the machine gun on the parked Urga Szturm 63A inside the police station to clear the militia, raise the Havoc Meter, and quickly destroy the three military targets. Open the gate Ⓐ to call in the Rebels.

PROVINCE: LITORE TORTO

GUARDIA LITORE TORTO I

SETTLEMENT TYPE: OUTPOST

MILITARY ASSETS:
- ☐ Antenna Tower (1)
- ☐ Doppler Radar (3)
- ☐ Satellite Dish (1)
- ☐ Transformer (1)

LIBERATION REWARDS
- ☐ Demolition Frenzy: 'Round the Bend Blast
- ☐ Sea Race: Regata Laco
- ☐ Flare/Beacon Resupply Point

Along with discipline, the secret to Di Ravello's constant victories over the Rebellion is constant, uninterrupted communication. Guardia Litore Torto I helps connect forces throughout Litore Torto.

Tips

This outpost has no surface-to-air defense. Annihilate this base in seconds with a well-armed aircraft.

GUARDIA LITORE TORTO II

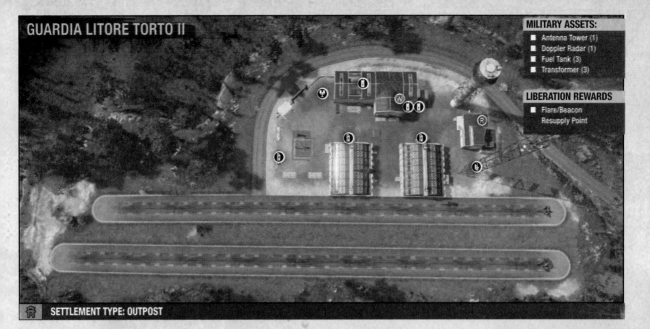

SETTLEMENT TYPE: OUTPOST

MILITARY ASSETS:
- ☐ Antenna Tower (1)
- ☐ Doppler Radar (1)
- ☐ Fuel Tank (3)
- ☐ Transformer (3)

LIBERATION REWARDS
- ☐ Flare/Beacon
  Resupply Point

Medici's skies are among the safest in the world, due in large part to airfields like Guardia Litore Torto II, which launches fighter jets, paratrooper carriers, and bombers to assist in frequent uprisings throughout Litore Torto.

Tips

This airport outpost is void of surface-to-air defense. A heavily armed helicopter can flatten this outpost in no time. Searching for one more military asset? Look inside the warehouse for the hidden transformer.

GUARDIA LITORE TORTO III

SETTLEMENT TYPE: OUTPOST

MILITARY ASSETS:
- ☐ Doppler Radar (2)
- ☐ Fuel Tank (1)
- ☐ Satellite Dish (1)
- ☐ Transformer (1)
- ☐ Water Tower (1)

LIBERATION REWARDS
- ☐ Flare/Beacon
  Resupply Point

Housing is cheap and easy to find in Medici, mostly thanks to outposts like Guardia Litore Torto III, which houses the large percentage of young Medicians lured by endless propaganda to serve in General Di Ravello's army.

Tips

If you attack this outpost without a helicopter, then steal the tank from the shelter just behind the guard tower. Use it to destroy the military assets. If you are attacking from an aircraft, take out the SAM site at the front gate first, and then shoot the soldier who calls for reinforcements. Afterward, concentrate your attacks on the key targets.

PLATTEFORMA LITORE TORTO I

MILITARY ASSETS:
- Fuel Tank (10)
- Generator (2)
- Substation Controls (2)
- Transformer (3)

LIBERATION REWARDS
- Flare/Beacon
  Resupply Point

SETTLEMENT TYPE: OUTPOST

Di Ravello's twin obsessions—maintaining order through military might and strip-mining Medici of all its precious Bavarium deposits—require thousands of barrels of petrol a year. Plattforma Litore Torto I works around the clock to provide fuel for the Medician war machine.

Tips

The best way to take out an oil platform is via attack helicopter. Take out the SAM site on the top level while looking for sea and aerial reinforcements. Circle the rig while shooting rockets into all layers. The more difficult-to-find military targets are the two fuel tanks on the support legs.

PLATTEFORMA LITORE TORTO II

MILITARY ASSETS:
- Doppler Radar (2)
- Fuel Tank (10)
- Satellite Dish (1)
- Transformer (3)

LIBERATION REWARDS
- Flare/Beacon Resupply Point

SETTLEMENT TYPE: OUTPOST

Di Ravello's twin obsessions—maintaining order through military might and strip-mining Medici of all its precious Bavarium deposits—require thousands of barrels of petrol a year. Platteforma Litore Torto II works around the clock to provide fuel for the Medician war machine.

Tips

As with any oil rig platform, the best tactic is to attack via helicopter. Take out the SAM site on the top level while watching for sea and aerial reinforcements. Circle the rig while shooting rockets into all layers. The more difficult-to-find military targets are the two fuel tanks on the support legs and a satellite dish on the end of the long extension arm.

PROVINCE: MAESTRALE

GUARDIA MAESTRALE I

MILITARY ASSETS:
- Fuel Tank (1)
- Satellite Dish (2)
- Transformer (1)
- Water Tower (1)

LIBERATION REWARDS
- Flare/Beacon
  Resupply Point

SETTLEMENT TYPE: OUTPOST

Medicians are fond of saying, "You can't drive two minutes without seeing a soldier." The roads of Maestrale stay full of rambling convoys and patrols, thanks to Guardia Maestrale I.

Tips

This outpost has little to no defense, and it falls in seconds when throttled from the air in an attack helicopter.

PLATTEFORMA MAESTRALE I

SETTLEMENT TYPE: OUTPOST

Di Ravello's twin obsessions—maintaining order through military might and strip-mining Medici of all its precious Bavarium deposits—require thousands of barrels of petrol a year. Platteforma Maestrale I works around the clock to provide fuel for the Medician war machine.

Tips

Take out the SAM site if you are attacking in an aircraft. Use the Capstone FH155s at the ends of the upper-level platform to help clear enemies, some military assets, attack boats, or air support. The trickiest targets to find are the fuel tanks on the support legs.

PORTO TRIDENTE

SETTLEMENT TYPE: BASE

Medici's oldest harbor, Porto Tridente, was long considered the nation's window to France and Spain. Now it's a window to nowhere, serving only to launch the zealous Medician fleet on endless patrols for pirates, Rebels, and spies.

Tips

This base is highly fortified with multiple surface-to-air missile launchers, snipers in towers, tanks, and heavily armored soldiers with powerful weapons. Attack boats can also be expected at this harbor base. The best approach is from the air in a helicopter equipped with rockets or heavy missiles. Carefully take out the six surface-to-air defense systems. Keep watching for arriving air and sea defense units, and take them out quickly; then return your focus to destroying the military asset targets.

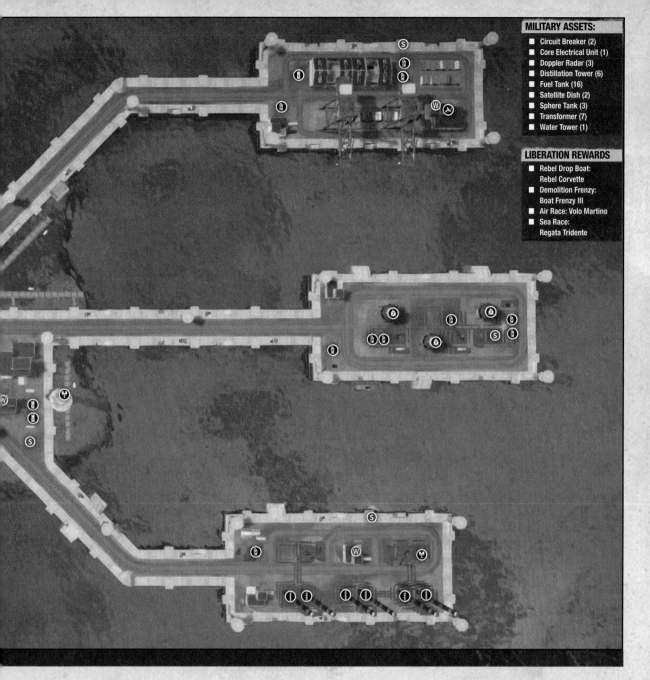

MILITARY ASSETS:

- Circuit Breaker (2)
- Core Electrical Unit (1)
- Doppler Radar (3)
- Distillation Tower (6)
- Fuel Tank (16)
- Satellite Dish (2)
- Sphere Tank (3)
- Transformer (7)
- Water Tower (1)

LIBERATION REWARDS

- Rebel Drop Boat:
  Rebel Corvette
- Demolition Frenzy:
  Boat Frenzy III
- Air Race: Volo Martino
- Sea Race:
  Regata Tridente

If you lose your helicopter or enter the battle without one, hijack the patrolling tank and use it to destroy the enemy forces and military asset targets. There's also an enemy attack helicopter with rockets on a helipad near the core electrical unit. Notice the many weapon caches on our map to help keep you armed. Hack the surface-to-air defense systems to turn on the enemy air support and allow your Rebel air support to assist you near the end of the battle.

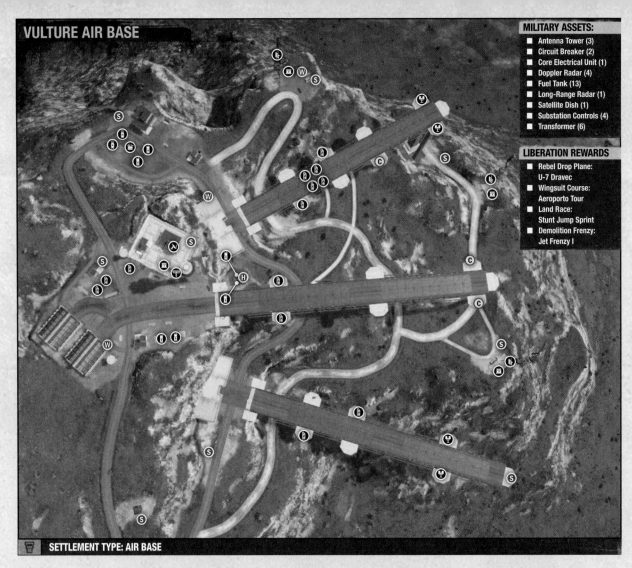

VULTURE AIR BASE

MILITARY ASSETS:
- Antenna Tower (3)
- Circuit Breaker (2)
- Core Electrical Unit (1)
- Doppler Radar (4)
- Fuel Tank (13)
- Long-Range Radar (1)
- Satellite Dish (1)
- Substation Controls (4)
- Transformer (6)

LIBERATION REWARDS
- Rebel Drop Plane: U-7 Dravec
- Wingsuit Course: Aeroporto Tour
- Land Race: Stunt Jump Sprint
- Demolition Frenzy: Jet Frenzy I

SETTLEMENT TYPE: AIR BASE

The military airport of Vulture stores a massive complement of jets and bombers in its underground hangars. The famous Hirundine Squadron, which has protected Medici's skies for 100 years, calls Vulture home.

Tips

This is an air base. It is more than adequately equipped to handle attacks from the air. So if you come into this battle in an attack helicopter or fighter jet, be prepared to battle with the many SAM sites positioned strategically around the base. The best tactic is to parachute in and hack the SAMs, then use the helicopters (on helipads) and fighter jets (in the hangars) to demolish the base. There are also plenty of Capstone FH155s to point back at the base and take out the many military assets. Remember that you can tether the Capstones to get them in better positions if necessary.

Commander Battle

The base commander comes riding to the rescue in a Bavarium-shielded Imperator Bavarium tank. Hijack the tank and throw the commander out when the shield goes down (which happens intermittently). Run over or blast the commander after throwing him out. Activate the Bavarium shields, then use his tank to destroy more military assets. Reference our map to find them all.

CAVA MONTANA

MILITARY ASSETS:
- Bavarium Dump Trailer (15)
- Bavarium Refinery Station (9)
- Excavator (2)
- Transformer (1)
- Water Tower (1)

LIBERATION REWARDS
- Rebel Drop Tank: Imperator Bavarium Tank
- Wingsuit Course: Snowy Slopes Tour
- Land Race: Grand Slalom Sprint
- Crash Bomb: Snowy Peak Blast
- Demolition Frenzy: Tank Frenzy III
- Air Race: Volo Campo

SETTLEMENT TYPE: BASE

Tips: Excavators

To destroy an Excavator, you must destroy its eight generators on the top platform. There are four on each side of the Excavator. Most Excavators are equipped with Capstone FH155s on each side, which allows you to destroy them pretty quickly. Just be aware that when you destroy the final generator that the main platform dangerously explodes, so clear out when you blow up the last one. Also, use the Capstones on military assets around the Excavators (such as the refinery stations) before you blow up the Excavator.

There's also the excavation arm that you must destroy. If destroying the eight generators does not destroy the Excavator, make sure that the excavation arm has been destroyed, as well. We typically attack the arm first. There are many target points there, but the two weakest are the joints on the extension closest to the platform. Target these with explosives or rockets to blow them up quickly. Sometimes these two joints aren't enough to bring the arm down and you must hit another target farther up the arm.

Bavarium Dump Trailers

Bavarium dump trailers, like a few other targets, blow up a lot quicker if you remove a certain panel first. In this case, shoot at the back door of the trailer and then shoot again into the trailer to explode the Bavarium. A rocket launcher does this all with one shot.

Commander Battle

The base commander flies into the scene with a Bavarium-shielded Urga MSTitel. If you hacked the SAM site, then every time his shields go down, that SAM will hit its mark. The easiest and quickest way to take him out is to grapple to the aircraft when the shields go down, enter it, and throw the commander out. Make sure he's dead when he hits the ground. And then use his helicopter to destroy the military targets.

GUARDIA MONTANA I

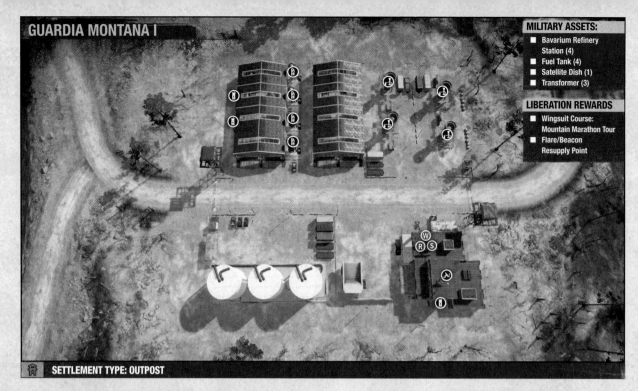

SETTLEMENT TYPE: OUTPOST

MILITARY ASSETS:
- Bavarium Refinery Station (4)
- Fuel Tank (4)
- Satellite Dish (1)
- Transformer (3)

LIBERATION REWARDS
- Wingsuit Course: Mountain Marathon Tour
- Flare/Beacon Resupply Point

Di Ravello mines mercilessly. The inability to build solid fortifications on ever-changing terrain spurs the need for quick-and-dirty outposts like Guardia Montana I, which supports the massive mines without wasting unnecessary resources.

Tips

Enter the settlement in an attack helicopter and get just within range to blow up the SAM on the resupply building rooftop before it shoots at you. Afterward, you can unload on all the military assets.

GUARDIA MONTANA II

SETTLEMENT TYPE: OUTPOST

MILITARY ASSETS:
- Antenna Tower (1)
- Circuit Breaker (2)
- Core Electrical Unit (1)
- Fuel Tank (6)
- Substation Controls (2)
- Transformer (6)

LIBERATION REWARDS
- Wingsuit Course: Cloudy Crevasse Tour
- Flare/Beacon Resupply Point

Di Ravello mines mercilessly. The inability to build solid fortifications on ever-changing terrain spurs the need for quick-and-dirty outposts like Guardia Montana II, which supports the massive mines without wasting unnecessary resources.

Tips

Approach this outpost in an aircraft, using the hill to prevent the SAM site from seeing you. Creep up (as pictured) until you can get the SAM in your sights, and then blow it up. Afterward, you can unload on all the military assets and liberate this outpost in seconds.

PROVINCE: PRIMA

ARGO

SETTLEMENT TYPE: TOWN

MILITARY ASSETS:
- Billboard (4)
- Police Station
- Fuel Tank (2)
- Projector (1)
- Speaker (3)
- Statue (1)
- Raise the Flag

LIBERATION REWARDS
- Argo Garage

The earliest known settlement of Insula Striate, Argo is known for its wheat fields and its rustic population. The farmers here seldom feel Di Ravello's pinch and go about their business as they have for millennia, making this sleepy village one of the more contented places in Medici.

Tips: Police Station

Strike the town and the police station in an attack helicopter. Raise the police station's Havoc Meter to 100% by blowing up all the military assets and doing some extra damage to vehicles or destructible walls. Land it and enter the police station on foot to hack or tether open the two gates (1) and (2) to call in the Rebels.

ARGO NOVE

SETTLEMENT TYPE: TOWN

MILITARY ASSETS:
- Billboard (2)
- Police Station
- Generator (1)
- Propaganda Van (1)
- Speaker (4)
- Statue (1)
- Water Tower (1)
- Raise the Flag

LIBERATION REWARDS
- Argo Nove Garage
- Crash Bomb: Metro Outskirts Blast

Over the course of centuries, this offshoot of nearby Argo grew into a larger, more progressive community. Young Medicians flock to Argo Nove to be closer to the land, to feel more "rustic" or "authentic." Modern apartments are decorated with wagon wheels and milk bottles. Young people grow herbs on their windowsills and have strong opinions about them.

Tips

Strike the town and the police station in an attack helicopter. Raise the police station's Havoc Meter to 100% by blowing up all the military assets and doing some extra damage to vehicles or destructible walls. Land it and enter the police station on foot to hack or tether open the two gates (1) and (2) to call in the Rebels.

Police Station

If you lost your helicopter to enemy air support, then steal one of the enemy's and bomb the crap out of the police station. Take down all the walls, assets, and vehicles to raise the Havoc Meter. There's only one gate (1) to open to call in the Rebels. Do this, then go raise the flag to liberate the town.

BELLEVIA

MILITARY ASSETS:
- ■ Billboard (2)
- ■ Police Station
- ■ Captain (1)
- ■ Fuel Tank (2)
- ■ Generator (1)
- ■ Satellite Dish (2)
- ■ Speaker (3)
- ■ Statue (1)
- ■ Transformer (1)
- ■ Water Tower (1)
- ■ Raise the Flag

LIBERATION REWARDS
- ■ Bellevia Garage
- ■ Land Race:
  Country Sprint

SETTLEMENT TYPE: TOWN

The broad white beaches of this breezy seaside town are ranked fourth most beautiful in the Mediterranean. Before the construction of Vigilator Nord, they were ranked second. Foreigners and those scant few Medicians still able to afford vacations flock to Bellevia and stroll down the beach until the General's voice no longer reaches them.

Tips: Police Station

If you aren't flying around, then grab and dismount the Urga Vulcan on the rooftop facing the police station gate ①. Use this to destroy the enemies and military assets and to raise the Havoc Meter. Open both gates (① and ②) to call in the Rebels. You are likely to have enemy air forces after you, so hijack a helicopter and take out all the assets in town; then raise the flag to liberate the town of Bellevia.

VISTA FONTE

MILITARY ASSETS:
- ■ Billboard (3)
- ■ Police Station
- ■ Fuel Tank (2)
- ■ Generator (1)
- ■ Monitoring System (6)
- ■ Satellite Dish (1)
- ■ Speaker (3)
- ■ Statue (1)
- ■ Raise the Flag

LIBERATION REWARDS
- ■ Vista Fonte Garage
- ■ Land Race: South Coast Sprint

SETTLEMENT TYPE: TOWN

A tiny fishing village only a decade ago, the up-and-coming town of Vista Fonte has ultimately benefited from Di Ravello's rule. The military's demand for grain and fish created thousands of stable jobs, and the burning of the north brought a fresh workforce south to fill them.

Tips: Police Station

Besides blowing up all the police station military assets and raising the Havoc Meter by going beyond asset destruction, you must also raise the gate Ⓐ to let in the Rebels and free some prisoners. There are three jail cells to hack to let prisoners out. There's a two-story jail cell Ⓑ whose doors you must hack, and you must hack the jail Ⓒ above the generator to complete the police station challenge. Use the Urga Vulcan gun on the militia. It's located on the second level of the prison building.

Disable Monitoring System
Time Limit: 1:19

There are six monitoring systems to disable. Start with the ones on the highest points in town. On this course, there are two very high ones, but we'll start on the hotel rooftop ①. Jump off the rooftop after pressing the button, then parachute and grapple directly to the rooftop of the lower resort's rooftop ②. From there it's residential rooftop skipping ③ and ④. From ④, turn, jump, and grapple to the side of the cliff; then parachute up to the white house on the hill. To reach monitoring system ⑤, grapple to the edge of the rooftop when you get close. From there, just jump, glide, and grapple to the last one on the residential rooftop ⑥.

PROVINCE: PROSPERE

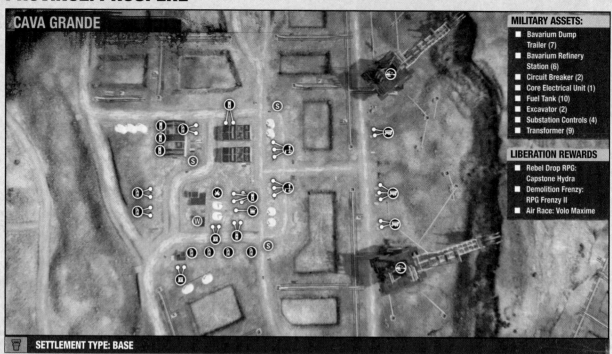

CAVA GRANDE

MILITARY ASSETS:
- Bavarium Dump Trailer (7)
- Bavarium Refinery Station (6)
- Circuit Breaker (2)
- Core Electrical Unit (1)
- Fuel Tank (10)
- Excavator (2)
- Substation Controls (4)
- Transformer (9)

LIBERATION REWARDS
- Rebel Drop RPG: Capstone Hydra
- Demolition Frenzy: RPG Frenzy II
- Air Race: Volo Maxime

SETTLEMENT TYPE: BASE

True to its name, Cava Grande is the largest single mine in Medici, visible even from space. Known for harsh conditions, it has become the final resting place of over 10,000 Medician souls in the past 50 years.

Tips

Check out our Excavator tips at the beginning of this chapter for help destroying these large mining machines. These particular Excavators do not have Capstones guarding them, so you must take out their generators an alternative way. Since this base is so spread out with assets distributed widely, we suggest hacking the SAMs and then using an air drop or hijacking an attack helicopter to make short work of what could be a long struggle to destroy very heavy machinery. The Bavarium refinery stations are also very difficult to destroy without multiple rockets. If you are going on foot (or gliding around), use our map to find the local weapon cache.

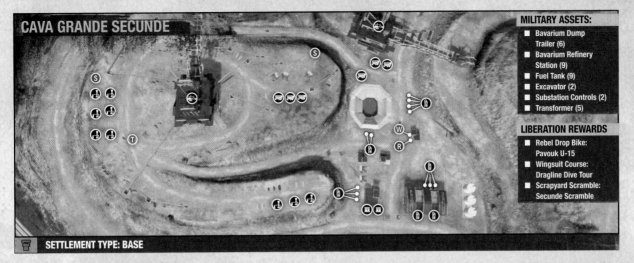

CAVA GRANDE SECUNDE

SETTLEMENT TYPE: BASE

MILITARY ASSETS:
- Bavarium Dump Trailer (6)
- Bavarium Refinery Station (9)
- Fuel Tank (9)
- Excavator (2)
- Substation Controls (2)
- Transformer (5)

LIBERATION REWARDS
- Rebel Drop Bike: Pavouk U-15
- Wingsuit Course: Dragline Dive Tour
- Scrapyard Scramble: Secunde Scramble

On a clear day, the great Excavators of Cava Grande Secunde are visible from Citate Di Ravello. Though smaller than its parent, Cava Grande, Secunde is just as successful a mine and leaves just as big a scar on the countryside.

Tips

If you liberate Guardia Prospera IV (the next settlement in this guide), then you can drive a Rebel tank (CS Odjur) right through this base and be the boss. You should also be able to find an enemy CS Odjur tank near the larger group of Bavarium refinery stations. Otherwise, we suggest using a Rebel Drop to attack in a helicopter.

For help with the Excavator, see our Excavator tips in the beginning of this chapter. This Excavator is not guarded by Capstones, so having an attack helicopter is helpful. Just make sure to hack the SAM sites first. You can also replenish your rockets (for your rocket launcher) at the nearby resupply building.

Di Ravello mines mercilessly. The inability to build solid fortifications on ever-changing terrain spurs the need for quick-and-dirty outposts like Guardia Prospere I, which supports the massive mines without wasting unnecessary resources.

Tips

If you are attacking via helicopter, first eliminate the SAMs on the rooftop of the resupply building. Otherwise, it's a small outpost with all military assets out in the open. The Bavarium refinery stations are the toughest to take out without a military vehicle, but there is a weapons cache nearby that will adequately supply you with the rockets or explosives you need.

GUARDIA PROSPERE I

SETTLEMENT TYPE: OUTPOST

MILITARY ASSETS:
- Bavarium Refinery Station (4)
- Fuel Tank (4)
- Satellite Dish (1)
- Transformer (3)

LIBERATION REWARDS
- Flare/Beacon Resupply Point

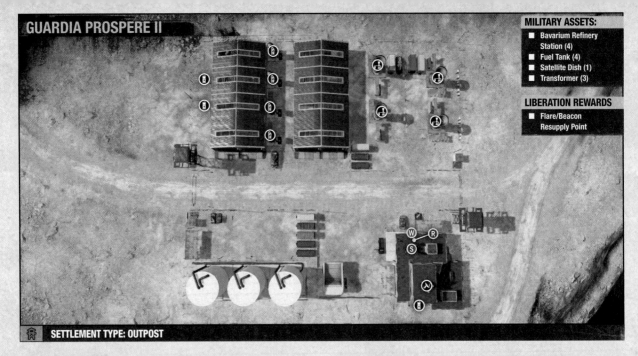

GUARDIA PROSPERE II

MILITARY ASSETS:
- Bavarium Refinery Station (4)
- Fuel Tank (4)
- Satellite Dish (1)
- Transformer (3)

LIBERATION REWARDS
- Flare/Beacon Resupply Point

SETTLEMENT TYPE: OUTPOST

Di Ravello mines mercilessly. The inability to build solid fortifications on ever-changing terrain spurs the need for quick-and-dirty outposts like Guardia Prospere II, which supports the massive mines without wasting unnecessary resources.

Tips

Guardia Prospere I and II have identical layouts. If you are attacking via helicopter, first eliminate the SAMs on the rooftop of the resupply building. The Bavarium refinery stations are the toughest to take out without a military vehicle, but there is a weapons cache at the resupply building that will adequately supply you with the rockets or explosives you need to take them out.

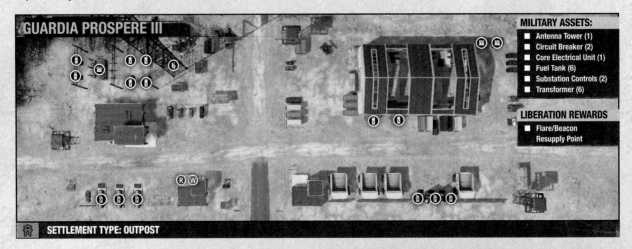

GUARDIA PROSPERE III

MILITARY ASSETS:
- Antenna Tower (1)
- Circuit Breaker (2)
- Core Electrical Unit (1)
- Fuel Tank (6)
- Substation Controls (2)
- Transformer (6)

LIBERATION REWARDS
- Flare/Beacon Resupply Point

SETTLEMENT TYPE: OUTPOST

Di Ravello mines mercilessly. The inability to build solid fortifications on ever-changing terrain spurs the need for quick-and-dirty outposts like Guardia Prospere III, which supports the massive mines without wasting unnecessary resources.

Tips

Similar to Guardia Prospere I and II, this outpost has a SAM site and many fuel tanks. However, this outpost supplies power, so there's a tall antenna tower standing tall above the core electrical unit and accompanying military assets. If you take out the legs of the antenna tower on the core electrical unit side, there's a chance the collateral damage will destroy all those assets in a huge cluster of explosions.

GUARDIA PROSPERE IV

MILITARY ASSETS:
- Antenna Tower (1)
- Circuit Breaker (2)
- Core Electrical Unit (1)
- Fuel Tank (6)
- Substation Controls (2)
- Transformer (6)

LIBERATION REWARDS
- Flare/Beacon Resupply Point

SETTLEMENT TYPE: OUTPOST

Di Ravello mines mercilessly. The inability to build solid fortifications on ever-changing terrain spurs the need for quick-and-dirty outposts like Guardia Prospere IV, which supports the massive mines without wasting unnecessary resources.

Tips

If you are attacking via helicopter, first eliminate the SAMs on the rooftop of the resupply building. Otherwise, it's a small outpost with all military assets out in the open. The Bavarium refinery stations are the toughest to take out without a military vehicle, but there is a weapons cache nearby that will adequately supply you with the rockets or explosives you need.

PROVINCE: REGINO

CITATE DI RAVELLO

SETTLEMENT TYPE: CAPITAL

An ancient seaside village persists as a small neighborhood in the city Di Ravello built as a testimony to his power. The greatest skyscraper in Medici anchors the expensive downtown district and the General's opulent palace crowns the ruins of an old Medician fortress from a bygone age.

Tips

Similar to Guardia Prospere I and II, this outpost has a SAM site and many fuel tanks. However, this outpost supplies power, so there's a tall antenna tower standing tall above the core electrical unit and accompanying military assets. If you take out the legs of the antenna tower on the core electrical unit side, there's a chance the collateral damage will destroy all those assets in a huge cluster of explosions.

You can catch the captain in a helicopter on a helipad atop a resort near the beach. If you're lucky, you can catch him before he takes off, making him a very easy target. Otherwise, shoot him down or grapple and take his helicopter, throwing him out of the cockpit to the ground.

MILITARY ASSETS:

- Billboard (8)
- Police Station
- Captain (3)
- Fuel Tank (7)
- Monitoring System
- Projector (2)
- Propaganda Van (2)
- Speaker (6)
- Sphere Tank (2)
- Statue (3)
- Transformer (8)
- Water Tower (1)
- Raise the Flag

LIBERATION REWARDS

- Citate Di Ravello Garage
- Wingsuit Course:
  Metropolis Tour
- Land Race: City Sprint
- Shooting Gallery: Burst
  Training Course
- Sea Race: Regata Citate

Police Station

This is one of the largest police stations in the game, as it should be, being in the capital. We suggest flying over and dropping missiles via helicopter; or you can commandeer a tank during a high heat level and blast everything in sight to raise the Havoc Meter. There are four gates to open to call in the Rebels. Having trouble finding them? Check out our map: Ⓐ, Ⓑ, Ⓒ, and Ⓓ.

Disable Monitoring System
Time Limit: 2:59

You have almost three minutes to disable eight monitoring systems in the downtown area. This is plenty of time. Check out our map for the best route through the course. See monitor numbers ① through ⑧ for a stress-free route that will have you completing the task with at least 30 seconds to spare.

PROVINCE: ROCCA BLAU

CAVA GEMINOS EST

MILITARY ASSETS:
- Antenna Tower (1)
- Circuit Breaker (2)
- Core Electrical Unit (1)
- Fuel Tank (15)
- Substation Controls (2)
- Transformer (16)

LIBERATION REWARDS
- Rebel Drop Military Car: Urga Fura 570

SETTLEMENT TYPE: BASE

The name Cava Geminos was given to the twin Bavarium mines before a third vein was discovered and Cava Geminos Est opened. The locals refer to it as "the third twin" as a wry poke at Medician military spending.

Tips

Liberate this base in an attack helicopter. Bring your own or hijack one when you get there and the heat is high. Either hack the SAM near the road and the one in the middle of the base before you get in the chopper or make them your first targets. However, you can take out most of the base assets without getting in range of the SAM site near the road. If you prefer to do your dirty work on the ground, then you will find a few tanks at this base that will help you liberate it quickly and easily.

CAVA GEMINOS NORD

MILITARY ASSETS:
- Bavarium Trailer (26)
- Bavarium Refinery Station (12)
- Fuel Tank (8)
- Excavator (2)
- Substation Controls (1)
- Transformer (3)

LIBERATION REWARDS
- Rebel Drop RPG: Fire Leech
- Scrapyard Scramble: Seismic Scramble
- Demolition Frenzy: RPG Frenzy III

SETTLEMENT TYPE: BASE

This Bavarium mine opened at the turn of the 20th century, when Salvatore Albano sold his hillside ranch to the Parvetalpo l'Obra Minerari. Di Ravello greatly expanded the mine and its neighbor, Cava Geminos Sud, near the turn of the 21st century.

These Excavators do not have Capstones on them, so taking out their generators with rockets or missiles from a helicopter is going to be the quickest process.

Commander Battle

Enemy reinforcements arrive via a battalion of three tanks. The base commander is in an Imperator Bavarium (shielded) Tank. Parachute above him until the Bavarium shield goes down and then grapple to the top of it and hijack it. The commander dies when you throw him out. Use his tank to finish off military assets.

CAVA GEMINOS SUD

- Antenna Tower (1)
- Bavarium Trailer (7)
- Bavarium Refinery Station (8)
- Circuit Breaker (2)
- Core Electrical Unit (1)
- Fuel Tank (5)
- Excavator (1)
- Substation Controls (2)
- Transformer (6)

LIBERATION REWARDS
- Rebel Drop Military Car: Urga Szturm 63A
- Wingsuit Course: Badlands Tour

SETTLEMENT TYPE: BASE

Bavarium was discovered here in the 1970s when a small team of French paleontologists unearthed blue rock near their camp. A meager quarry ("Mine your own Bavarium!") served as a tourist attraction until Di Ravello militarized the mine shortly after coming to power in Medici.

Tips

There are no SAM sites at this base, so assaulting in an attack helicopter is a no-brainer. If you are on foot, notice that there are Capstone FH155s near each group of Bavarium refinery stations. This will help make short work of these well-armored machines. You can also find enemy tanks to commandeer and use for a ground assault. For Excavator tips, see the beginning of this chapter.

GUARDIA ROCCA BLAU I

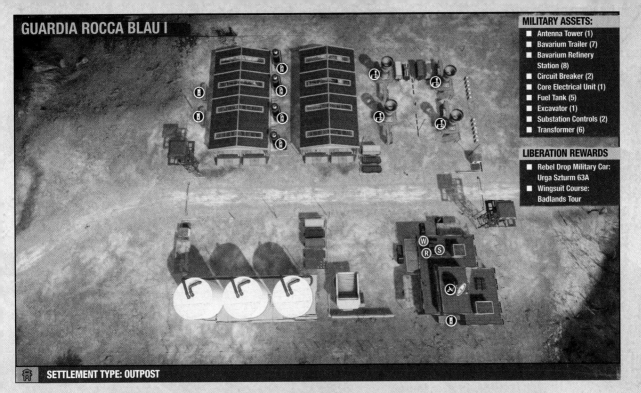

MILITARY ASSETS:
- Antenna Tower (1)
- Bavarium Trailer (7)
- Bavarium Refinery Station (8)
- Circuit Breaker (2)
- Core Electrical Unit (1)
- Fuel Tank (5)
- Excavator (1)
- Substation Controls (2)
- Transformer (6)

LIBERATION REWARDS
- Rebel Drop Military Car: Urga Szturm 63A
- Wingsuit Course: Badlands Tour

SETTLEMENT TYPE: OUTPOST

Di Ravello mines mercilessly. The inability to build solid fortifications on ever-changing terrain spurs the need for quick-and-dirty outposts like Guardia Rocca Blau I, which supports the massive mines without wasting unnecessary resources.

Tips

Take out the SAM on the rooftop of the resupply building and then safely attack the rest of the outpost using aircraft missiles. If you do not attack by air, commandeer the enemy tank near the warehouses and use this to flatten the outpost.

PROVINCE: VAL DE MAR

Reliable energy is hard to come by for the Medician people, but not for the Medician military. Larger power plants route through smaller outposts like Guardia Val De Mar I to keep the lights on for monitoring devices, propaganda, and the military.

GUARDIA VAL DE MAR II

MILITARY ASSETS:
- Fuel Tank (4)
- Sphere Tank (1)
- Transformer (2)

LIBERATION REWARDS
- Flare/Beacon
  Resupply Point

SETTLEMENT TYPE: OUTPOST

The sheer size of Medici's ever-expanding military spurred demand for storage and refueling facilities like Guardia Val De Mar II.

Tips

Destroy the SAM site at the outpost entrance if you are arriving via aircraft. Flatten the outpost in seconds with a few well-placed missiles.

VAL DE MAR

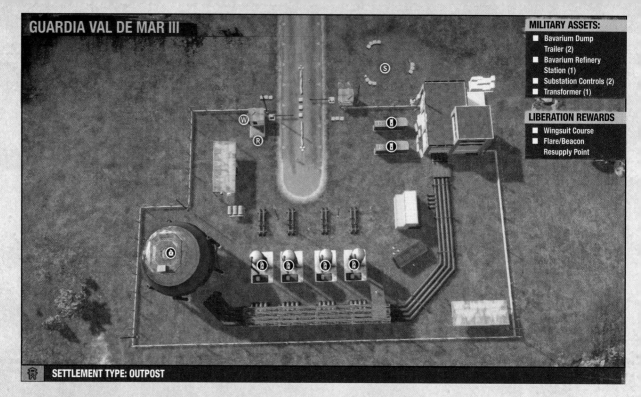

GUARDIA VAL DE MAR III

MILITARY ASSETS:
- Bavarium Dump Trailer (2)
- Bavarium Refinery Station (1)
- Substation Controls (2)
- Transformer (1)

LIBERATION REWARDS
- Wingsuit Course
- Flare/Beacon Resupply Point

SETTLEMENT TYPE: OUTPOST

The mines of Insula Striate produce roughly 80% of Medici's Bavarium stockpile, most of which goes to military use. Smaller operations like Guardia Val De Mar III send their resources to scientists like Dimah, who toil under threat of torture to create weapons and military equipment.

Tips

This outpost has no SAM sites, but a couple targets are trickier to hit from the air. There's a Bavarium refinery station and a transformer inside the warehouse. You can send rockets in through the open skylights or go in on foot.

GUARDIA VAL DE MAR IV

MILITARY ASSETS:
- Fuel Tank (3)
- Long-Range Radar (1)
- Transformer (2)

LIBERATION REWARDS
- Flare/Beacon Resupply Point

SETTLEMENT TYPE: OUTPOST

Medici's skies are among the safest in the world, due in large part to airfields like Guardia Val De Mar IV, which launches routine patrols and scrambles choppers to assist in frequent uprisings throughout Val De Mar.

Tips

There's a SAM site right in the middle of the outpost. If you don't have a helicopter, hack the SAM and take the one from this base—before or after you flatten this outpost.

GUARDIA VAL DE MAR V

MILITARY ASSETS:
- Circuit Breaker (2)
- Core Electrical Unit (1)
- Transformer (4)

LIBERATION REWARDS
- Flare/Beacon Resupply Point

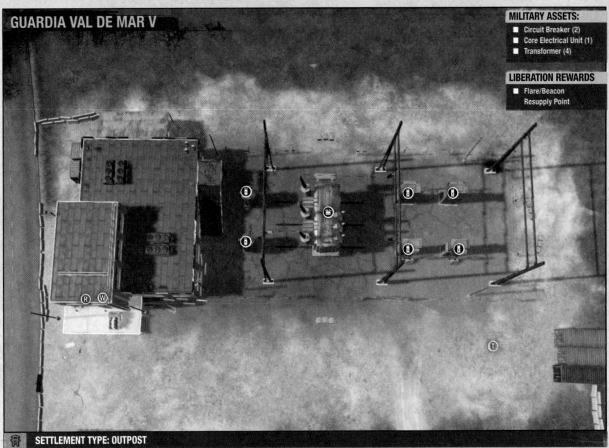

SETTLEMENT TYPE: OUTPOST

Reliable energy is hard to come by for the Medician people, but not for the Medician military. Larger power plants route through smaller outposts like Guardia Val De Mar V to keep the lights on for monitoring devices, propaganda, and the military.

Tips

If you are without a military vehicle or aircraft when near this outpost, steal the tank parked on the grounds and destroy this power plant with a few cannon shells.

PORTO COCLEA

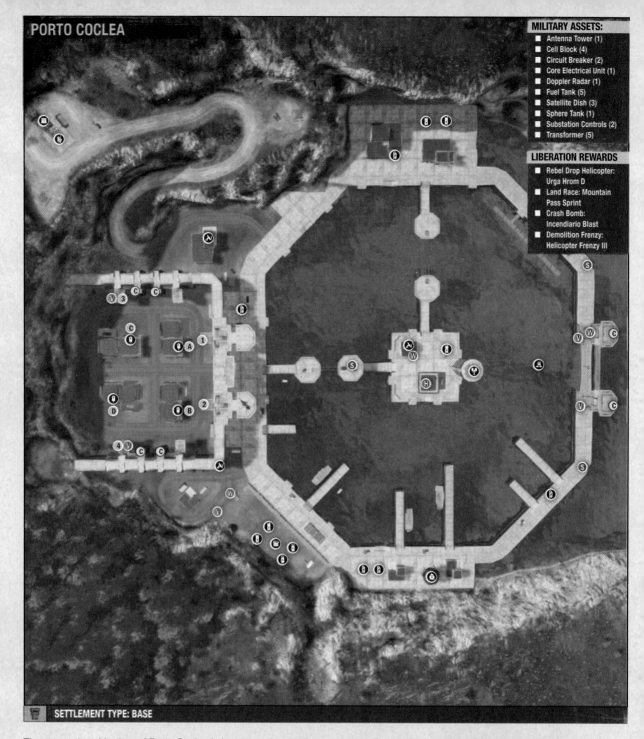

MILITARY ASSETS:
- Antenna Tower (1)
- Cell Block (4)
- Circuit Breaker (2)
- Core Electrical Unit (1)
- Doppler Radar (1)
- Fuel Tank (5)
- Satellite Dish (3)
- Sphere Tank (1)
- Substation Controls (2)
- Transformer (5)

LIBERATION REWARDS
- Rebel Drop Helicopter: Urga Hrom D
- Land Race: Mountain Pass Sprint
- Crash Bomb: Incendiario Blast
- Demolition Frenzy: Helicopter Frenzy III

SETTLEMENT TYPE: BASE

The sequestered harbor of Porto Coclea is home to a large prison complex. Smugglers who fail to elude capture on their way to or from Spain, France, or Monaco spend time here before either bargaining for their freedom or being transferred to one of Insula Striate's monstrous Bavarium mines.

Tips

Approach the base from the water in a CS Navajo and surgically remove the SAMs from the first pier. Then take out any enemy aircraft and remove any attack boats from the water. If you lose your chopper, mount one of the Capstones on the bridge towers and delete enemy targets and military assets in the area. Remember you can tether the guns and move them to get a better view if necessary.

Cell Blocks

Toward the back of the base is a large network of multistory scaffolding with locked cell blocks on the ground level. All this is surrounded by castle walls equipped with Capstones and Vulcan guns. First, clear the riffraff out with the Capstones and Vulcan guns; you could also commandeer a tank and take out groups of enemies.

After the area is relatively clear of military, press the buttons on the ledges to open the cell block doors. You have a limited amount of time to destroy the generator inside before the door closes again, so use a rocket launcher or the Vulcan guns that are nearby. Button ① unlocks cell block door Ⓐ; button ② unlocks cell block Ⓑ, and so on.

Commander Battle

The commander appears in a military attack boat near the watery entrance to the base. Glide to him and either rocket him from your parachute or mount a Capstone and blast him out of the water.

CHALLENGE TIPS

Getting the maximum number of gears is key to quickly unlocking all of the options in each Gear Mod sub-section. While it's not necessary to achieve a five-gear rating on each of the Challenges, you will need five gears on them all to achieve 100% completion. Use the tips in this chapter to achieve perfection. Once you've unlocked a few gear mods, these Challenges will be even easier!

WINGSUIT

Wingsuit races have you falling out of the sky a great distance away from your final destination. Simply flying through all the rings is not enough for a full five gears on these challenges; you must also increase your point total in two ways:

AIM FOR THE CENTER

- Try to fly through the red ring in the center of the white ring. This grants a large number of points.
- Sometimes it's better to avoid a red ring if it seems hard to reach; you don't need to hit every red ring to get all five gears.

FLY LOW

- Skimming low to the ground provides bonus points at the end of the course. These points are not displayed on screen as you earn them. The total appears only after you've completed the course.

- If you get too close to the ground and you're slowing down, use your tether to pull yourself forward, providing an immediate boost of speed.
- Use of the Parachute is restricted. If you use it at any time, the challenge immediately fails.
- You'll still be in your wingsuit at the end of the course, so pull your parachute to avoid hitting anything after seeing your rewards and closing that screen.

RACING

Race through the way points as fast as you can to earn gears! The number of waypoints remaining appears at the top of the screen, next to the amount of time that has elapsed.

Checkpoints

Races start once you go through the first checkpoint. Use this to your advantage by moving yourself further away from the first checkpoint, then building up extra speed before hitting it.

- Once you've completed the race, you will still be in the same vehicle that you ran the race in, so you can use this as a "free" Rebel Drop!
- Speed Boosts from the Gear Mods help with all of these races, allowing you to gain much faster times with the default vehicles suggested.
- If you're struggling to get decent times, try capturing a good vehicle in the class that's the same at the race you're struggling with, then select that vehicle by pressing Square/X at the Challenge menu.
- Any vehicle you've unlocked for Rebel Drops is available, as long as it's in the class of vehicle allowed for that specific race.

AIR

In Air Races you're allowed to select either helicopters or planes, depending on the race (you can't select a jet to use for a helicopter race).

- When flying planes use Square/X and Circle/B to turn. Steering this way is much easier. It does, however, make turning much slower so you may need to use the Left Stick for sharper turns.
- Managing your speed is key. You want to go fast, but aren't on a road, so missing a checkpoint is very easy and results in a few lost gears on your final rating.
- Keep an eye on your altitude when flying in the helicopters. You can easily get too close to the ground while concentrating on moving forward! Don't forget about your rotor blades. They extend past the body of your helicopter, so getting too close to trees or other objects can easily throw your helicopter off course!

LAND

Land Races send you down hills, around tight corners, and occasionally off jumps.

Use Your Brakes!

Damaging your car in any way significantly lowers its top speed and handling performance, so hit your brakes before you take sharp corners to avoid sliding off the road.

- Always try to reverse as far as the game will let you from the starting checkpoint before driving through it. This allows you to hit the starting line at a much higher speed than you would have if you started from the spawn point.
- When crossing a busy intersection, always pass cars on the trunk side. This prevents them from clipping your car as you speed by.
- Use the standard brake L2/LT instead of the E-Brake Square/X when taking corners to maintain traction on the road. It allows you to accelerate much faster out of the turn.

⚓ SEA

Setting good times on Sea Races is heavily determined by the lines you draw to get from each objective. Try to take the most direct path possible. This may be hard to decipher due to the waves moving your boat from side to side as you navigate.

- Once you've unlocked jumping in the Gear Mod menu, you can use it to jump over mines in the water, greatly increasing your time on a few courses.
- Speed boats and Jet Skis are pretty easy to find in the resort towns of Medici, so take a little trip to town and bring a new boat to your dock to be stripped down if you're struggling to get a good time.

🔀 SCRAPYARD SCRAMBLE

Scrapyard Scramble requires you to collect massive amounts of Bavarium and deposit it in a large silo.

- Before you begin collecting Bavarium, you must connect your Bavarium Attractor to the vehicle you've picked. Attach it fairly close to the end of your car to make it easier to gather Bavarium.
- Bavarium comes in two quality grades, and each grants a different number of points. While grabbing better quality Bavarium is useful, don't make it your focus; instead, just grab as much as possible before depositing it.

- Large quantities of Bavarium are stored inside big metal cargo containers. A close pass near one of the container's ends rips the doors off and chunks of Bavarium begin to spill out.
- Once you've entered the pit, shut off the Attractor to drop all of the Bavarium before driving back out of the pit.
- Bring enough Bavarium to reach the bonus number and you are granted a time bonus, allowing you even more time to reach the amount needed for five gears.

Keep it Close

If you attach the Bavarium Attractor too far from the car, press L2/LT to bring it closer.

Follow Me!

If any enemies are chasing you, have them follow you into the pit, then let them fall down into the depths with the collected Bavarium.

💣 CRASH BOMB

Once you hit the gas in a Crash Bomb car, there's no stopping. That is, unless you want to blow up. You need to get to the objective marked on the map and blow up everything in the area surrounding it.

'63 AUTOSTRAAD WELTBUS

Hurry!

The minimum speed to avoid exploding is marked as a small bar on the speedometer in the bottom-left corner of your HUD.

■ You must bail out just before hitting the target or you'll blow up with the car and fail the mission. This isn't hard, but make sure your car is lined up for the perfect hit on the target as the amount of damage applied affects your score toward the gears at the end.

■ Enemies begin to pop up and chase you down the road. Hitting anything drastically slows down your vehicle, so just tap your brakes to avoid hitting a pedestrian or enemy vehicle.

■ Keep enemy vehicles behind you. If they catch up, they try to grind you to a stop.

■ Be careful when bailing out. If you do it too close, you'll be caught up in the blast. If you're using your parachute to jump out of the car, make sure to turn away from the explosion. The blast has a large horizontal and vertical radius, making it dangerous even if you're above it.

■ You can use a Crash Bomb car to explode something else other than your target. Vehicles equipped with a Crash Bomb damage a much larger area than the ones without.

⊕ SHOOTING GALLERY

Speed and accuracy are critical to gaining five gears in each Shooting Gallery. Aim for the bullseyes without hitting blue "X"s or missing to keep your multiplier up! The first time you play a Shooting Gallery, you are without the Precision Aim Weapon Mod. Precision Aim requires three gears to unlock. Getting these gears is a simple task.

MACHINE GUN

■ Always aim for the center of the target, don't be afraid to miss a bullseye every now and then. Keep firing your gun as often as possible, but be prepared for the target to disappear when it reaches the end of its path. If you focus too much on just hitting the center, you'll end up with fewer points than if you aimed a little more freely at the target.

Control Your Fire!

While you may be used to running and gunning around the world, use short, simple bursts on your targets as any shot missed reset your multiplier.

■ Missing the targets resets your multiplier, so stop shooting before the target drops out of sight. The multiplier bonus counts for any spot on the target hit, including the center.

SHOTGUN SHOOTING GALLERY

■ Accuracy is much less important here. Your goal is to hit as many targets as possible. Aim for the center of all the targets you're trying to hit, then fire while taking a step to the left or right. Taking the step adds additional spread on the bullets, allowing you to hit a greater number of targets for a higher bonus.

HANDGUN

The Handgun Challenge pits you against mostly moving targets with plenty of the blue "X" targets tossed in to make things interesting.

■ A large group of targets are turned around at the far side of the range. Keep an eye on them as they are your key to achieving a five-gear rating.

■ Once you've worked about halfway through the challenge, three of the back targets flip around. Work to take them out quickly, then shoot the targets that come across the middle. There's a green bullseye target right in the center of the bottom row of the back targets. Shooting it unlocks even more stationary targets to hit.

■ Avoid hitting any of the blue "X" targets while aiming for the back set of targets. It's easy to get "tunnel vision" and accidentally hit one as they move in from the left or right side.

REVOLVER

- Targets disappear after being hit once, so always aim for the bullseye. When the match starts, targets begin to move from right to left across the screen with each target appearing after the one before it is shot.

Avoid the Blue "X"

Watch out for targets with a blue "X." These not only reset your multiplier, they also subtract 100 points from your total!

- Look for the two stationary target boxes that appear in the back of the room. As you shoot each target, a new set branches off of each of the boxes. Once you've cleared all of the targets, a row of targets with a special green bullseye appears.

- The targets with green bullseyes grant a lot more points when hit in the center, so take your time to aim for perfect aim before shooting at these.

BURST

Each pull of the trigger fires four shots in this challenge. All three shots hit almost on top of each other, but it's still a good idea to aim low in the center of the bullseye to guarantee all shots grant maximum points.

Take Your Time

Don't move to the next target too quickly. Missing a single shot of the burst resets your multiplier.

- As your multiplier increases, take a few extra seconds to aim for the bullseye, keeping your eye out for the green bullseyes. Hitting all four shots with full multiplier on the green bullseyes grants 6000 points, making a five-gear rating pretty manageable.
- Targets fall over after the fourth shot of the burst hits, so pull the trigger only once on each target.

- Completing a set of targets quickly sometimes causes an extra green bullseye target to appear. These are not necessary for a five-gear rating, but are great for setting high scores!

💥 DESTRUCTION FRENZY

Destruction Frenzies require you to rack up points by exploding everything in sight. Explosions can be linked together to maximize the number of points given via a multiplier that can grow up to eight times. If you take too much time between explosions, your multiplier divides in half until it's back down to x1.

The timer starts counting down once you've set off the first explosion, so use that to you advantage. Take some time to scout out the area, and set up a few explosions. Check out our maps of each outpost for a quick overview of all of the destructible objects in the area. Explode smaller objects first to build your combo meter, then go for the big stuff.

While your weapon selection may be restricted to just a few options in each of the Frenzies, you can use any vehicle inside the area to help you reach your goal. So if you're struggling to complete a certain mission, grab a helicopter or tank from inside the Destruction area and go to work.

SNIPER RIFLE FRENZY

Spend some time dealing small amounts of damage to all of the objects in the area. This allows you to keep your multiplier much higher as you will not have to take multiple shots to blow things up once the first explosion happens. Target the weak points of objects; for example, target the panels of a transformer instead of just a plain side. Some larger objects cannot be destroyed by your sniper rifle, so ignore them. Once you've eliminated all other objects, use your grenades or tethers to take the remaining stuff down.

JET FRENZY

Take a look around before getting in the jet. Search for small and large groups of items. Target the small groups of items first, then turn around and bomb the larger ones. The overhead maps for each area help you precisely target each group of objects.

HELICOPTER FRENZY

You're the eye in the sky, with bullets and rockets. Check out our Challenges Map at the end of this chapter to plot your attack. Some targets may be hidden behind small buildings or inside large warehouses. Make a mental note of this while planning your attack.

If your helicopter only has miniguns, fire a few bursts on the larger objects, being careful not to destroy them outright. This makes keeping your multiplier up easier since you won't spend as much time grinding away on each target.

GRAPPLE FRENZY

Much like other Frenzies, start out by setting up a few explosions with your tethers.

Connect explosive barrels to the power supplies around the compound, saving your grenades for the fuel tanks.

Grapples

This challenge becomes much easier if you have unlocked 3x grapples by completing a few Scrapyard Scrambles.

After you've set off you initial explosions, take down anything left in sight by either grappling the object to the ground, wall, or any explosive in the area.

Speed it Up

To speed things up, press and hold L2/LT while you attach the tethers. This immediately begins to pull the objects together.

If you don't have Tether Strength upgrades, you may need to attach two tethers to an object to bring it down. This makes using other objects with some momentum in the environment, such as explosives or even a cement barricade, a much better choice than trying to take something down by grappling it to a wall.

BOAT FRENZY

The boat missions are much like the Support Vehicle Frenzies. In essence, you cannot shoot and move the vehicles. However, unlike the Support Vehicle Frenzy, you are able to switch the starting vehicles to one that has the ability to shoot from the driver's seat.

If you haven't advanced far enough to unlock this vehicle, you can still beat this challenge. It just requires a bit more planning.

Get Tricky

You can attach a tether to the front of your boat with the other side hooked into something down the way from it. This allows you to move the boat while you're on the guns. Be warned that you cannot reverse, so doing this requires precise timing.

Check the map and determine where the groups of destructive items are, then set up some explosions with your grappling hook. Pull the shields off of power sources. With everything exposed and some explosions set up, get in one of the boats with a good number of targets to shoot at, then trigger your explosions.

Alternatively, you can save the tether explosions for when you want to move from boat to boat. Tethering to a different boat is much faster than attempting to drive the boat and switch back to the gunner's seat.

RPG FRENZY

Every shot counts when using the standard RPG. You must reload every time, making it a little tricky to take down successive targets.

The Hydra is the best option, hands down. Why fire one rocket when you can fire three, right? This allows you to fire and forget at targets, knowing that it will blow up whether you've hit its weak point or not.

Some non-explosive chaos objects may require more than one rocket to disable. To avoid losing your multiplier, fire a shot at the harder target, aim for an explosive object, like a gas tank or transformer, to keep your score up, then fire the second shot at the tougher object.

TANK FRENZY

Elevated objects are a tank's worst enemy. Look for weak points or support beams of a different chaos object. For example, a tank cannot hit the top of the water tower, but it has no problem destroying the lower support beams.

Tether It!

If you're having trouble taking something down, tether it to your tank and pull it down manually!

Plan out your driving route before you start destroying all the chaos objects in sight. This helps you to keep your multiplier up and also prepares you for any tougher shots you may have to make when facing taller objects.

FOW FRENZY

If you love destruction, you'll really love the FOW Frenzy. Use your FOW weapon of choice to take down a base as quickly as possible. Getting yourself into the sky before starting is a great idea, unless you're using the Dionysus PLDS-H.

When using the PLDS-H, acquiring targets from the air is inconsistent, and for the most part they will be out of range. So grabbing a vehicle inside the base to drive you quickly around may be your best bet at quickly destroying all chaos objects in the area.

MORTAR FRENZY

Learning how to aim the mortar is the most challenging part of the Mortar Frenzy.

If you don't want to spend the time learning how to aim the mortar, just position yourself close to the objects that need to be taken down. The mortar generally destroys the target on the way up into the sky, instead of on the way down. This also decreases the amount of time between effective hits, which help keep your multiplier up.

Beware of the Blast

Be cautious when using the mortar at close range. It's incredibly easy to hit a small roof over your head, which will knock you over and take away precious time while effectively killing your multiplier.

SUPPORT VEHICLE FRENZY

Support vehicles do not allow you to drive and shoot at the same time. That said, you must arrange for a few things to be destroyed before starting this mission. It makes the task much easier. Use the tethers to attach explosive barrels to a few objectives, then start on either side of the set of three cars that the game has spawned for you.

Placement is Important

If you feel that the support cars may not be in a good position, move them before setting off the first explosion. Moving items before the first explosion does not start the timer.

Start destroying objects from the first car's gun. Once you've hit everything you can, launch yourself to the middle car on the high ground.

While you're transferring to the second vehicle, tighten your tethers, triggering explosions you have already set up. This keeps your multiplier up.

If you've accomplished the sets of targets available from the first two cars quickly enough, you have plenty for all five gears.

Continue to the third car, eliminating the few remaining targets. Toss grenades if necessary while you transfer to the final shooting position.

GRENADE LAUNCHER FRENZY

Grenade Launcher Frenzies are pretty manageable. Just stay high in the sky and rain down grenades from above. Once you've cleared out an area, activate your wingsuit to fly to the next area, using your tether for a boost of speed.

Aiming for critical points is helpful, but not necessary, when using explosives, so there's no reason to slow down. When searching for targets, look for small vehicles. The light vehicles can be blown up with just one hit, granting you a few extra points while you work toward other objectives.

MACHINE GUN FRENZY

While it's possible to accomplish this challenge with a machine gun, there's a much easier way without even firing a shot from your provided weapon. There's a helicopter armed with dual miniguns right in front of the challenge's starting position. Hop in and take out everything in the area around it!

Once you've eliminated all the targets, follow the road around to the other side of the base, taking out any of the possible targets (like electrical boxes).

You eventually discover the larger area with more items to explode. If you've kept your multiplier up, you'll land all five gears!

STUNT HANG FRENZY

Helicopters patrol the area, so tether onto one and let it take you to the end of its patrol before opening fire on the area below. If you don't wait for it to start returning to the center before opening fire, you end up losing your multiplier while you work your way back to the other areas of the map.

Use your wingsuit to quickly travel between areas and onto other choppers. Take out all of the base that resides above ground before cleaning up the area below. Moving from the top side of the base to the bottom is much easier than trying to tether and parachute your way into position to grab a higher helicopter, so stay on top until you've cleared the whole area.

SHOTGUN FRENZY

Shotguns are a bit tricky to use. They allow you to get in close to destroy things easily, but also knock you around a bit.

Keep a little bit of distance; missing isn't an entirely bad thing, especially if there are other targets around.

Remember that you still have your tethers and grenades. Use grenades on bigger targets as shooting them with the shotgun does not help.

Always aim for the weak points of objects and use the explosives in the environment to help speed up the destruction of all the targets around you.

CHALLENGES WORLD MAP

Here's your one-stop resource to finding every Challenge in Medici. There's so much to do besides the Main Story and the seriously explosive business of Liberation: Air Races, Boat Races, Crash Bomb, Destruction Frenzy, Land Races, Scramble, Shooting, Gallery, Wingsuit—get out there and have fun!

✈	**AIR RACES**
⚓	**BOAT RACES**
💣	**CRASH BOMB**
✵	**DESTRUCTION FRENZY**
◉	**LAND RACES**
↷	**SCRAMBLE**
✛	**SHOOTING GALLERY**
🖝	**WINGSUIT**

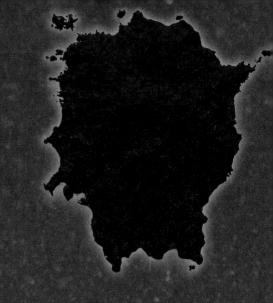

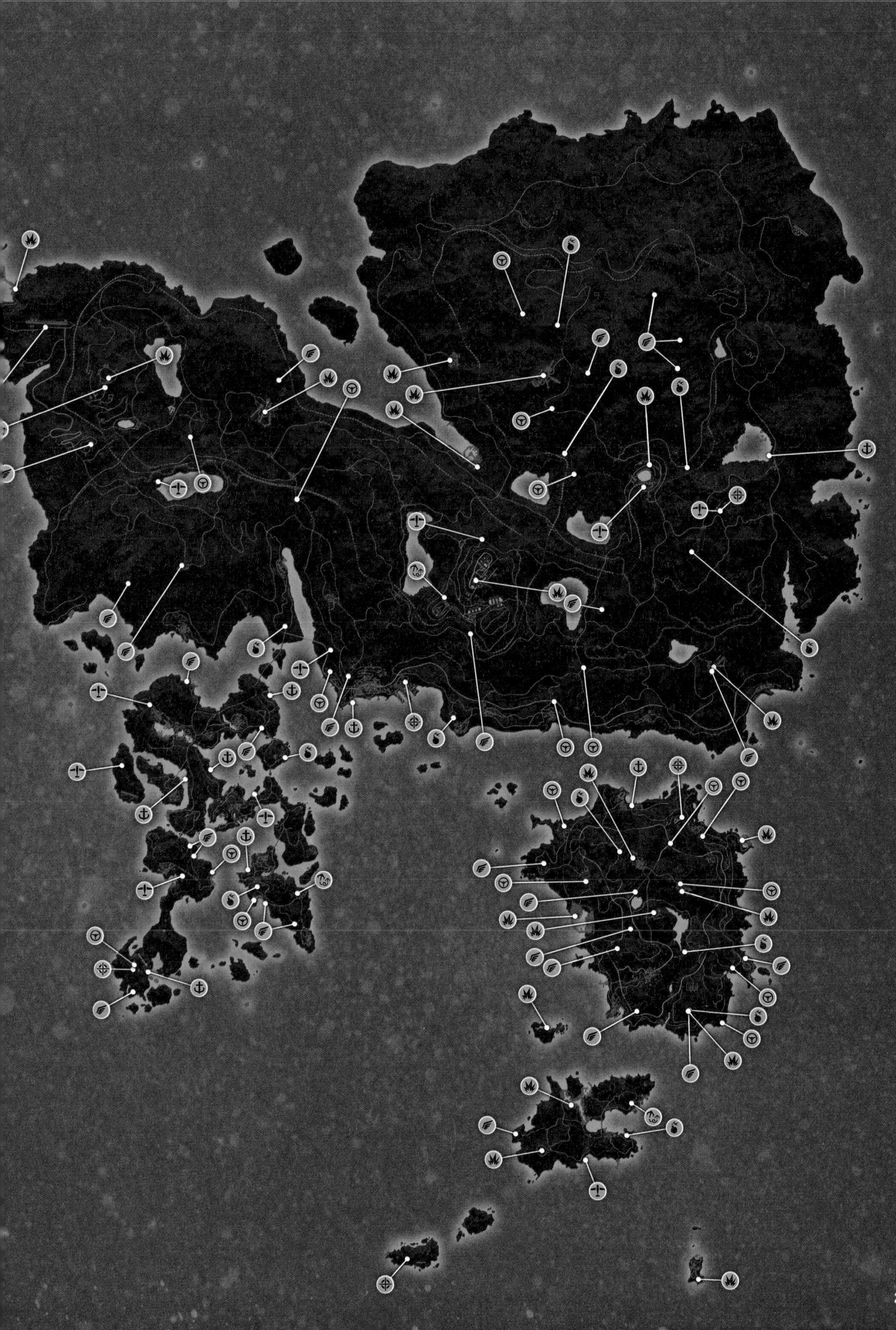

COLLECTIBLES

There are five different types of collectibles scattered around the three regions: Ancient Tombs, Daredevil Jumps, Di Ravello Tapes, Rebel Shrines, and Vintage Parts. This chapter provides detailed maps and locations for them all!

ANCIENT TOMBS

Ancient tombs are easily found from the sky. They appear as a large mound covered with light blue flowers. To "collect" each one you must Pay Respects by finding the door and holding Y/Triangle. An Urga Stupka-210 (handheld mortar) is found behind each tomb after you do this. Once you've Paid Respects at all of the Ancient Tombs, the Urga-Supka-210 becomes available for Rebel Drops.

INSULA STRIATE

MAP NUMBER	PROVINCE	COORDINATES	
		N 40	E 5
1	Litore Torto	50.48	45.10
2	Grande Pastura	51.54	44.60
3	Grande Pastura	50.67	41.79
4	Grande Pastura	49.94	41.84
5	Grande Pastura	49.65	42.93
6	Val De Mar	47.10	41.19
7	Val De Mar	46.79	40.78
8	Maestrale	47.20	39.02
9	Maestrale	47.14	38.06
10	Maestrale	47.18	36.89
11	Maestrale	47.71	35.08
12	Maestrale	48.52	36.04
13	Maestrale	48.79	35.44
14	Maestrale	48.82	34.57
15	Maestrale	49.47	34.26
16	Maestrale	49.07	33.08
17	Libeccio	45.89	32.75
18	Libeccio	45.98	33.68
19	Libeccio	46.37	36.94
20	Maestrale	45.75	38.74
21	Prospere	44.605	40.03
22	Litore Torto	46.91	45.68
23	Costa Sud	46.46	46.69

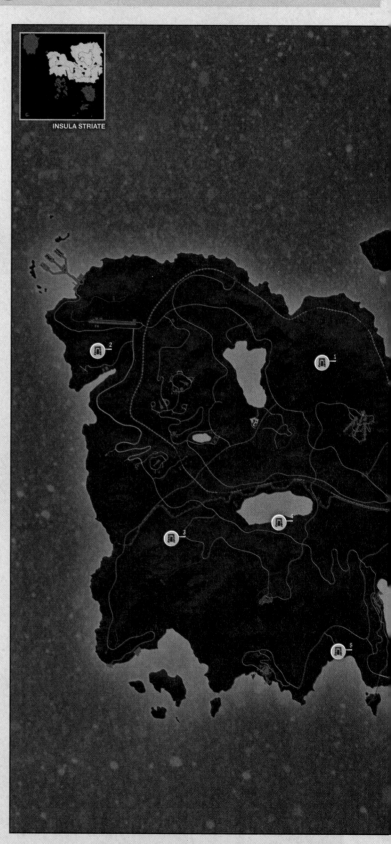

INSULA STRIATE

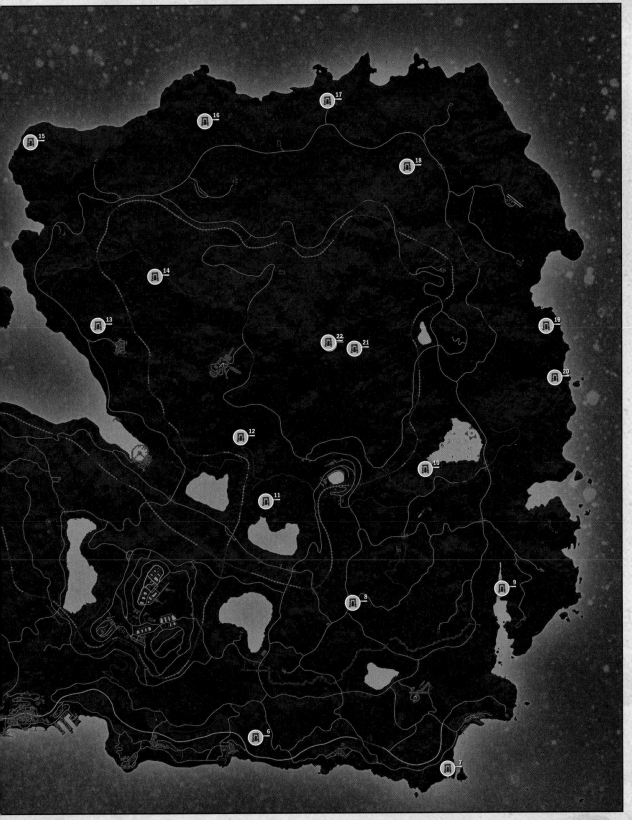

DAREDEVIL JUMPS

Take a perilous jump off of the different marked ramps all around Medici. The car doesn't need to survive the jump, just Rico.

INSULA DRACON

INSULA DRACON

Complete all 10 of the Daredevil Jumps in Insula Dracon to unlock the Custom Kletterer 300 (Quad) in the Rebel Drop list.

Insula Dracon – Daredevil Jumps

MAP NUMBER	PROVINCE	COORDINATES		DESCRIPTION
		N 40	E 5	
1	Petra	41.24	37.34	A car can be found in the small guarded area to the north of the jump. Take the ramp south of the landing in Puncta Sud. If you haven't yet liberated Puncta Sud, the guard tower you land beside may attack.
2	Petra	42.06	36.76	You need some serious speed to land this jump, so plan accordingly. The jump sends you south over the large open area in Espia Bassa. If you don't want to end up at the bottom, pull your parachute and grapple to the other side after the jump.
3	Petra	42.15	36.83	Follow the road to the upper-north side of Espia Bassa. The road dead ends into the ramp, so maintain your speed to land on the road below to the north. If you don't have enough speed, you may crash into one of the buildings below.
4	Corda Dracon	42.79	36.59	Follow the road east out of Corda Dracon: Centcom, hitting the ramp that the road eventually dead ends into. Landing the jump is very easy as the road below lines up with the jump perfectly.
5	Corda Dracon	42.89	36.29	Take the north road out of Corda Dracon: Centcom, following it around to the jump that lines up with the road leading to Jump 4. If you can cleanly land it on the road below, you'll easily continue straight on to Jump 4.
6	Trio	42.40	35.37	Take the east road out of Guardia Trio I and follow it north as it begins to shift into a dirt road. The landing for this one is a bit tricky as you attempt to land on a two-lane bridge. As you launch off the jump, begin to shift your car to the left in air. It's easy to under or overshoot this jump, but hitting a speed of 140 km/h should land you right on the bridge.
7	Capite West	43.49	35.58	A dirt road leads up to the jump. Since there generally aren't any cars lining this road, it may be easier to start Jump 8 and launch the car over to the ramp for Jump 7. To land either one, you need a good amount of speed to clear the gap and land it. If you fail you'll end up in the shallow water below.
8	Capite West	43.51	35.60	This jump is very easy as cars are plentiful and a long paved road lines the way to the jump. The ramp on the other end is the same ramp that you would use to initiate Jump 7.
9	Capite Est	43.79	36.15	The road to this jump is east of Espia Alta. If you haven't liberated Espia Alta yet, be ready for a fight when you land as you'll be right in the heart of the base. If you don't want to fight, you can use your parachute once you've gone far enough to complete the jump, then glide away from the base, landing on the road to the south.
10	Capite West	43.80	34.94	Launch this jump from the south end of the air strip in Porto Cavo. There's nowhere to land safely since you're jumping into the large body of water below. Pull your chute early, then steal a car on either side of this lake and make your get away. This jump is much easier to complete when the Base is liberated since the water below contains boats armed with cannons and other weapons.

INSULA FONTE

Completing all 13 of the Insula Fonte Daredevil Jumps unlocks the Custom Geschwind (Motorcycle) as a Rebel Drop.

INSULA FONTE

Insula Fonte – Daredevil Jumps

MAP NUMBER	PROVINCE	COORDINATES N 40	COORDINATES E 5	DESCRIPTION
1	Feno	42.68	42.87	Blocked by a few barricades that can be simply avoided, follow the dirt path off the main road and head toward Babica. If you hit this jump with too much speed, you'll end up inside the police station. Ease off and lower your speed to land safely on the road below to the east of the jump.
2	Plagia	42.54	43.30	Break off the north side of the highway and follow the dirt road west that leads toward the ramp. The jump takes you west, landing you in Feno. If you've got a decent amount of speed, you easily land on some flat land just before the road below.
3	Feno	42.13	42.44	A car can usually be found right at the start of this ramp. If not, hijack one from the nearby outpost. Follow the dirt road up away from the outpost and take the jump south out of Feno and into Lavanda. This jump is easy to land; the slope below isn't very steep and the ground levels out quickly, so keep your car level midair to assure a safe landing.
4	Lavanda	41.89	42.61	This jump branches off of the main road just north of the small dirt road leading to Sancte Lucas. Take the jump north. It's an easy landing thanks to the road below that's perfectly in line with the jump.
5	Feno	41.68	43.05	Grapple up from the base of the mountain below the ramp. A car can be found at the bottom, since this ramp has a long downhill dirt road. Even a slower car can clear this jump. If you can't find a car, steal one from the outpost to the north and quickly take it down the dirt path to the jump. Landing this one isn't terribly hard, with a road and a small slope below there aren't many obstacles to get in your way.
6	Lacos	40.76	43.47	This jump leads you south off the paved road, launching right next to a large wind turbine. Cars are rare on the road that takes you to the jump, so steal one from the main road to the north, or the outpost further down the road to the west. This jump is a bit tricky to hit with speed, so be ready to bail out of your car and parachute to the city below.
7	Lacos	40.87	43.74	Grab a fast car off the main road to the north of the jump, then follow the trail down to the ramp. Line up on the dirt road, being careful on the long turn leading up to the jump. Amass a fair amount of speed to land on the road to the east and continue on.
8	Lacos	41.01	44.41	Heading east out of Fortalessa, this ramp heads straight off the main road as it begins to curve. Be careful when transitioning onto the dirt road; there's a small bump that may send your car flying early, and not in the direction of the ramp. Once you've launched off the ramp, hit the brakes and to stick a landing on the road below.
9	Baia	40.30	44.62	There are cars on the dirt road or at any of the houses along it on the way to the jump. This one is easily survived as you land straight on the road to the south.
10	Baia	40.15	44.56	Find a car near the base of the wind turbine, then take the car off the ramp to the south east and land safely on the road.
11	Baia	40.02	43.77	Take this ramp at the highest speed you possibly can if you're aiming to land this jump. You cross over a large chasm, so be prepared to bail out of your car and parachute to finish crossing the gap or you'll end up in the water below.
12	Sirocco Nord	39.04	42.87	This jump takes you south off the main road. A short dirt path leads up to the ramp. The only obstacle to an easy landing is a large tree right where you're likely to land. To avoid it, stick to the left or right of the ramp. Be ready to turn when you hit the ground or you'll plunge into the ocean.
13	Sirocco Nord	38.51	42.50	Follow the dirt road up from Cirilla or from the main road to the east of the jump. The jump launches you west into an open field or road, so keep your car level to survive with your car in good shape.

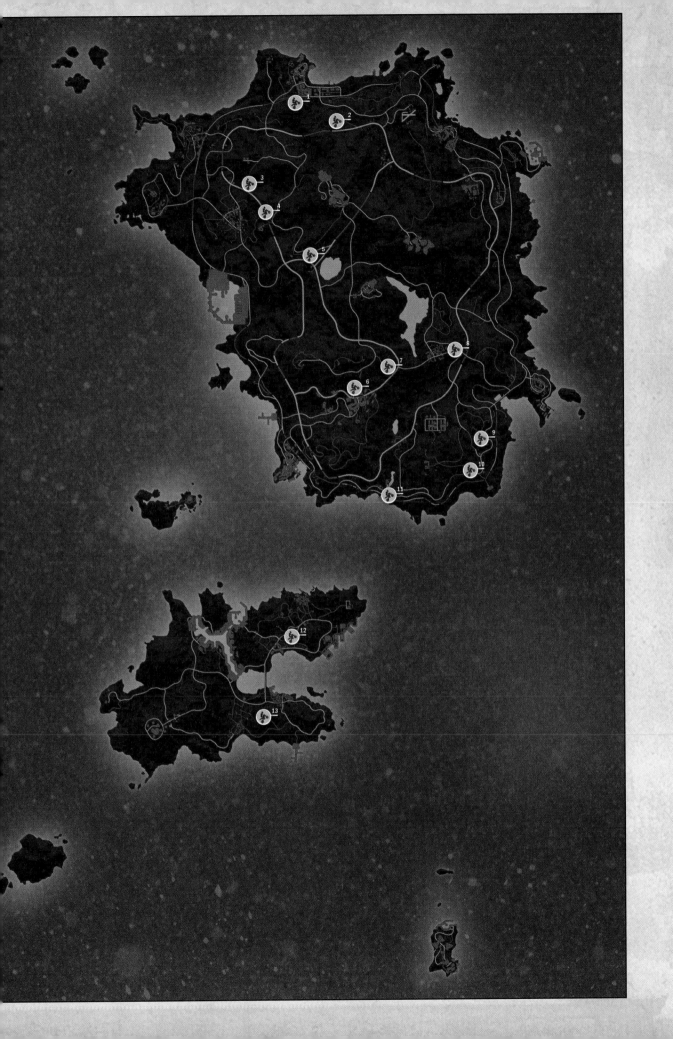

INSULA STRIATE

Completing all seven Daredevil Jumps in Insula Striate unlocks the Incendario Monster Truck.

Insula Striate – Daredevil Jumps

MAP NUMBER	PROVINCE	COORDINATES		DESCRIPTION
		N 40	E 5	
1	Libeccio	45.74	35.18	A dirt road on the west side of Vista Dracon leads up to the jump that takes you straight off of a cliff. You must break through a barrier at the end of the ramp, so make sure you're in a car with enough speed to do this.
2	Val De Mar	44.73	42.36	Steal a car from Guardia Val De Mar IV and run it through the chain fence to the west. Then find the path that leads you to the jump. It sends you west, landing just before the exit of the outpost.
3	Costa Sud	44.30	45.45	This jump is just off the main road and takes you south into Perla Est. Use your parachute to avoid meeting your end in the buildings below.
4	Costa Sud	46.12	44.42	You jump off the ramp just east of Sancte Evita at the top of the mountain. It launches you over the snow covered slope to the north, lining you up with the road below. If you have enough speed and the skills to land, you won't even need your parachute.
5	Val De Mar	46.73	42.06	Take the small dirt road that branches off the main road east of the Mountain Pass Sprint. If you have too much speed going off the ramp, you end up crashing into the top of the tunnel that the railroad tracks lead into, so be prepared to pull your chute.
6	Litore Torto	47.42	45.72	Grab a car on the main road in the small city directly south of the jump. Then follow the dirt path east out of the city, watching your speed as you ascend the mountain. The road takes you all the way to the jump. Amass enough speed to clear the trees and make it all the way to the road below.
7	Litore Torto	49.22	45.05	This jump splits off of the road that leads up to Sancte Malco. There may be cars up near the spot of the jump, but the main paved road below is a better spot to find them. The jump launches you east over the railroad tracks and down the canyon, giving you the choice of crashing into the mountain or ditching your car and keeping yourself alive.

INSULA STRIATE

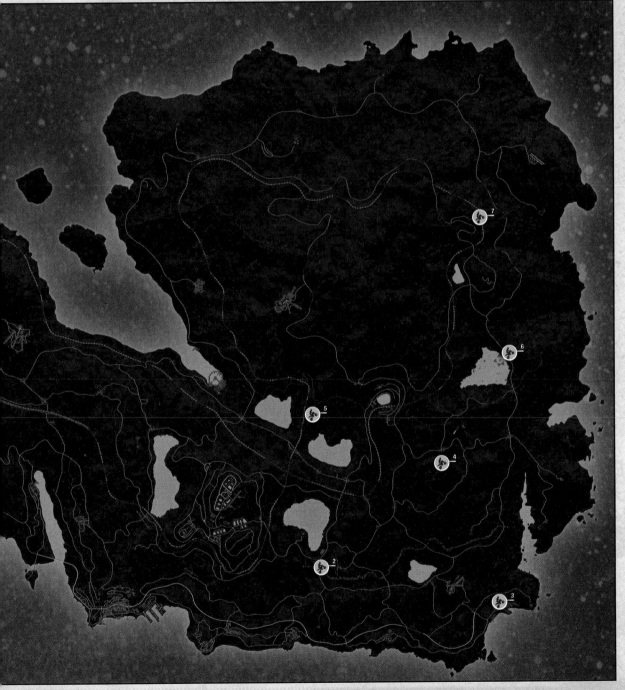

DI RAVELLO TAPES

Di Ravello has recorded his journey into his role as Dictator as he saw it happen. Find the tapes to hear every step of his rise.

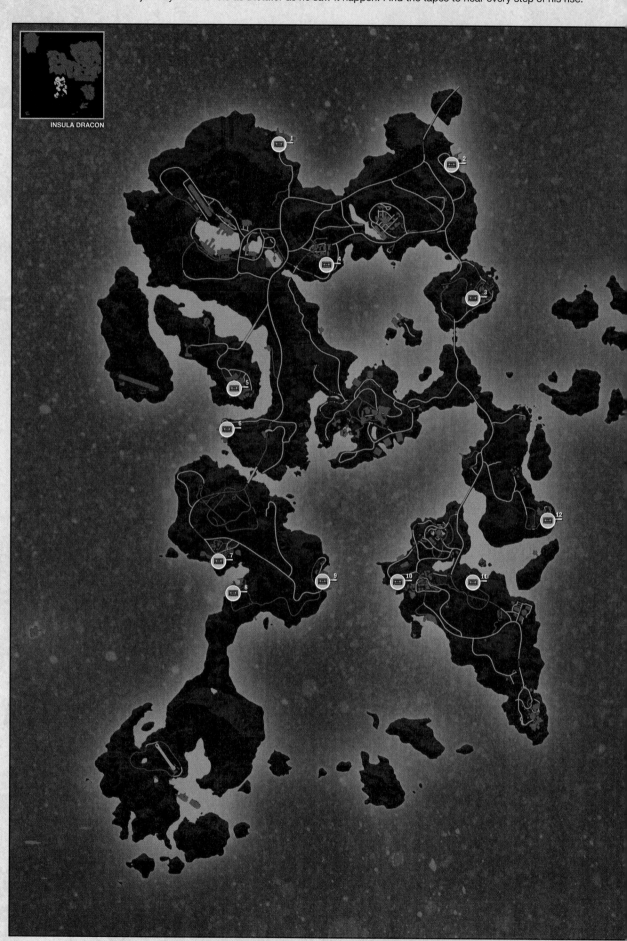

INSULA DRACON

Collecting all of the tapes unlocks the Golden Urga Mstitel, a deadly attack chopper.

Tape Unlocks

The tapes are unlocked in order, regardless of which ones you pick up.

INSULA DRACON

Insula Dracon – Di Ravello Tapes

MAP NUMBER	PROVINCE	COORDINATES N 40	E 5	DESCRIPTION
1	Capite Est	44.25	35.49	On the second level of the ruins before the third set of stairs leading up to the top.
2	Capite Est	44.13	36.80	Near a bunch of trash between the bottom of the yellow building and a large wall.
3	Massos	43.39	37.05	On a pile of rubble in a graveyard of cars.
4	Capite Est	43.60	35.84	Mixed into a pile of trash on the porch of the building with the national flag hanging in the front.
5	Capite West	42.93	35.18	On the porch of the darker stone building displaying the national flag.
6	Trio	42.69	35.07	On the top walkway of the lighthouse facing the ocean.
7	Trio	41.93	35.03	In the ruins before the church, underneath some wooden scaffolding.
8	Trio	41.77	35.14	At the bow of a white sail boat next to a red paddle boat.
9	Trio	41.87	35.79	Next to a bench underneath a lamp that sticks out on the west side of the red building with green shutters.
10	Petra	41.80	36.47	At the top of the tower in the ruins, in the corner of two standing walls.
11	Petra	41.84	36.97	Behind a dumpster, underneath the wooden scaffolding behind Sancte Cinta.
12	Massos	42.19	37.60	Near some trash cans in a small alley with flowered covered stairs leading in from the road to the west.

INSULA FONTE

INSULA FONTE

Insula Fonte – Di Ravello Tapes

MAP NUMBER	PROVINCE	COORDINATES		DESCRIPTION
		N 40	E 5	
1	Sirocco Sud	38.40	42.37	On the porch of the small house facing the ocean.
2	Sirocco Sud	38.65	42.65	Between two benches in front of a small planter box facing the water to the north.
3	Sirocco Nord	38.95	42.66	Next to a tool box on the east side of the gas station.
4	Sirocco Nord	39.29	42.87	On a north facing balcony with a clothes line and a few trees planted in pots.
5	Lacos	40.07	43.71	On a small hidden balcony that extends into the hill from the white house with the red roof.
6	Lacos	40.16	42.76	Beside a bench on the east, facing balcony that makes up the roof of the yellow building below it.
7	Lacos	40.69	43.53	On the other side of the white fence with red shingles in the northeast side of Alba.
8	Lacos	40.95	44.18	Behind a few umbrellas and tables next to a black metal fence.
9	Baia	40.76	45.20	On the balcony of the orange building facing the ocean. The balcony has a bench and a few tree boxes.
10	Plagia	41.58	44.68	To the left of the doors leading into the gas station.
11	Plagia	42.36	44.37	Through a metal gate in the white wall that lines the east side of the road, next to some broken cars.
12	Plagia	42.47	44.20	Down the stairs on the pathway leading into the vineyards from the east side.
13	Plagia	42.51	43.95	At the top of the air traffic control tower, near the locked door.
14	Plagia	42.25	43.78	Just on the other side of the metal gates that face the road to the east.
15	Feno	42.37	42.86	On the east balcony of the yellow house, facing a large field of sunflowers.
16	Feno	42.73	43.29	On the rooftop garden of the furthest east building in Babica.
17	Feno	42.88	43.00	Set on the balcony of the building across the street from the church with the large tower.
18	Feno	42.42	42.03	On the balcony of the brick building facing the road to the east.
19	Lavanda	41.95	41.59	East facing balcony of the building north of the Police Station.
20	Lavanda	41.84	42.34	In front of the door to the women's restroom, around the back side of the gas station.

Di Ravello Tape

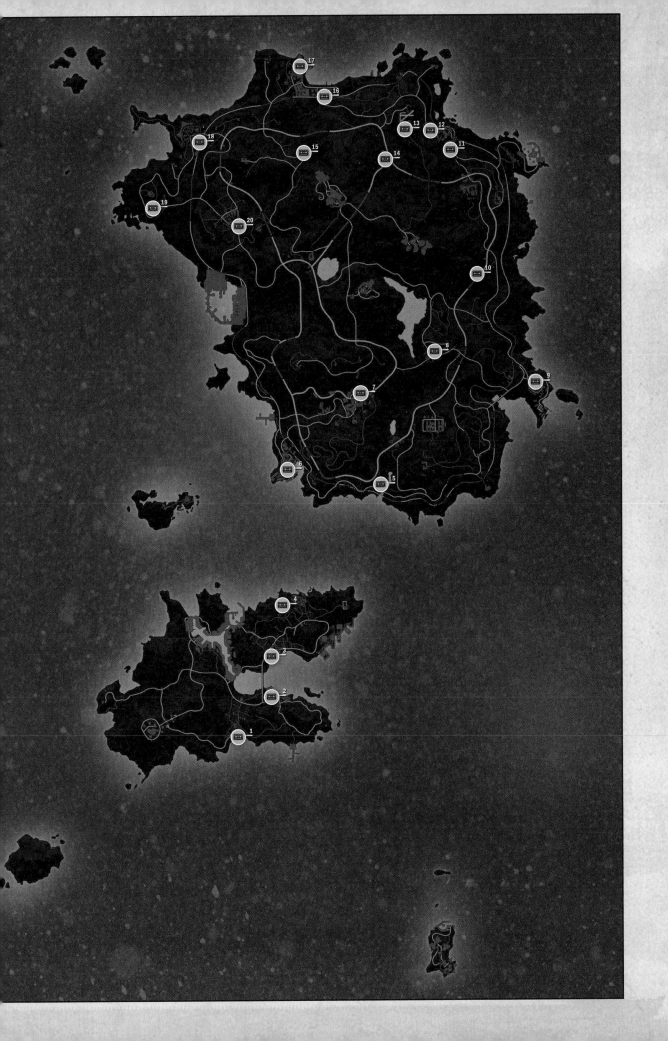

INSULA STRIATE

INSULA STRIATE

Insula Striate – Di Ravello Tapes

MAP NUMBER	PROVINCE	COORDINATES		DESCRIPTION
		N 40	E 5	
1	Montana	48.09	43.36	On top of the mountain, east of the tallest point in the world.
2	Litore Torto	49.26	46.25	North building on the south end of the catwalk.
3	Litore Torto	50.31	44.98	In a pile of trash in the rubble on the west side of the road.
4	Grande Pastura	50.93	41.21	Next to a fountain with a bull's head in the ruins.
5	Grande Pastura	49.97	40.11	In the middle of the ruined house on the north side of the road going east to west.
6	Grande Pastura	48.52	40.75	Near some knocked down trees and a rock on the west edge of a crater in the mountain.
7	Val De Mar	47.51	39.93	At the edge of the dock.
8	Val De Mar	45.98	42.16	You must grapple into this roofless ruin as there are no doors in. The correct building has a metal door next to a lantern. Just grapple to the top of the wall and drop in. The tape is on a pile of rubble inside.
9	Val De Mar	44.91	42.22	Inside the factory at the top near the control room.
10	Maestrale	45.38	39.07	At the top of some stairs in the ruins that point west to the large checkpoint wall.
11	Maestrale	46.18	39.16	On top of the tower inside the ruined village.
12	Maestrale	46.99	38.30	Inside the ruins between a free standing pillar and a wall.
13	Maestrale	47.54	37.78	At the top of some stairs in the ruins.
14	Maestrale	47.40	36.05	On the north side of the arch below a lamp.
15	Maestrale	48.22	35.34	Inside a ruined building. The entrance is on the west side.
16	Maestrale	48.57	34.83	Near some trash inside the factory, near the opening that faces the water.
17	Maestrale	48.30	32.87	On the catwalk in the center of the building.
18	Libeccio	45.18	33.39	On the catwalk to the south of the small office.
19	Libeccio	44.98	35.24	Second level from the top in the building that's being constructed. On a ledge facing back toward the city.
20	Libeccio	44.88	35.36	On a balcony next to a sun chair.
21	Libeccio	45.83	35.42	Fenced in on the north side of the small farm house.
22	Libeccio	45.72	37.15	South side of the roof on the building with the green blinds.
23	Libeccio	45.25	37.87	Behind two burned out buses.
24	Regno	44.41	37.82	On the top of the crane between the counterweights and a coil of cable.
25	Regno	44.07	38.17	East side of the large orange temple in a small walled off garden.
26	Regno	44.35	38.45	Near some bundles of lumber next to a construction site.
27	Regno	44.22	38.68	Next to some portable restrooms on the roof of the building that a crane built off the top.
28	Regno	44.21	39.30	On the blue crane of the east dock closest to land.
29	Prima	43.94	39.99	South balcony of the house closest to the road.
30	Prima	43.71	40.15	Underneath the walkway below a building's 2nd floor, next to a sign for "Soda Salate."
31	Prima	43.94	40.66	Inside the playground behind a large red building.
32	Prima	43.76	41.60	In the lounging area on the roof of the building on the southeast side of Vista Fonte.
33	Prima	43.91	41.65	Near a dumpster and trash bin on the north side of town, behind a red white and yellow building.
34	Prima	43.82	43.38	On the balcony across from "Kool Kebabs" between two pots with white flowers.
35	Prima	43.77	43.50	West corner of the building with green blinds, on a balcony below a clothesline.
36	Costa Sud	44.54	44.18	On the northwest balcony of the corner house.
37	Costa Sud	44.15	45.36	Beside a table with a blue and white umbrella, on the balcony of a white building with a "Pulvere De Fee" sign.
38	Costa Sud	44.25	45.59	Between two clotheslines on the balcony of the yellow building.
39	Costa Sud	45.23	46.21	On the south catwalk of the broken down factory near the west corner.

REBEL SHRINES

Small shrines to Rebels who have sacrificed their lives for the people of Medici are scattered along roads, in towns, and some on cliffs. Light the shrine to collect it.

Lighting all of the Rebel Shrines unlocks free Fast Traveling from anywhere in the world.

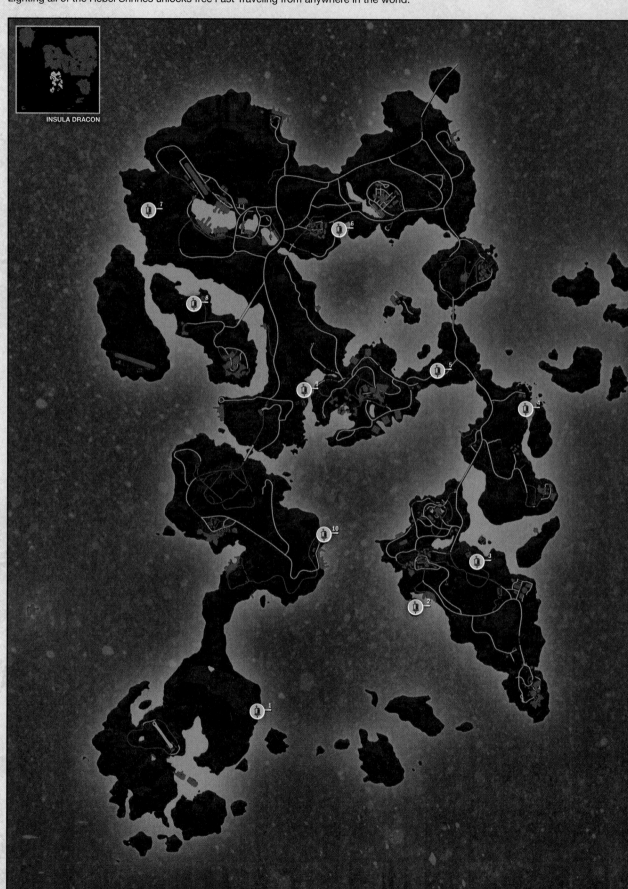

INSULA DRACON

INSULA DRACON

Igniting all of the Rebel Shrines in Insula Dracon unlocks free Fast Traveling for the Province.

Insula Dracon — Rebel Shrines

MAP NUMBER	PROVINCE	COORDINATES		DESCRIPTION
		N 40	E 5	
1	Cauda	40.95	35.36	On the east side base of the mountain, just before the cliffs leading to the water.
2	Petra	41.52	36.54	Near some ruins at the base of a tree on the peninsula to the west of Vico Tructa.
3	Petra	41.83	37.05	East of Sancte Cintia, next to a tree at the end of a sunflower field just before the cliffs.
4	Massos	42.75	37.40	South of Guardia Massos II, at the top of the east facing cliffs.
5	Massos	42.86	36.74	Just off the north side of the road on the cliffs before the beach.
6	Capite Est	43.62	35.98	East of Vinialetta, just off the road before the cliffs.
7	Capite West	43.76	34.52	On the south side of a field of sunflowers.
8	Capite West	43.29	34.87	North of Sancte Antonio, on the edge of the dock near the water.
9	Trio	42.78	35.71	Hidden in the trees near the cliff just before the water.
10	Trio	41.96	35.86	Near the lighthouse north of Vico Maquerello. Easily visible from the road.

INSULA FONTE

Igniting all of the Rebel Shrines in Insula Fonte unlocks free Fast Traveling for the Province.

INSULA FONTE

Insula Fonte – Rebel Shrines

MAP NUMBER	PROVINCE	COORDINATES		DESCRIPTION
		N 40	E 5	
1	Lavanda	41.62	42.85	On the balcony of a large house, facing down to the road and fields of sunflowers and lavender to the west.
2	Lavanda	41.76	42.14	In a small villa to the west of Lantuina, in a small break in the fence that looks back toward the city.
3	Lavanda	42.14	42.25	At the base of a tree on the east side of the road. There's a large lavender field north of it.
4	Feno	42.60	41.40	To the right of the entrance for the blue and white striped lighthouse, near the start of the stone fence.
5	Feno	42.58	42.92	South of Babica, in a small clearing near a group of trees.
6	Plagia	42.80	43.90	Against the stone fence near the house of a small vineyard. A large field of lavender lines the road leading to the house.
7	Plagia	42.46	43.93	South of the control tower in the airport of Plagia.
8	Plagia	42.00	44.75	Off the highway on the border of a large grassy field and a field of hay.
9	Baia	41.31	44.60	On the north side of a wall near a house at the end of a large field of sunflowers.
10	Lacos	41.04	43.89	Northeast of the main road near the water.
11	Baia	40.24	44.05	Head up to Sancte Rita and find the shrine on a view point to the north.
12	Lacos	40.31	43.51	On a cliff above the main road facing a bridge to the east.
13	Lacos	40.63	43.22	Take the main road directly east out of Alba and find the Shrine on the cliff to the south, near a house.
14	Lacos	40.75	42.48	In the yard of the south house, behind two orange trees.
15	Lacos	40.08	43.05	In the broken part of a fence south of a small house facing the water and road below.
16	Sirocco Sud	38.61	41.13	North of the blue and white lighthouse against the wooden fence.
17	Soros	37.60	40.47	On the north island of the Soros area, near a house and a memorial to Tae 'Jina' Stevenson.
18	Soros	37.14	39.54	On the east side of the house where the road dead ends at the top of the hill.

Rebel Shrine

INSULA STRIATE

Lighting all of the Rebel Shrines in Insula Striate unlocks free Fast Traveling for the Province.

INSULA STRIATE

Insula Striate – Rebel Shrines

MAP NUMBER	PROVINCE	COORDINATES N 40	E 5	DESCRIPTION
1	Litore Torto	50.20	45.55	In a clearing north of the road in front of a group of scattered rocks.
2	Litore Torto	49.12	45.02	On the mountain with Sancte Malco, on the southeast corner of the ruins.
3	Montana	49.15	42.59	On the east side of a warehouse that contains a few supercars and a tank.
4	Val De Mar	47.43	39.53	Against a stone wall behind some trees in the ruins north of the road.
5	Maestrale	48.99	35.60	North of the railroad tracks facing the ocean.
6	Maestrale	49.12	33.17	Through the fence at the end of the trail, just north of the trails end.
7	Rocca Blau	47.80	33.19	West of the railroad tracks in an area that looks like the trees have been burned down.
8	Libeccio	46.79	34.91	On the west side of the lake, on the edge of a group of ruins looking down toward the lake.
9	Libeccio	45.80	37.92	Behind a stone fence that connects to a house on the east side of the road.
10	Maestrale	46.49	39.37	Near the base of a wind turbine on the north side of the lake.
11	Val De Mar	45.99	42.13	A few steps north off the road behind some bushes, just before a bunch of broken trees.
12	Costa Sud	45.92	44.17	In the ruins to the southwest of Sancte Evita, at the start of a stone fence.
13	Umbra	46.50	44.73	Inside Refugio Umbra in one of the cutouts on the east side of the hangar. This is easy to grab once the Safehaven is liberated.
14	Umbra	46.54	44.81	Northeast out of Refugio Umbra, up the path to the north of the tower.
15	Costa Sud	45.93	45.76	At the northwest corner of the bay in the playground of a ruined house.
16	Costa Sud	44.25	46.00	To the north of the entrance to Sancte Galile.
17	Costa Sud	43.44	44.67	On the cliffs facing the water near the southernmost tip of Costa Sud.
18	Costa Sud	43.69	44.33	Behind a building on the south side of the road, east of the large sunflower field, against a wooden fence.
19	Prima	44.48	43.57	On the south side of the road, behind a stone fence next to a tree. A lavender field is on the opposite side of the fence.
20	Prima	44.46	42.72	Behind a building on the north side of the road, next to a tree.
21	Prima	44.54	39.73	On a green strip of land, between hay fields just north of the road.

VINTAGE PARTS

Vintage parts for different guns and an old fighter plane are buried in various locations around Medici. They are marked as a shovel stuck into the ground.

Collecting all of the Vintage Parts from every area unlocks "Noir Mode." When activated, this gives the game a Film Noir (Black & White) look. To activate Noir mode, pause the game, then go to options, select gameplay, and toggle Noir to On.

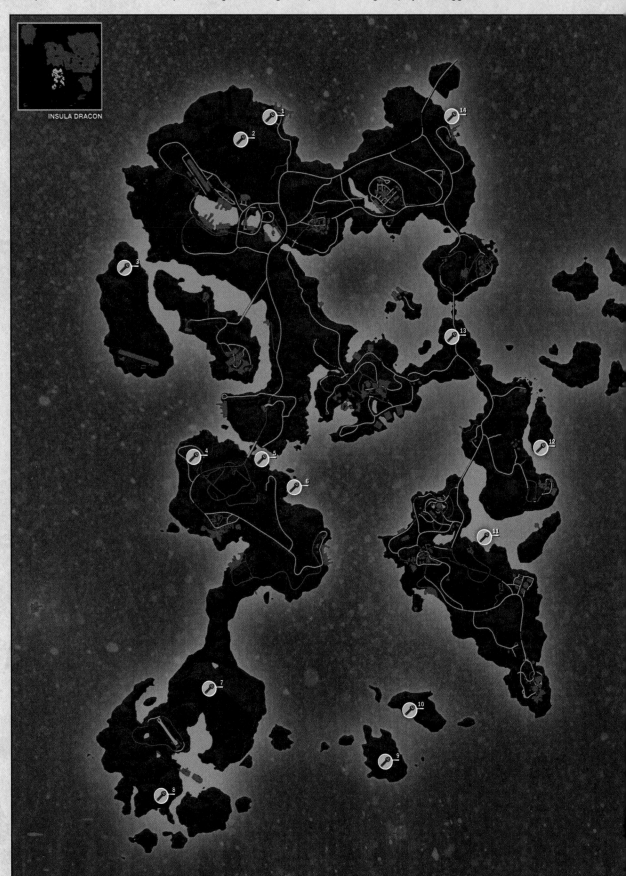

INSULA DRACON

INSULA DRACON

Once all of the Vintage Parts are retrieved in Insula Dracon, the CS44 Peacebringer (Revolver) is unlocked and appears in your Rebel Drop list.

Insula Dracon – Vintage Peace Bringer

MAP NUMBER	PROVINCE	COORDINATES		DESCRIPTION
		N 40	E 5	
1	Capite Est	44.25	35.43	Enter through the vine covered door into the cave. The part is right in front of a statue.
2	Capite West	44.14	35.16	On a cliff facing southeast toward Porto Cavo.
3	Capite West	43.40	34.32	On a cliff facing south toward Volo Dracon.
4	Trio	42.37	34.83	On the north side of the tunnel. Climb the hill to the west.
5	Trio	42.35	35.31	On the south side beach, on the east side of the bridge.
6	Trio	42.20	35.61	On the raised beach, facing east.
7	Cauda	41.10	34.96	In the small cavern between the two mountain peaks.
8	Cauda	40.55	34.53	Inside a small tunnel that leads to Grotta Contrabandero, a beach entrance can be found at N 40.45, E 34.64
9	Petra	41.15	35.15	On the south slope of the mountain facing Platteforma Petra I.
10	Petra	40.98	36.53	On top of the mountain facing the Puncta Sud Radar.
11	Petra	41.91	37.07	In the southwest corner of the ruins on the small island.
12	Massos	42.43	37.50	On the south side of the island facing Cinta.
13	Massos	43.04	36.82	In the small cave underneath a north facing cliff.
14	Capite Est	44.24	36.83	On the small peninsula next to the only tree.

INSULA FONTE

Once all of the Vintage Parts are retrieved in Insula Fonte, the Vintage U-24 Zabijak (Shotguns) is unlocked and appears in your Rebel Drop list.

MAP NUMBER	PROVINCE	COORDINATES		DESCRIPTION
		N 40	E 5	
1	Plagia	42.85	43.69	On the north side of the set of ruins.
2	Feno	42.56	42.45	North side of the valley between the two hills.
3	Feno	42.27	43.20	On the north slope of the mountain in a group of trees.
4	Plagia	42.18	43.98	North side of the road at the west entrance to the tunnel.
5	Aspera	41.75	44.08	On the north side of the base, at the bottom of a ruin wall. Beware of airstrikes if you have not yet cleared Cima Leon: Centcom!
6	Lavanda	41.84	42.59	In the cavern north of Sancte Lucas, near the arch that leads the road into the church.
7	Lavanda	42.10	41.31	On the beach below the cliffs.
8	Lavanda	41.96	41.45	In the cavern that's parallel to the road to the east.
9	Lavanda	41.25	42.94	Under the center of the bridge.
10	Lacos	40.75	42.17	On the south side of the island, tucked between a few boulders in a small cove.
11	Lacos	40.64	43.98	At the end of a small cave. The cave entrance can be found at N 40.65 E 44.01
12	Sirocco Nord	39.40	42.15	On the northwest side of the small island.
13	Sirocco Nord	39.24	43.40	In a cave below Guardia Sirocco II. The entrance can be found to the north at N 39.28 E 43.42
14	Sirocco Sud	38.52	42.65	In a cave. The entrance can be found underneath a cliff at N 38.53 E 42.68
15	Sirocco Sud	38.04	41.39	On the west side of the small island.
16	Soros	37.35	40.08	On the southwest side of the island.
17	Soros	37.03	38.31	Inside a cave. The entrance of the cave is found at N 37.03 E 39.50
18	Soros	37.12	38.98	Inside a cave that leads to Cava De Rebelles. The entrance of the cave can be found at N 37.06 E 39.01

Insula Fonte – Vintage U-24 Zabijak Parts

COLLECTIBLES: VINTAGE PARTS, INSULA FONTE

INSULA STRIATE

Once all of the Vintage Parts have been excavated in Insula Striate, the Vintage Carmen Albatross (Old Fighter Plane) is unlocked and appears in your Rebel Drop list.

Insula Striate – Vintage Carmen Albatross Parts

MAP NUMBER	PROVINCE	COORDINATES		DESCRIPTION
		N 40	E 5	
1	Maestrale	48.55	36.22	On top of the mountain, just east of a tomb.
2	Maestrale	48.50	32.74	South of the airstrip, on top of the mountain, between some trees.
3	Libeccio	46.37	33.79	On a north facing cliff on the mountain.
4	Libeccio	46.65	35.61	Behind some trees on the slope leading down to the lake.
5	Libeccio	45.18	36.48	On a small plateau in the cove south of Sancte Elena. A few cliff divers may spawn on the same spot as the Artifact. Grapple up from below for easy access.
6	Prima	44.03	42.11	West of the main door to Sancte Federico.
7	Costa Sud	43.63	44.98	In the corner of one of the walls that leads into the ruins to the east.
8	Val de Mar	45.48	43.59	Hidden in some bushes on the hill east of the ruined town.
9	Costa Sud	45.64	45.89	Inside the small inlet, near a snowman on the small beach.
10	Litore Torto	46.94	44.73	On the small hill below the mountain, facing the flooded city to the northeast.
11	Val De Mar	46.52	42.25	Next to some broken rocks, due north from the northernmost tip of the small lake.
12	Val De Mar	47.32	41.98	On the southern slope of the mountain. Drop in from the sky or grapple your way up the mountain to reach it.
13	Grande Pastura	48.62	39.73	Between two peaks of the lower mountain on the south side of the larger mountain range.
14	Grande Pastura	49.17	40.67	In the valley between two mountain peaks. The lower road dead ends just above the Artifact.
15	Grande Pastura	50.72	38.67	On a cliff that faces the ocean to the north.
16	Grande Pastura	50.80	41.34	Tucked in the corner of the stairs connected to the east wall of this ruined amphitheater.
17	Grande Pastura	51.40	43.10	Next to a boulder where some small shrubs meet the sand of the beach.
18	Grande Pastura	50.34	44.35	Northeast of the snowy mountain at the top of a cliff.
19	Litore Torto	48.72	46.69	In a shadowed crevasse below a large cliff.
20	Litore Torto	47.97	46.67	Between two mountains in the valley that runs east into the ocean. Next to some tall bushes and trees.
21	Montana	48.27	43.62	In a snowy crevasse that leads west in the area containing the "Mountain Marathon Tour" Wingsuit Course.
22	Montana	48.32	43.23	In a small, dark rocky area below a large cliff on the north side of the snowy mountain range.

INSULA STRIATE

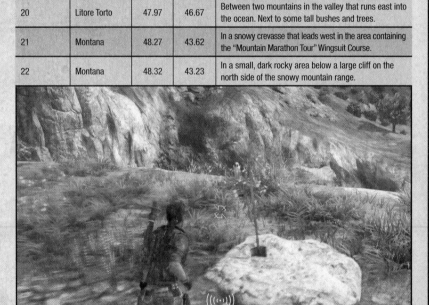